The State in
Shakespeare's Greek and Roman Plays

NUMBER 149 OF THE COLUMBIA
UNIVERSITY STUDIES IN ENGLISH
AND COMPARATIVE LITERATURE

The State
in Shakespeare's Greek
and Roman Plays

By JAMES EMERSON PHILLIPS, Jr.

1972

OCTAGON BOOKS

New York

822.33
P561s
1972

Reprinted 1972
by special arrangement with the Columbia University Press

OCTAGON BOOKS
A DIVISION OF FARRAR, STRAUS & GIROUX, INC.
19 Union Square West
New York, N. Y. 10003

LIBRARY OF CONGRESS CATALOG CARD NUMBER: 79-159249

ISBN 0-374-96427-0

Manufactured by Braun-Brumfield, Inc.
Ann Arbor, Michigan

Printed in the United States of America

To My Mother and Father

Preface

THE PRESENT STUDY is the outcome of an investigation that began as an attempt to determine what Shakespeare has to say about kings and kingship. In an effort to secure a more precise understanding of the terms and concepts involved in Renaissance thinking about governors of states, I turned to the political literature, both learned and popular, of the dramatist's own day. The results of this approach were to a certain degree successful in clarifying Shakespeare's treatment of kingly figures. Theories of royal conduct and authority implicit in many of the plays emerged as significant criteria determining the dramatist's handling of his characters and his attitude toward them.

It became increasingly evident, however, that little could be understood of Shakespeare's thinking about kings and kingship without reference to an even more fundamental concept in Renaissance political reasoning, namely, the concept of the whole nature of the state. For in the dramatist's works, as in the political literature of his day, the king was consistently presented not as an isolated phenomenon, but as an integral part of the larger political pattern. Theories of his prerogatives and functions were inextricably linked with theories of the purpose and nature of the commonwealth, and only by reference to the concept of the state could his authority and duties be properly understood and criticized. Particularly interesting in this connection were the elaborate analogies drawn by Shakespeare between the commonwealth and the human body, the bee hive, and the solar system, in which the king is made "semblable" to the head, the queen bee, and the sun, respectively. For it became evident in the light of prevalent Renaissance practice that these passages were written not simply as rhetorical decorations, but as keys to the true dignity and authority of political society as it was conceived to be by Shakespeare's contemporaries. Facts such as these directed my attention from the problem of kingship to the more fundamental problem of the idea of the state.

Because this idea seemed to be most clearly and fully worked out in the political action of Shakespeare's Greek and Roman plays, and because these plays offered a body of material well suited to the restrictions of a study of this sort, the subject and the limits of the present work were defined.

A word must be said in explanation of the term "Renaissance" as it is used in this study. To maintain that certain concepts were generally prevalent in the sixteenth century, and accordingly to label them with the term "Renaissance," is not to assert that they were peculiar to that period. The principles of order, degree, and unitary sovereignty, and the use of analogical argument have a long and full history extending back through medieval and classic periods. Indeed, they flourish under frequently thin disguises at the present time. I have tried to indicate something of the nature of the earlier history as it concerned the currency of specific terms and ideas. But the main objective in the first half of this study has been not a historical survey of political theories, but an examination of theories as they were known and understood in Shakespeare's era. My interest has been to determine the Renaissance way of thinking about certain problems of the state and society. In many respects my problem has been one merely of interpreting a forgotten terminology in an attempt to arrive at the full significance of Shakespeare's political expression.

In turning to contemporary modes of thought and expression to secure a more complete understanding of Shakespeare's concept of the state I have naturally been guided in my selection of correlative materials by those problems and theories which are suggested in the plays themselves. Consequently the picture of the state drawn in the preliminary chapters of this study is by no means to be considered a complete account of sixteenth century theories of the state and society. It represents, rather, the concept which seems largely to have influenced Shakespeare's own thinking. But it represents also, I am convinced, the concept most widely prevalent and generally accepted in his day.

Adequately to acknowledge my indebtedness for assistance received in preparing this study would be impossible; I can only single out the few whose contributions are representative of invaluable aid given by many. Practically all of the material upon which the first half of the work is based was courteously and generously made available to me by the Huntington Library in San Marino, California. To the librarians there, as to those at Columbia University and the University of California at Los Angeles, I am grateful for many favors. Miss Lily B. Campbell, under whose guidance I began the study of Shakespeare's political thinking at the University of California, has shown continued interest in the work which has been a source both of inspiration and of valuable aid. A University Fellowship granted by Columbia University for the academic year 1938–39 made it possible for me to complete the work. The faculty of Columbia University have offered helpful criticism throughout. I am particularly indebted to Professor R. M. MacIver for much needed advice concerning the treatment of Renaissance political theory, to Professor Ernest Hunter Wright for suggestions about the material on *Timon of Athens,* and to Professor John L. Gerig for pointing out interesting and important parallels between French and English political thinking in the period. Many pertinent criticisms were the result of careful reading of the manuscript by Professors H. M. Ayres, R. S. Loomis, Ralph L. Rusk, and Dino Bigongiari, and by Dr. Henry W. Wells. I am grateful to Miss Matilda L. Berg, of Columbia University Press, for her work in preparing the manuscript for publication. For Professor Oscar James Campbell must be reserved my chief thanks, however; his contribution extended beyond critical direction of the study to that encouragement and friendship essential to an undertaking of this sort.

JAMES EMERSON PHILLIPS, JR.

University of California at Los Angeles
July, 1940

Contents

The State in

Shakespeare's Greek and Roman Plays

CHAPTER I

The Problem

IN SHAKESPEARE's *Henry V*, the Archbishop of Canterbury, seeking
to prove to the king that all the elements of his realm work for
the success of the French campaign, describes in detailed figurative
language the structure and functioning of civil societies. He says:

> Therefore doth heaven divide
> The state of man in divers functions,
> Setting endeavor in continual motion,
> To which is fixed, as an aim or butt,
> Obedience; for so work the honey-bees,
> Creatures that by a rule in nature teach
> The act of order to a peopled kingdom.
> They have a king and officers of sorts,
> Where some, like magistrates, correct at home,
> Others, like merchants, venture trade abroad,
> Others, like soldiers, armed in their stings,
> Make boot upon the summer's velvet buds,
> Which pillage they with merry march bring home
> To the tent-royal of their emperor;
> Who, busied in his majesty, surveys
> The singing masons building roofs of gold,
> The civil citizens kneading up the honey,
> The poor mechanic porters crowding in
> Their heavy burdens at his narrow gate,
> The sad-eyed justice, with his surly hum,
> Delivering o'er to executors pale
> The lazy yawning drone. I this infer,
> That many things, having full reference
> To one consent, may work contrariously.
> As many arrows, loosed several ways,
> Come to one mark; as many ways meet in one town;

> As many fresh streams meet in one salt sea;
> As many lines close in the dial's centre;
> So may a thousand actions, once afoot,
> End in one purpose, and be all well borne
> Without defeat.[1]

Canterbury here presents as his concept of the state a stratified, integrated political society in which all the parts function for the welfare of the whole under the administration of a single, sovereign governor. Numerous plays in the canon bear testimony to the fact that Shakespeare brought to his dramatic examination of states principles of political organization and social conduct similar to these suggested by the Archbishop in *Henry V*. The English chronicle history plays, and particularly *Henry VI*, Parts II and III, offer evidence of these principles, as does *Measure for Measure*. The satire on the ideal commonwealth portrayed by Gonzalo in *The Tempest* is a further indication of the nature of Shakespeare's interest in the problem of the state.[2]

I

The present study is concerned with Shakespeare's concept of the state as it is manifested in his five plays based on Greek and Roman history. Here the idea of political society embodied in Canterbury's analogy receives perhaps its fullest dramatic exposition. In three of these plays, *Timon of Athens, Julius Caesar,* and *Antony and Cleopatra,* the concept is clearly built up in numerous references which appear throughout the dramas. In *Troilus and Cressida* and in *Coriolanus* a similar idea of the state is embodied in extended analogies which are practically identical with Canterbury's in their method of presentation

---

[1] *Henry V,* I, ii, 183–213. With this should be compared Exeter's speech immediately preceding Canterbury's discourse:

> While that the armed hand doth fight abroad,
> The advised head defends itself at home;
> For government, though high and low and lower,
> Put into parts, doth keep in one consent,
> Congreeing in a full and natural close,
> Like music.

(Throughout this study all Shakespearean quotations are from *The Complete Works of William Shakespeare,* edited by W. A. Neilson, Student's Cambridge Edition (1910).

[2] See, for example, *Henry VI,* Part II, IV, ii, 35 *et seq.,* and all of scenes vi–x, the episode of Cade's rebellion. For the passage in *The Tempest* see p. 56, below.

and analysis. Because of their importance as evidence of the dramatist's theory of the state these latter passages must be quoted here at length.

Ulysses, in *Troilus and Cressida,* analyzes the lethargy of the Greeks in terms of the principles which, he maintains, should govern the conduct of any human society, political or military:

> Troy, yet upon his basis, had been down,
> And the great Hector's sword had lack'd a master,
> But for these instances:
> The specialty of rule hath been neglected;
> And, look, how many Grecian tents do stand
> Hollow upon this plain, so many hollow factions.
> When that the general is not like the hive
> To whom the foragers shall all repair,
> What honey is expected? Degree being vizarded,
> The unworthiest shows as fairly in the mask.
> The heavens themselves, the planets, and this centre
> Observe degree, priority, and place,
> Insisture, course, proportion, season, form,
> Office, and custom, in all line of order;
> And therefore is the glorious planet Sol
> In noble eminence enthron'd and spher'd
> Amidst the other; whose medicinable eye
> Corrects the ill aspects of planets evil,
> And posts, like the commandment of a king,
> Sans check to good and bad. But when the planets
> In evil mixture to disorder wander,
> What plagues and what portents! what mutiny!
> What raging of the sea! shaking of earth!
> Commotion in the winds! Frights, changes, horrors,
> Divert and crack, rend and deracinate
> The unity and married calm of states
> Quite from their fixture! O, when degree is shak'd,
> Which is the ladder to all high designs,
> Then enterprise is sick! How could communities,
> Degrees in schools, and brotherhoods in cities,
> Peaceful commerce from dividable shores,
> The primogenitive and due of birth,
> Prerogative of age, crowns, sceptres, laurels,
> But by degree, stand in authentic place?

Take but degree away, untune that string,
And, hark, what discord follows! Each thing meets
In mere oppugnancy. The bounded waters
Should lift their bosoms higher than the shores
And make a sop of all this solid globe.
Strength should be lord of imbecility,
And the rude son should strike his father dead.
Force should be right; or rather, right and wrong,
Between whose endless jar justice resides,
Should lose their names, and so should justice too.
Then everything includes itself in power,
Power into will, will into appetite;
And appetite, an universal wolf,
So doubly seconded with will and power,
Must make perforce an universal prey,
And last eat up himself. Great Agamemnon,
This chaos, when degree is suffocate,
Follows the choking.
And this neglection of degree is it
That by a pace goes backward, in a purpose
It hath to climb. The general's disdain'd
By him one step below, he by the next,
That next by him beneath; so every step,
Exampled by the first pace that is sick
Of his superior, grows to an envious fever
Of pale and bloodless emulation;
And 't is this fever that keeps Troy on foot,
Not her own sinews. To end a tale of length,
Troy in our weakness stands, not in her strength.[3]

Menenius, in the familiar belly passage in *Coriolanus*, suggests in a manner similar to Ulysses' the political and social relationships which should exist among the various elements in a state; attempting to reason with the rebellious populace he says:

MEN.   There was a time when all the body's members
       Rebell'd against the belly, thus accus'd it:
       That only like a gulf it did remain
       I' the midst o' the body, idle and unactive,
       Still cupboarding the viand, never bearing

---

[3] *Troilus and Cressida*, I, iii, 75–137.

Like labour with the rest, where the other instruments
Did see and hear, devise, instruct, walk, feel,
And, mutually participate, did minister
Unto the appetite and affection common
Of the whole body. The belly answer'd—

. . . .

2. CIT.   Your belly's answer? What!
The kingly-crowned head, the vigilant eye,
The counsellor heart, the arm our soldier,
Our steed the leg, the tongue our trumpeter,
With other muniments and petty helps
In this our fabric, if that they . . .

. . . .

Should by the cormorant belly be restrain'd,
Who is the sink o' the body,—
MEN.   Well, what then?
2. CIT. The former agents, if they did complain,
What could the belly answer?

. . . .

MEN.   Note me this, good friend;
Your most grave belly was deliberate,
Not rash like his accusers, and thus answered:
"True is it, my incorporate friends," quoth he,
"That I receive the general food at first
Which you do live upon; and fit it is,
Because I am the store-house and the shop
Of the whole body. But, if you do remember,
I send it through the rivers of your blood,
Even to the court, the heart, to the seat o' the brain;
And, through the cranks and offices of man,
The strongest nerves and small inferior veins
From me receive that natural competency
Whereby they live. And though that all at once,
You, my good friends," —this says the belly, mark me,—
2. CIT. Ay, sir; well, well.
MEN.   "Though all at once cannot
See what I do deliver out to each,
Yet I can make my audit up, that all
From me do back receive the flour of all,
And leave me but the bran." What say you to 't?
2. CIT. It was an answer. How apply you this?

MEN.   The senators of Rome are this good belly,
       And you the mutinous members; for examine
       Their counsels and their cares, digest things rightly
       Touching the weal o' the common, you shall find
       No public benefit which you receive
       But it proceeds or comes from them to you
       And no way from yourselves.[4]

Certain striking likenesses between these two speeches justify us in considering them as expressions of a well-rounded and well-developed theory of the nature and structure of political society similar in every respect to the state-concept set forth by Canterbury. In the first place, both passages are characterized by figurative language and analogical argument closely similar in nature and purport. As does Canterbury from the beehive, so Menenius from the human body and Ulysses from a variety of natural phenomena, draw by analogy the principles which should determine political form and action in the world of men. In the second place, the civil order so described is in each case basically the same; the analogies consistently suggest a divinely ordained social and political structure in which vocationally determined degrees of ascending merit function coördinately under a sovereign governor for the welfare of the whole organization. This is the clear import of such phrases as Ulysses' "The heavens themselves, the planets, and this centre, Observe degree, priority and place" marked by a "noble eminence"; and as Menenius' "My incorporate friends." Both resemble Canterbury's "therefore doth heaven divide the state of man in divers functions." In the third place, Shakespeare in each instance introduces this political concept early in the action of the play; it appears in the third scene (but the first camp scene) of *Troilus and Cressida,* and in the opening scene of *Coriolanus.* This initial position enhances the significance of the passages as keys to the political action which follows in each case; the discourses seem to establish the principles by which the action of the political characters is to be judged. Finally, the passages are presented by characters who have been generally recognized by critics as the spokesmen for intelligence and reason in the plays, if not for Shakespeare himself.

The common elements in these passages suggest that the analogies

---

[4] *Coriolanus,* I, i, 99–158.

embody a concept of the state, similar to that found elsewhere in the Shakespearean canon, which is fundamental in the political action of plays in which they occur. *Coriolanus*, for example, illustrates vividly how a clear understanding of this concept of the state can aid materially in the solution of certain dramatic problems. Critical opinion, after a long struggle over the structure and meaning of the play, has divided itself into three camps. One of these is composed of commentators who believe that the dramatic interest centers in the common people. Stopford Brooke represents those critics in this group who find Shakespeare's sympathy to lie with the oppressed masses.[5] The majority, however, consider the play to be Shakespeare's last and strongest word of contempt for the common people; this contempt, they assert, is the theme of the drama, and the evolution of the tragic consequences of mob action its structural unity.[6] Another group maintains that the title figure himself is the center of interest and that the play is a tragedy of the noble but tragically flawed hero.[7] A third group, the largest of the three, unwilling or unable to reconcile these apparent irreconcilables, follows Coleridge in acclaiming the "wonderfully philosophic impartiality of Shakespeare's own politics." [8]

Such division of critical opinion merely emphasizes a problem which confronts any reader of *Coriolanus*. If he concludes that the consul, a victim of himself and of his people, is the center of the play, he recalls that almost equal attention is devoted to the mob, and that no little time is spent in justifying its behavior on the basis of Coriolanus' arrogance and apparent lack of concern for its welfare. This division of the reader's sympathy and interest between Coriolanus and the mob not only obscures the point of the drama, but sadly impairs its structural unity.

If, however, we take Menenius' speech on the belly as a key to the

[5] Stopford Brooke, *On Ten Plays of Shakespeare* (1905), p. 226.

[6] Cf. Georg Brandes, *William Shakespeare: a Critical Study*, translated by William Archer, *et al.* (1935), p. 537 *et seq.*

[7] Cf. A. C. Swinburne, *Shakespeare*, p. 187. (Quoted in *Coriolanus*, p. 661, edited by H. H. Furness, Jr., 1928, The New Variorum Shakespeare) : "It is from first to last . . . rather a private and domestic than a public or historical tragedy."

[8] S. T. Coleridge, *Notes and Lectures upon Shakespeare* (1874), IV, 100. (Quoted in *Coriolanus*, p. 19, note, edited by H. H. Furness, Jr., 1928, The New Variorum Shakespeare.)

political structure and action of the play, we see immediately that this is not the tragedy of a ruler alone or of a people alone, but a picture of the threatened disintegration of an institution including and yet superior to them both—the state. In its terminology, as in the ideas it embodies, the passage outlines the political organization of civil society within which a ruler, such as Coriolanus, and a subject people, such as the mob, must function. With equal clarity Menenius asserts that when this order is preserved, the health of the whole body will be effected, but when it is destroyed, political tragedy—the failure of the state to achieve the ends for which it is established—will ensue. In the course of the play Shakespeare examines the conduct of Coriolanus and the plebeians and shows how in each case failure to observe fundamental principles of political action set forth in the first scene threatens to destroy the social organism designed by nature for the welfare of all. The impartiality of Shakespeare's treatment of ruler and ruled, which Coleridge admired, is the consequence of his definite partiality for the whole state and its well-being.

In other instances, notably in *Troilus and Cressida,* an identical concept of civil society, embodied in extended analogies, similarly affords a basis for determining the dramatic significance of the political action of the play. Although the state is not explicitly described in *Timon of Athens, Julius Caesar,* and *Antony and Cleopatra,* I hope to make clear that the same basic principles govern the political action in these dramas as well.

2

The concept under consideration in this study is Shakespeare's answer to the question, "What is a state?" Broadly speaking, the state, or body politic, is the framework, or constitution, of a human society within a nation. It is concerned, as Professor J. W. Allen remarks, with "the actual structure of society—how its parts are related and what binds it together and what should be its animating purpose." [9] Thus the main features of the social structure and its governmental machinery are the materials from which Shakespeare, like his contemporaries and like most political thinkers, constructed a concept of civil

[9] J. W. Allen, *A History of Political Thought in the Sixteenth Century* (1928), p. 135.

society. It includes not only the source and form of government in a state, but also the organization, conduct, and contribution of all the individuals who comprise the state. Accordingly, although it is essentially a political concept, it is not solely one, for it embraces certain fundamental social and economic problems as well.

To judge from the passages which have stimulated this investigation, Shakespeare clearly thought of the state as a well-defined entity, and so presented and employed it in his plays. The principal elements of this concept which will require careful analysis may be defined in terms of these dramatic utterances.

At the outset we must give some consideration to the origin of the state and to the source of its authority over the individual. Canterbury touches the issue when he mentions the "heaven" which divides men according to degree and vocation; Ulysses and Menenius indicate in their natural analogies a law of nature which suggests the same problem. What power draws men together into civil societies and establishes the pattern of their communal life? What basis is there for the assumption that one pattern is superior to others and that men are obliged to adhere to this order in preference to any other?

These questions involve a second fundamental problem of state-theory, a determination of what Professor Allen calls the "animating purpose" of political society. In the beehive of Canterbury's parable this purpose is the production of honey; in the human body of Menenius' discourse, physical health; and in the natural phenomena of Ulysses' analogies, the peace and harmony of the universe. What is the corresponding aim of the state, and what achievements for man's welfare justify its existence? What are the ends for which God, or Nature, or man himself, set up the order of civil society?

It is next necessary to discover the nature of the structure so authorized and so justified. This consideration leads to the essence of the state-concept itself, to the arrangement and function of its component parts. Detailed analysis of the order of the beehive, of the solar universe, and of the human body in the Shakespearean passages indicates the relevance of the problem to the dramatist's theory of the state. How are men organized within the structure of civil society? How are these elements of organization defined, and what is the nature and activity of each in relation to the whole state? The problem requires a discussion not only of the relation of individuals, or groups of individuals, to each other, but to the community as a whole.

The most important single feature of this structure is perhaps the authority which governs and controls it. A political thinker must determine the form of government best suited to the purposes for which states are established and most agreeable to the power which established them. A sovereign, governing authority is indicated in the body politic depicted in each of the plays under consideration. Ulysses points to the "noble eminence" of the sun in the solar system; and Menenius observes the parallel between certain governmental functions of the belly in the body and the Senate in the state. These parallels recall Canterbury's account of the king and emperor of the hive. What is the source of this political authority, and what form—monarchic, aristocratic, or democratic—should it take? What is its function in the state-structure? What is the extent of its power? As one historian of political theory puts the problem, "The first and most simple question is, who has the right to rule, to govern his, or their, fellow men, and why?" [10]

These problems, as the student of political science will only too readily perceive, by no means cover the whole subject of state-theory. They constitute, however, the essential features of the state-theory which Shakespeare employed for dramatic purposes, and hence comprise the subject matter of the present study. Naturally, even the problems involved by implication in the Shakespearean idea of the state are enormous in number. But in order to see clearly the dramatic function of the concept as a whole, as well as to keep the subject within practical limits, we must in the ensuing discussion adhere rigorously to the basic idea itself and leave to other investigators the details of its far-flung social, economic, and political implications.

3

The existence of a definite theory of the state in Shakespeare's plays has not been hitherto unrecognized. Professor Dover Wilson has observed in Shakespeare's plays a "concern for politics, or rather for the dramatic possibilities of political life." [11] His statement bears testimony

[10] Thomas I. Cook, *History of Political Philosophy from Plato to Burke* (1936), p. 6.

[11] John Dover Wilson, *The Essential Shakespeare* (1932), p. 92.

to De Selincourt's conviction that Shakespeare "was profoundly impressed, in a way that the modern artist is seldom impressed, with the essential relation of the individual to that larger society which is called a nation; and with the influences which a man's feelings towards the community have upon his whole life and character." [12] This critic more specifically describes the dramatist's concept of political society as "a complicated human machine, in which each separate part contributes its quota to the general efficiency, and it may at any one time be thrown out of gear by the failure of one part to perform its allotted functions." [13] A similar concept in the plays, which the critic attributes to the influence of Hooker's *Laws of Ecclesiastical Polity*, has been analyzed by Professor Gayley.[14] Dr. Kohler, in "Die Staatsidee Shakespeares in 'Richard II,' " describes the same principles. He observes that

das Abbild des Staates entnimmt er dem Bienenvolke und seiner Gliederung, worin jedes Wesen seine. besondere Bestimmung erfüllt, jedes nach festgesetzter Richtung hin das Ganze fördert. . . . In gleicher Weise steht ihm das Bild des Himmelsgewölbes vor Augen, wie sich hier alles nach einer bestimmten Regel, nach Ordnung und Unterordnung vollzieht, da nur durch die Gesetzmässigkeit das grosse Universum erhalten wird.[15]

These studies, products of the years from 1914 to 1918, were less concerned with the dramatic significance of the concept of the state than with the lessons it held for war-harried Europe. The same concept is interpreted, according to the sympathies of the particular critic, as Shakespeare's approval or disapproval of the democracy for which the world was at that time being made safe. Such an attitude results not only in an incomplete and distorted presentation of the problem, but in neglect of the body politic as a dramatic element.

Shakespeare's theory of the state has been treated from various points of view in a number of more recent studies. Professor Hart believes that he has discovered the source of the concept, along with that of other elements of political theory, in the *Homilie agaynst Disobedi-*

---

[12] Ernest De Selincourt, *English Poets and the National Ideal* (1915), p. 10.

[13] *Ibid.*, p. 21.

[14] Charles Mills Gayley, *Shakespeare and the Founders of Liberty in America* (1918), Chapters V and VI.

[15] Josef Kohler, "Die Staatsidee Shakespeares in 'Richard II,' " *Shakespeare Jahrbuch*, LIII (1917), 1, 2.

ence and Wylfull Rebellion, published in 1571.[16] The same concept is among the large number of political subjects which Grosse, in a comprehensive investigation, finds reflected in the drama of the Tudor period.[17] His primary interest, however—"aus dieser Synthese einer Beitrag zum Staatsgedanken der englischen Renaissance zu geben" [18] —is political rather than literary. The conclusions of Professor Draper, based on a similar investigation of Shakespeare's political ideas in the light of contemporary sixteenth-century thought, bear further witness to the presence of a theory of the state as the core of interest in politics in the plays.[19] He remarks:

surely Shakespeare could not write at length about the fall of princes and the catastrophes of government without consistently implying the principles by which a government was believed to prosper or decline. . . . Shakespeare shows us in comparison the three types of government recognized in the Renaissance, monarchy, oligarchy, and democracy, and he analyses in detail the diseases of the state, and shows the causes and the degrees by which civil government disintegrates.[20]

Professor Draper's emphasis is on the governmental problem of state-theory; the state as a whole, with its social and economic elements, he does not consider. His investigation is further limited by an unwillingness to recognize a "sense of the body politic and of the principles that govern it" in any of the plays written by Shakespeare before the accession of James I.[21]

While differing in method and purpose, the foregoing studies concur in finding a definite theory of the state to be fundamental in Shakespeare's political ideology, and in suggesting the significance of the problem as a subject for investigation. They have been supplemented by a host of studies of the dramatist's attitudes toward related individual problems of political science. Shakespeare's kings have received the largest share of this attention, but the counselor, the common peo-

---

[16] Alfred Hart, *Shakespeare and the Homilies* (1935), "A New Shakespearean Source-Book."

[17] F. Grosse, "Das englische Renaissancedrama im Spiegel zeitgenössischer Staatstheorien," *Sprache und Kultur der Germanischer und Römanischer Völker,* A, XVIII (1935).

[18] *Ibid.,* p. 2.

[19] John W. Draper, "Political Themes in Shakespeare's Later Plays," *Journal of English and Germanic Philology,* XXXV (1936).

[20] *Ibid.,* p. 70.   [21] *Ibid.,* p. 88.

ple, the forms of government, and similar problems have been discussed as elements of Shakespeare's political theory.[22] In a word, the subject is by no means a neglected one in Shakespearean criticism.

These investigations, while illuminating the general subject of the nature and sources of Shakespeare's political ideas, fail for the most part adequately to reveal the dramatic functions of these ideas. The concept of the state which these scholars consider is isolated and analyzed rather for its bearing on non-dramatic problems—on Shakespeare's sources, on his message to the twentieth century, on his manner of alluding to political events of his own day. Professor Charlton is among the few who have suggested that problems of political theory may constitute a vital factor in dramatic technique; what he writes of the English history play he applies later to the Roman history play:

> But just as the author of tragedy, moving his hero from predicament to predicament and at last to his ruin, weaves into the design of his play his apprehension of the ultimate forces which sway the life of individual man in our universe, so in the history play. At its beginning England is presented in such and such condition. As the action proceeds, there are changes in the protagonist's welfare; and at the end . . . the state of affairs ensues as the inevitable outcome of what has gone before. But to give such conviction to his ending the dramatist must have apprehended the fundamental principles conditioning the form of life he is displaying. In the history play it is the welfare of a nation as a nation; that is, it is a specifically political interest. . . . A better name would be political plays, for they are plays in which the prevailing dramatic interest is in the fate of a nation. Since that is their nature there will be in them much of what Shakespeare's insight had apprehended of the forces which shape a nation's destiny.[23]

These forces which Professor Charlton describes are embodied in their clearest form in the concept of political society outlined in the foregoing pages. In the passages referred to, Shakespeare gives con-

---

[22] Cf. for example B. Tschischwitz, *Shakespeares Staat und Königthum* (1866); F. Tupper, "The Shaksperean Mob," *PMLA*, XXVII (1912), 486; W. Keller, "Shakespeare's Königsdramen," *Shakespeare Jahrbuch*, LXIII (1927), 35; W. Clemen, "Shakespeare und das Königtum," *Shakespeare Jahrbuch*, LXVIII (1932), 56; F. T. Wood, "Shakespeare and the Plebs," *Essays and Studies by Members of the English Association*, XVIII (1932), 53; C. R. Sleeth, "Shakespeare's Counsellors of State," *Revue anglo-américaine*, XIII (1935), 97. Similar works on subjects more closely connected with the present study will be found listed in the bibliography.

[23] H. B. Charlton, *Shakespeare, Politics and Politicians* (1929), p. 11.

crete expression to the principles which he recognized as governing the destiny of states. Any consideration of the dramatic significance of these political plays must accordingly begin with a clear understanding of the theory of the state so presented. The concept is a key not only to the interpretation of the plays primarily concerned with the welfare of nations, but also to the solution of dramatic problems in the many instances where political figures and activities are involved. Such an approach must not be mistaken for an attempt to explain what Shakespeare the man thought about this particular theory. Nor should the state-theory be analyzed as principally a Shakespearean commentary on actual political events of his day or ours. Its dramatic function and not its ideological value to Shakespeare will be the subject of the present investigation.

4

An accurate definition of terms and concepts involved in the Shakespearean conception of civil society is essential to a critical approach of this sort. If such an investigation were conducted on the basis of evidence found in the plays alone, the results would necessarily be fragmentary and conjectural. For Shakespeare, in a majority of cases, merely implies or suggests problems of state-theory, relying, perhaps, on the political knowledge and attitudes manifestly widespread among Elizabethan playgoers to provide the complete meaning and effect intended.[24] Rarely does he present a political concept in explicit and fully rounded form, and when he does, his terminology is such that it holds little meaning for present day readers. Monarchy, aristocracy, and democracy as forms of government in a state are terms which have undergone radical change in meaning since the sixteenth century. Shakespeare's use of them, therefore, cannot safely be interpreted on the basis of their modern connotation alone. Similarly, Hector, in a passage in *Troilus and Cressida*, employs the term "law of nations" in such a manner that much of the meaning of the passage hinges on a clear understanding of the phrase.[25] In the sixteenth century the con-

---

[24] See Chapter II, below.
[25] *Troilus and Cressida*, II, ii, 183:

> If Helen then be wife to Sparta's king,
> As it is known she is, these moral laws
> Of nature and of nations speak aloud
> To have her back return'd. . . .

cept of a law of nations was a familiar one, but it has long since merged
with and become lost in the totally different modern concept of international law. Insofar as Shakespeare's term is misunderstood, the
passage will remain correspondingly obscure. For the purposes of this
investigation, then, we must adopt a method which will afford an
accurate understanding of the political terms and concepts involved in
the dramatist's description of organized society.

Shakespeare's expression may be clarified if it is studied in the light
of the theories of the state prevalent in sixteenth-century political
thought. Such a procedure requires that we accept the premise that
Shakespeare thought and wrote essentially in the language of his day,
that the raw materials of his expressions, however refined the latter,
were those of his own time and place. Certain resemblances, apparent at
first glance, indicate that Shakespeare's concept of the state is in its essential outline that which was accepted by the majority of his politically
orthodox contemporaries. His use of natural analogy in describing the
body politic can be paralleled in writers on state theory from Elyot, in
the opening chapters of *The Boke Named the Gouernour* to Bodin, in
the *Six livres de la république* (translated, 1606, as *The Six Bookes of a
Commonweale*). Order and degree in the structure of states received
in a host of political writers—the homilists, Sir John Cheke, Bodin, and
Hooker, to name only a few of the more prominent—the same emphasis
which it received in Shakespeare. Bodin, Merbury, Hayward, Craig,
and even the Jesuit Parsons argue as do Canterbury and Ulysses in
favor of monarchy as the most desirable form of government in a
political society. Sir Leslie Stephen, in defending the approach through
contemporary materials as a basis for critical investigation, remarks that

every man is an organ of the society in which he has been brought up,
since the material upon which he works is the whole complex of conceptions, religious, imaginative and ethical, which forms his mental atmosphere. . . .[26]

And elsewhere he declares:

If any man ever imitated and gave full utterance to the characteristic ideas
of his contemporaries, it was certainly Shakespeare.[27]

---

[26] Quoted by Brander Matthews in *Shakspere as a Playwright* (1923), p. 296.
[27] *Ibid.*

By so analyzing Shakespeare's political expressions in the light of Renaissance thought Miss Henneke and Dr. Grosse have remarkably clarified certain elements of the dramatist's political theory.[28] Their success in this respect seems to justify adoption of a similar method in an investigation of Shakespeare's idea of the state. If, on the basis of contemporary writings, we can determine with some accuracy and fullness the prevalent Elizabethan ways of thinking about the state, we shall have at hand the materials for interpreting and discussing the idea as it is employed with its manifold dramatic implications by Shakespeare.

The English scholar quoted just above once said, "I am reluctant to break the rule—or what ought to be the rule—that no one should write about Shakespeare without a special license." [29] The possibility of throwing some new light on certain aspects of the dramatist's work by developing the problems, materials, purposes and methods suggested in the foregoing pages perhaps provides the necessary license in this instance. The study so licensed will, accordingly, describe at the outset the widespread interest in Tudor England in problems of political theory and the circumstances which made the subject particularly appropriate for dramatic treatment. A detailed analysis of the body politic itself and a description of it in terms of contemporary Renaissance political thinking will follow. How this concept finds dramatic expression particularly in Shakespeare's Greek and Roman plays will be the purpose of the concluding chapters.

[28] Agnes Henneke, "Shakespeares englische Könige im Lichte staatsrechtlicher Strömungen seiner Zeit," *Shakespeare Jahrbuch*, LXVI (1930), 79; Grosse, *op. cit.*

[29] Sir Leslie Stephen, "Shakespeare as a Man," *Studies of a Biographer* (1907), IV, 1.

CHAPTER II

The State in Tudor Political
Thought and Discussion

SPECULATION about controversial political actualities in the six-teenth century was a matter of very real concern not only to theorists, but to all Englishmen whose material and spiritual welfare was vitally affected by the course of politics. Dramatic use of political theory in general and of the state-concept in particular was one manifestation of the active and widespread popular interest which Englishmen of the Renaissance took in problems of this sort. Some understanding of the nature of this interest, and of the circumstances of its popular expression, is essential, therefore, to an appreciation of the important influence which it had on the drama of the day.[1]

I

The idea of the state, as a fundamental concept of political theory, shared the popularity and attention enjoyed by the larger subject in the sixteenth century. And among the fields of intellectual activity in Tudor England few received more extensive development than po-litical theory. Such interest was largely the result, directly or indirectly, of the dictatorial rule which the Tudors established in their realm. The attempts of Henry VII to repair the ravages of one hundred years of civil war necessitated a consolidation of power in the throne which created an absolutism in government such as England had not experi-enced in centuries. The gains made by Henry VII in this respect were amplified during the reign of his son, who added supremacy in church

---

[1] In the present chapter I am indebted chiefly to J. W. Allen's *A History of Political Thought in the Sixteenth Century* (1928) and to his *English Political Thought, 1603 to 1660*, Vol. I (1938). Other general histories of political theory employed in this study will be found listed in the bibliography.

affairs to the powers of the crown, and were maintained with new additions during the reign of Elizabeth. This centralization of authority was not achieved without changes in the political, social, economic, and religious institutions of English life. And changes were not brought about without widespread controversy and debate which focused national attention on the issues at stake. Principally from attempts to justify or assail the policies of the Tudors arose the large body of sixteenth-century political theory.[2]

Such controversy and speculation found innumerable channels of expression in Tudor England. The bulk of the political writing in the period was concerned primarily with only one element in the state, namely, the governor, his position, authority and duties. Of such a nature were the principal writings of the Tudor proponents of absolute monarchy and their chief adversaries, the Jesuit and Calvinist advocates of limited, elective monarchy. That class of conduct literature concerned with the education of princes was also in this category. Embodying many of the attitudes and principles found in the foregoing works, but dealing more comprehensively with the state as a whole, are those political documents, prominent throughout the century, which attempt to portray an ideal commonwealth. But whatever their primary interest, common to all these types of Renaissance political literature as a starting point for discussion was a concept of the whole state, its structure and its purpose. Briefly suggested by some and fully described by others, it usually followed the same general pattern. It presented the state as a structure established by God or by natural reason, designed for the common good of all its members, governed by a sovereign authority, and composed of functionally determined ranks and degrees each of which, performing its appointed task, contributed to the welfare of the whole. In learned treatises and popular pamphlets alike this was the framework within which a variety of theories and attitudes were developed concerning such individual political problems as the authority of the king, the function of law, the duties of subjects, and the right of rebellion. Theorists disagreed in their conclusions regarding these particular problems, but with few exceptions they all accepted the same general pattern of the state. Almost

---

[2] See J. W. Allen, *A History of Political Thought in the Sixteenth Century*, pp. xiv–xv.

unanimously they acknowledged stratification and monarchy as essential to the structure of the state, obedience to vocation and order as essential to its successful operation, and common justice and welfare as its aim and purpose.

As has been suggested, this concept of organized society found its most complete expression in the type of literature which Professor Allen has labeled "the very and true commonweal." [3] As a genre it is best exemplified in the *Utopia* of Sir Thomas More (1516), the *Dialogue between Cardinal Pole and Thomas Lupset* by Thomas Starkey (c. 1538), and *The Way to Wealth* by Robert Crowley (1550). All of these works appeared before the mid-century mark, after which "the very and true commonweal" as a distinct genre begins to disappear. However, the theories of political and social purpose and organization which they embody remain fixed in the currents of political discussion.

Of the three works, More's *Utopia*, though most important for posterity, is of least importance as a clue to the characteristic thought of his own century. As Professor Allen concludes, More was isolated not only, or chiefly, by time.[4] In constructing a fantastic realm completely removed from the actual structure of Renaissance English society, More failed to impress his contemporaries as a serious commentator on social and political problems. Bodin's attitude toward utopian literature is typical of the age; he writes in Book I of the *République:*

Yet it is not our intent or purpose to figure out the only imaginary forme and idea of a commonwealth without effect, or substance, as have Plato, and Sir Thomas More Chancellor of England, vainly imagined; but so nere as we possibly can precisely to follow the best laws and rules of the most flourishing cities and commonweales.[5]

---

[3] *Ibid.*, Chapter III, "The Very and True Commonweal."

[4] *Ibid.*, p. 135. E. Routh in *Sir Thomas More and His Friends* (1934) observes that More himself recognized the impracticality of his plan and in general accepted the established order of monarchy and degrees in his political writings outside the *Utopia*. Cf. also Karl Kautsky, *Thomas More and His Utopia* (1927), pp. 125, 190.

[5] Jean Bodin, *The Six Bookes of a Commonweale* (1606), p. 3. John Hayward, in *An Answer to the First Part of a Certaine Conference Concerning Succession* (1603), p. 36, asks of his opponent, the Jesuit Robert Parsons, "But what a shame is it for us, to open our eares to these Utopicall state writers? who being mellowed in idleness, and having neither knowledge nor interest in matters of government, make new models upon disproportioned ioints, borrowed from nations most different in rule."

It is significant to observe, as does Professor Allen, that the extensive publication of the *Utopia* on the continent had no parallel in Tudor England.[6] Crowley and Starkey, on the other hand, were convinced "that the existing form of society must, substantially, be accepted."[7] In this respect their works are more representative; they discussed the principles and ideals of civil organization in terms of institutions and problems actually present in sixteenth-century England.

In their emphasis on order and degree, on vocation and obedience, these principles and ideals were, as Professor Allen points out, a heritage of medieval social and political thought:

It is true to say that under Henry VIII and Edward VI, there was formed a conception of what the commonwealth should be, or, if you like to put it so, of what it really is. It would be more fully true to say that medieval conceptions received at that time a fresh expression. The writers who furnished that expression were, in the main, reproducing medieval conceptions of the meaning and purpose of the social and political order, and of the duty of every man in his station to see to it that his activities were strictly related to that end.[8]

These doctrines, as manifested in Crowley and Starkey "and indicated and implied in many others,"[9] dealt with the stratified organization of society according to vocational classes, the obedience which each class should pay to those above it, and the functioning of each class, unselfishly and in Christian love for the good of the whole. The concept is summarized by Starkey when he writes:

As we may also see by commyn experyence, al laburys besnys, and trauayle of wyse men, handeled in matyrs of the commyn wel, are ever referryed to thys end and purpos, that the whole body of the commynalte may lyue in quyetnes and tranquylyte; every parte dowynge hys offyce and duty; and so much as the nature of man wyl suffer, al to attayne to theyr natural perfectyon.[10]

---

[6] Allen, *op. cit.*, p. 153, note 2.

[7] *Ibid.*, p. 153. "It is essentially this lack of faith in the possibility of actually constructing a very and a true commonwealth that isolates More and separates him from Crowley and Starkey."

[8] *Ibid.*, p. 134.   [9] *Ibid.*, p. 138.

[10] Thomas Starkey, *A Dialogue between Cardinal Pole and Thomas Lupset* (c. 1538), p. 5, "Early English Text Society," Extra Series, Vol. XXXII (1878).

Monarchy, as the form of government which keeps this state-society in order, was accepted at this time without much argument, although Crowley and Starkey differed, as did the proponents of absolutism and limited monarchy respectively, on the source and scope of the governing authority.[11]

"The very and true commonweal," as it was developed by English political thinkers in the Renaissance, was characterized, therefore, by social and economic elements as well as political.[12] The same basic principles can be traced in English discussions of state and society throughout the century. How these ideas appeared in the various streams of political thought will be suggested below. They are also apparent in the few late-century works whose primary interest is the whole nature of political society, notably Sir Thomas Smith's *The Commonwealth of England* (1589), William Blandy's *The Castle, or Picture of Pollicy* (1581), John Case's *Sphaera civitatis* (1588) and, to a degree, Bacon's *New Atlantis*. Bodin's "république bien ordonnée," in the principal elements of its outline, is not vastly different from the English concept of the state structure. Order, degree, vocation, authority and obedience are as essential in Bodin's theory of the state as they are in contemporary English conceptions.[13] Unlike Crowley and Starkey, who took government more or less for granted and discussed the body politic primarily in relation to social and economic problems, the later writers, possibly under the influence of classic theories, discussed political society in relation to the form of government best suited to its nature and purpose. The relative advantages of monarchy, aristocracy, and democracy emerge, therefore, as cardinal issues in the latter part of the century.[14] But the change is largely one of emphasis;

[11] Crowley asserted that the ruler is appointed by God and is responsible to none but Him; "For the king is Goddes minister to revenge the wronges done unto the innocent." (*The Way to Wealth*, 1550, p. 134, in *Select Works*, "Early English Text Society," Extra Series, Vol. XV.) Starkey, on the other hand, maintains that a ruler is subject to the will of those whom he governs, and may be deposed by them when he fails to govern justly according to the laws of his realm. (*Dialogue*, p. 167.)

[12] Allen, *op. cit.*, p. 134.

[13] Cf. Bodin, *op. cit.*, Book III, Chapter VIII, "Of the Orders and Degrees of Citizens."

[14] Bodin's primary concern in *The Six Bookes of a Commonweale*, for example, is with the nature of sovereignty in a state. Case considers at length the question,

throughout the period the problems of state theory remain essentially the same—the origin and purpose of the state, the nature of its structure, and the form of its government.

These works in the tradition of "the very and true commonweal" construct a pattern of political and social organization similar to the state-concept which appeared, in some degree, throughout English political thinking in the sixteenth century. In the larger body of thought, the concept played a role of unusual importance. For it was in relation to the welfare and maintenance of political society as so conceived that theories on the individual political problems of ruler, subject, law, church, rebellion and the like were developed and evaluated. Hence essentially the same description of the body politic is found at the outset of such otherwise divergent political treatises as Elyot's on the humanistic education of a prince, the Homily of 1571 on obedience and rebellion, the work of Parsons on limited elective monarchy and of Wentworth, Hayward and Craig on unlimited hereditary monarchy, and others too numerous to cite specifically. A brief review of these latter types of political argument will indicate the fundamental and widespread importance in Renaissance political thinking of the concept of a stratified, monarchic society.

Arguments for the unlimited and hereditary authority of kings and for passive obedience by subjects constitute by far the largest part of Tudor political expression. Because of the support it gave to the autocratic government characteristic of Renaissance states, this type of political argument came to be the theory officially adopted and encouraged by established authority. In England especially, thanks to Tudor patronage, the doctrines of absolutism were widely promulgated not only in political treatises, but in sermons, histories, plays, romances, and a variety of other media.[15] As a result of such diffusion the political

---

"An populus, vel tyrannus, divites, vel probi viri, optimus unus, vel lex rempublicam administrare debeat?" (*Sphaera civitatis*, 1588, p. 251.) Smith similarly considers the problem of government, discussing the relative merits of monarchy in its various forms, of aristocracy or oligarchy, and of democracy. (*The Commonwealth of England*, 1589, Chapters XII–XV in particular.)

[15] Sermons constitute one of the most important means of popular dissemination of these political concepts. *Fiftie . . . Sermones Divided into Five Decades*—or sets of sermons—by Henry Bullinger (translated in 1587), a disciple of Calvin, contain a complete exposition of the theories supporting absolutism, obedience, and related doc-

attitudes of the absolutists and the scriptural terminology they employed became the most familiar of the current modes of political thinking.

The principles of absolutism and obedience, though originally set forth by the early church fathers, were primarily the product of struggles for supremacy between secular and ecclesiastical power, and had their immediate origins in the medieval clash between empire and papacy.[16] The Reformation intensified the quarrel between national and papal authority and provided stimulus for further elaboration of royal authority not only in secular matters, but also in spiritual and ecclesiastical matters. The desire to throw off papal control, combined with the practical need for justifying *de facto* autocracy, kept officially inspired theorists at work throughout the sixteenth century. But from the advent of Luther until the last two decades of the century the advocates of authority and obedience added little to the fundamental doctrines established in the middle ages.[17]

These early exponents of royal absolutism, primarily concerned as

---

trines. See particularly the Second Decade: "Of Laws, and of the Law of Nature, Then of the Laws of Men." In 1586 at the Convocation of the Province of Canterbury Archbishop Whitgift introduced "Orders for the better increase of learning in the inferior ministers," which stipulated, among other things, that all ministers were to study Bullinger's *Decades* weekly and submit notes on them monthly. (*Decades*, Parker Society, 1849, Vol. I, Introduction, p. viii.) By such orders as these, preachers sent out all through England were well informed on matters of official political theory. Cf. also the officially inspired homily books noted below.

[16] Dante, for example, attempting to deny the secular authority of the Pope, argued that temporal power is delegated by God directly to the ruler of a state, and not indirectly through His spiritual vicar. (*De monarchia*, edited by Aurelia Henry, 1904, p. 206.) For more extended accounts of the development of concepts of royal sovereignty in this period see R. G. Gettell, *History of Political Thought* (1924), Chapter VI, and R. W. and A. J. Carlyle, *A History of Medieval Political Theory in the West* (1903-36), the most adequate treatment of the whole subject.

[17] These doctrines are based on the thirteenth chapter of Paul's epistle to the Romans, verses 1-5, which may be quoted in part to indicate the principal points in the absolutist's argument: "Let every soul be subject unto the higher powers. For there is no power but of God; the powers that be are ordained of God. Whosoever therefore resisteth the power, resisteth the ordinance of God: and they that resist shall receive to themselves damnation. . . . For he is the minister of God to thee for good. But if thou do that which is evil, be afraid; for he beareth not the sword in vain; for he is the minister of God, a revenger to execute wrath upon him that doeth evil. Wherefore ye must needs be subject, not only for wrath, but also for conscience sake."

they were with teaching obedience to constituted authority, gave little attention to the nature of that authority or to the political structure of which it was a part. The Homilies of 1547 [18] and Sir John Cheke's *Hurt of Sedicion* (1549) indicate, however, the presupposition of a stratified society governed by a single monarch, and the Homily of 1571 expands this concept.[19] After 1580, largely because of the influence of the French theorist Jean Bodin, the principles of absolutism were amplified into a more consistent and well-developed body of political theory. Bodin's *Six livres de la république* (1576) introduced concepts, drawn largely from classic thought, pertaining to the nature of the state and of sovereignty in the state, the type of government best suited to such a state, the restraints of law and custom on royal authority, and the hereditary nature of such authority.[20] As Professor Allen has pointed out, Bodin's influence was immediately manifested in England.[21] Among the most notable of Elizabethan treatises which show this influence are Merbury's *A Briefe Discourse of Royall Monarchie* (1581), Wentworth's *A Pithie Exhortation to Her Majestie for Establishing Her Successor to the Crowne* (1598), Hayward's *An Answer to . . . R. Doleman* [Robert Parsons?] (1603) and Craig's *Concerning the Right of Succession to the Kingdom of England* (1603). Although not directly in this tradition, Hooker's monumental *Of the Laws of Ecclesiastical Polity* (1594 *et seq.*) embodies a similarly expanded concept of the whole structure of states.[22]

Whenever a sovereign monarch claimed unrestricted authority for

[18] *Certayne Sermons or Homilies, Appoynted by the Kynges Maiestie to be Declared, and Redde by All Persones, Vicars, or Curates, Every Sundaye in Their Churches, Where They Have Cure* (1547). Most important among these is Homily X, "An Exhortation Concerning Good Order and Obedience," in which the order of degrees and vocations established by God is described as the basis of all organized human society. (See below, Chapter V.)

[19] *An Homilie agaynst Disobedience and Wylfull Rebellion* (issued singly, 1571). Here is a more elaborate account of social and political order in terms of the universal order established by God for all things. (See below, Chapter V.)

[20] Cf. Allen, *op. cit.*, Part III, Chapter VIII, "Jean Bodin."

[21] *Ibid.*, p. 250. "It would seem, indeed, that the publication of Bodin's *Republic* in 1576 must be seriously regarded as one cause of the new direction taken by thought in England towards the end of Elizabeth's reign."

[22] Book I, Chapter IX, "Human Laws of States and Societies," edited by Ronald Bayne, Everyman's Library (1907). Allen (*op. cit.*, p. 185) declares that Hooker owes little or nothing to Bodin, but rather "was intensely and typically English."

himself in all matters over his subjects, however, he was bound to encounter opposition minorities who evolved arguments designed to protect their rights and limit the power of the ruler. From such circumstances arose the theories of restricted monarchy, popular sovereignty, and the right of rebellion which characterize Jesuit and Presbyterian attitudes toward Tudor political problems.

The concept of a ruler whose authority is subject to the sovereign will of the people of a state and limited by the laws of God and man had figured prominently in Greek and Roman political thinking and remained the dominant theory of medieval Europe.[23] In the latter period it was the particular doctrine of the papacy in its struggle against the rising power of temporal rulers, for as Baker points out, "Monarchy limited by the people was a powerful buttress to monarchy limited by the church; and *libertas populi* and *libertas ecclesiae* were good allies." [24]

Baker's statement applies fundamentally to the attitude of sixteenth-century religious minorities and the political theories which they developed in an attempt to resist royally imposed creeds and churches. Catholic and Protestant minorities argued along different lines but had come by the end of the century to basically similar conclusions.[25] They

[23] "The theory, if not the practice, of the consent of the governed, insofar as the governed were Roman citizens, was preserved in ancient Rome. Law itself became more and more the orders of the ruler. . . . Nevertheless this was qualified by the statement that the ruler received his authority to make law by the *lex regia;* and *lex* . . . was the enactment of popular legislative bodies. If the qualification was easily forgotten, the principle was nevertheless admitted, and at a later date was to be revived as the legal basis for theories of consent." (Thomas Cook, *History of Political Philosophy,* 1936, p. 150.) Of the prominence of this doctrine in the middle ages Carlyle writes, "We venture to say . . . that the proper character of the political civilization of the Middle Ages is to be found in the principle that all political authority, whether that of the law or of the ruler, is derived from the whole community, that there is no other source of political authority, and that the ruler, whether emperor or king, not only held an authority which was derived from the community, but held this subject to that law which was the embodiment of the life and will of the community." (*A History of Medieval Political Theory in the West,* V, 474–75.)

[24] E. Baker, in F. J. C. Hearnshaw (editor), *The Social and Political Ideas of Some Great Medieval Thinkers* (1923), Introduction, p. 22.

[25] Jesuit theorists in the sixteenth century stressed the contractual right of popular sovereignty and of limited monarchy. "The divine right of kings, the chief theoretical basis for secular sovereignty at the time, was held to be erroneous. The king was merely a delegate of his people and of God. The sovereignty of the people was pro-

asserted that rulers exercise authority as the result of a contract, by which the sovereignty belonging to a people is transferred to one man on condition that he fulfill specified obligations and respect the laws of God, of nature, and of the state which he governs. His abrogation of the contract entitles the people to revoke their delegated authority, remove and punish the offender, and grant the ruling power to another.

Opponents of absolutism, although they differed on the source and scope of the ruler's authority, agreed with their adversaries that monarchy was the form of government best suited to the purpose and structure of the state. The Calvinists and the Jesuits alike stress order and degree in the social structure and monarchy in the government of a state as strongly as does any defender of absolutism. Thus Knox, in his *First Blast of the Trumpet against the Monstrous Regiment of Women* (1558), reiterates ideas found frequently in his political arguments, when he describes the order of degrees and vocations which constitute a political society, and draws an illuminating analogy between the body of the state and the body of the individual man.[26] The Calvinist John Ponet, in his *Short Treatise of Politike Power* (1556), defended this concept of political society and monarchic government,[27] as did Buchanan in *De iure regni apud Scotos* (1579).[28] The Jesuit Robert Parsons held similar convictions; an entire chapter of the *Conference about the Next Succession to the Crowne of England* (1594), a work generally attributed to him, is devoted to a defense of monarchic

---

claimed as part of the law of peoples, which sprang from the law of nature and was based on custom and consent." (Cook, *op. cit.*, p. 351.) The Calvinists, however, in the beginning at least, emphasized the divine right of popular resistance and limited monarchy. John Knox, for example, believed that the state was divinely ordained and that the authority of the ruler was directly delegated by God; thus far he closely agreed with the absolutists. But Knox asserts that this authority is revoked by God and that the people have the right and obligation to depose such a ruler when the conditions upon which God delegated His power are violated. Cf. *An Apology for the Protestants in Prison at Paris* (1557), *Works*, edited by Laing, IV, 297. Later in the century, however, Puritan writers began to incorporate the contractual theory of the Jesuits into their own arguments. Buchanan's *De iure regni apud Scotos* (1579) clearly reveals this trend. As Professor Gerig points out, Estienne La Boetie's *Le Contr'Un*, written before 1568 and published after his death by Montaigne, possibly exerted some influence on English theories of the right of rebellion.

[26] *Works*, edited by Laing, IV, 390.   [27] 1642 edition, p. 3.
[28] Translated by "Philalethes," 1689, pp. 7–9.

government and a stratified society of naturally ordained vocations and degrees.[29] These writers aroused the antagonism of proponents of royal absolutism because of the limitations which the former placed on the king and because of the liberties which they granted subjects—not because they rejected the essential order and elements of the state.

Meantime, the humanistic "institution" of princes was expounding a concept of the state similar in essentials to that found in politico-theological discussion. Sixteenth-century interest in the "institution" does not represent so much the recovery of a lost classic genre as the renewal of interest in a form showing a continuous history through the middle ages from Greek and Roman times.[30] Its main features, as Dr. Born indicates in his survey of the type, remained fundamentally unaltered from their initial appearance in Isocrates' *To Nicoles* down through the period with which this study is concerned. The basic outline begins with a brief résumé of the purpose and nature of the state. A defense of monarchy as the form of government best suited to the state as so defined leads to a discussion of the duties and qualities desirable in the head of such a government. The exposition is generally developed around the four cardinal virtues of classic moral philosophy, justice, fortitude, temperance and prudence. Medieval "mirrors for princes" added to these the three Christian virtues of faith, hope, and charity. Emphasis is placed on the evils of flattery, to which a prince is especially susceptible, and copious advice is given regarding the choice and use of counselors. The military duties of a prince generally figure in the discussion, and among the more advanced thinkers, notably Aristotle, the duties pertaining to the economic administration of a realm are suggested to the ruler. Finally, to emphasize by contrast the nature and function of an ideal prince, the writers of "institutions" define in detail the character and conduct of a tyrant.

First and most important among such works in the Renaissance was Erasmus' *The Education of a Christian Prince*, written for the young prince who was to become Charles V, and published in 1516. It aroused widespread and lasting interest; Sir Thomas More wrote to Erasmus,

---

[29] Chapter II, "Of the Forme of Monarchies and Kingdoms in Particular." See Allen, *op. cit.*, p. 260, for the attribution, generally accepted, of "Doleman's" work to Robert Parsons.

[30] This history is traced by Lester K. Born in the Introduction to his edition, published in 1936, of Erasmus, *The Education of a Christian Prince* (1516).

"You have done well in writing on the instruction of a Christian prince. How I wish Christian princes would follow good instructions. Everything is upset by their mad follies." [31] And as if following the implication in More's words, Erasmus promptly sent a copy of his work to Henry VIII.[32] The *Education* went through numerous editions in the sixteenth century [33] and was frequently drawn upon and referred to by subsequent writers of similar treatises. Thus the greatest English example of the genre, Sir Thomas Elyot's *The Boke Named the Gouernour* (1531), not only drew heavily on Erasmus, but openly acknowledged the debt and recommended the *Education* to all princes and their tutors.[34] A complete treatise on princeship, closely following in form and substance the traditional model, was inserted by Castiglione in Book IV of *Il Cortegiano* in 1528,[35] and became, through Thomas Hoby's translation in 1561, an important source of ideals of kingship in England. As a result of the popularity of these three works the outline and concepts of the "institution" came to be firmly established in the political thinking of Renaissance Europe. In England translations and original works contributed to the spread of such ideals of kingship. The treatise by Tigurinus Chelidonius, *A Most Excellent Historie of the Institution and First Beginning of Christian Princes and the Originall of Kingdomes* . . . , translated in 1571, followed the familiar outline, and in 1580 appeared a translation of *To Nicoles*, the prototype of the genre, in Isocrates' *A Perfite Looking Glasse for All Estates*. William Alexander's *A Paraenesis to the Prince* (1604),

[31] Quoted by Born, *op. cit.*, p. 27.   [32] *Ibid.*, p. 28.

[33] See *Bibliotheca Erasmiana*, Ghent, 1893. Forty-three editions of the *Education* were published in Europe before 1584.

[34] Sir Thomas Elyot, *The Boke Named the Gouernour* (1531), p. 48, edited by Foster Watson, Everyman's Library (1907): "It wolde nat be forgoten that the lytell boke of the most excellent doctour Erasmus Roterodamus, (whiche he wrate to Charles, nowe beynge emperour and then prince of Castile) whiche booke is intituled the Institution of a christen prince, wolde be as familyare alwaye with gentilmen, at all tymes, and in euery age, as was Homere with the great king Alexander, or Xenophon with Scipio; for as all men may iuge that haue radde that warke of Erasmus, that there was neuer boke written in latine that, in so lytle a portion, contayned of sentence, eloquence, and vertuous exhortation, a more compendious abundance."

[35] Baldassare Castiglione, *The Book of the Courtier*, pp. 273–93, translated by Sir Thomas Hoby (1561), edited by W. B. Drayton Henderson, Everyman's Library (1928).

Barnabe Barnes's *Foure Bookes of Offices* . . . (1606), George More's *Principles for Yong Princes* . . . (1611), and Francis Bacon's *XVI Propositions Concerning the Raign and Government of a King* (1647) are later examples of political treatises which carry on in many respects the traditions and ideals established by the classic "institution."

Practically all these Renaissance educators of princes follow the classic model and incorporate some discussion of the nature and structure of political societies into the opening sections of their treatises. Consistently the body politic which they describe is a stratified society controlled by one sovereign governor. Readers of Elyot's *Boke Named the Gouernour* will recall, for example, the elaborate analogies with the beehive which he draws in an attempt to make clear his theory of the state.[36] In their insistence on vocation, order and degree, and monarchy, these political and social ideals appearing in the treatises reveal their fundamental similarity to the concept of the state which seems basic in the greater part of Tudor political theorizing. The unanimity of the "institutions" on this point will become evident in the following pages of this study.

The realist Machiavelli drew no such ideal picture of the state as is found in the classic institution, but in his insistence on a strong ruler obligated to keep subjects in their proper places he gave support to the monarchic concept fundamental in Tudor theories of the state. Where his own writings were known, the Florentine was recognized as an advocate of resolution, promptness, and severity in government for the good of the commonwealth. According to his view, the prince is not to concern himself with traditional moral and ethical standards of private conduct, as are the princes described by Erasmus and Elyot. For Machiavelli believed that human nature is essentially bad and requires any means, even force if necessary, to keep it in line. Machiavelli's prince is rather to substitute the higher and more realistic standard of morality, the welfare of the state and the common benefit of all its citizens.[37] Machiavelli agreed, therefore, with more idealistic

[36] Elyot, *op. cit.*, p. 9.

[37] "Therefore a prince, so long as he keeps his subjects united and loyal, ought not to mind the reproach of cruelty; because with a few examples he will be more merciful than those who, through too much mercy, allow disorders to arise, from which follow murder or robbery; for these are wont to injure the whole people,

theorists of the Renaissance that the good of society must be the first consideration of every individual in it. The influence of Machiavelli's ideas about monarchy and the supremacy of the state must, however, insofar as Tudor England is concerned, be considered slight. There is evidence, in editions, translations, and scattered references, that the true Machiavelli was known in sixteenth-century England.[38] But the investigations of Meyer and Praz establish beyond question the fact that this knowledge was overshadowed to a great extent by the influence of "machiavellism," the popular concept of what the Florentine represented.[39] According to this impression, fostered by Innocent Gentillet's *Discours sur les moyens de bien gouverner et maintenir en bonne paix un royaume . . . contre N. Machiavel* which appeared in Paris in 1576, Machiavelli was an exponent of a villainous, atheistical tyranny designed solely for the malicious pleasure and selfish advancement of the prince.

As the common concern of practically all schools of thought, therefore, the concept of the state received its share of the attention devoted to political theory in the sixteenth century. And the interest was by no means confined to the abstract treatises reviewed above, extensive as such expression was. Political actualities such as state control of religion, women on the throne, frequent rebellion, and the choice of Elizabeth's successor vitally touched the welfare of every Englishman and gave him cause for real and lively interest in the theories and principles involved in these problems. The popular concern with theories of government which such issues aroused was nourished by dissemination of political ideas through a number of popular channels; as has been suggested, sermons, pamphlets, and other media served to familiarize the general public with the concepts and terminology of

---

whilst those executions which originate with the prince offend the individual only." (Machiavelli, *The Prince*, p. 133, translated by W. K. Marriott, Everyman's Library, 1908.) "For that reason, let a prince have the credit of conquering and holding his state, the means will always be considered honest, and he will be praised by everybody." (*Ibid.*, p. 144.)

[38] See J. W. Horrocks, *Machiavelli in Tudor Opinion and Discussion* (1908), and L. A. Weissberger, "Machiavelli and Tudor England," *Political Science Quarterly,* XLII (1927). Among the more prominent Elizabethan men of letters apparently familiar with Machiavelli's works were Spenser, Raleigh, and Chapman.

[39] E. Meyer, *Machiavelli and the Elizabethan Drama* (1897); Mario Praz, "Machiavelli and the Elizabethans," *Proceedings of the British Academy* (1928).

political thinking. Among the manifestations of this lay concern with political theory the drama, for reasons now to be described, was one of the most significant.

2

In order to understand how and why this very real interest in problems of political theory was reflected in the drama, it is necessary to discuss the role played by history in political thinking. By theorists of all schools, history was regarded as the final and authoritative textbook of political science. In history's account of the rise and fall of nations, men could discover the principles which controlled the destiny of states. Professor Lily B. Campbell, writing of "Elizabethan Historical Patterns," remarks that

it is necessary to remember that history during the Tudor-Stuart period was increasingly consulted for its political precedents, not only in the law courts, but also in everyday life. Nations and rulers might, it was believed, perceive in history the path of political virtue that led to national peace and prosperity.[40]

The method employed in this use of history was more often deductive than inductive. In general theorists sought to draw from history examples supporting preconceived doctrines, rather than to formulate doctrines on the basis of historical evidence. As Elyot wrote of those who criticize history as "leasinges and fantisies," "Lete them revolve in their myndes generally that there is no doctrine, be it eyther diuine or humaine, that is not eyther all expressed in historie or at the leste mixte with historie."[41] Thus proponents of absolutism and passive obedience cited cases from history to prove that nations prosper under these conditions alone.[42] Defenders of limited monarchy found

[40] L. B. Campbell, "The Use of Historical Patterns in the Reign of Elizabeth," *Huntington Library Quarterly*, I (1938), 137.

[41] Elyot, *op. cit.*, pp. 280–81.

[42] Cf., for example, Thomas Craig, *Concerning the Right of Succession to the Kingdom of England . . .* (1703), p. 65: "I have brought these historical Instances, for these Electors to ruminate on, and all such as desire above all things, to Alter and Subvert the present Constitution and Government of the Kingdom, and of an Hereditary to make an Elective Monarchy, that they may be convinced that such Innovations may happen not only to fall short of their expectations, but also may be of very Fatal consequences to themselves and Families, and that at the last, they may

equally authoritative precedent for successful resistance to established government.[43] History, therefore, was employed to show that nations and rulers conforming to the particular theories of the writer enjoyed prosperity and success, while those failing to conform met with disaster.

Sixteenth-century political theory, primarily interested in the nature and duties of rulers, used history for the most part as a "mirror for magistrates" showing the principles involved in the rise and fall of noble men.[44] But history was also recognized as a mirror for states. Elyot writes:

For it nat onely reporteth the gestes or actes of princes or capitaynes . . . but also it bringeth to our knowledge the fourmes of sondry publike weales with augmentations and decayes and occasion thereof; . . .[45]

Amyot's preface to Plutarch's *Lives,* translated in 1579 by North, clearly states the same purpose of history:

To be short, it may be truly sayd, that the reading of histories, is the schole of wisedome, to facion mens understanding, by considering advisedly the state of the world that is past, and by marking diligently by what lawes, maners and discipline, Empires, Kingdomes and dominions, have in old time bene stablished and afterward maintayned and increased: or contrariwise changed, diminished and overthrown.[46]

This emphasis on historical exemplification of theories of political society in one of Shakespeare's most important source books is of par-

come to read their Sin in their Punishment, when God who is a most just Judge, takes Vengeance on them, for violating the Fundamental Constitution of the Kingdom."

[43] Cf., for example, Parsons, *op. cit.,* Chapter III, "Of Kings Lawfully Chastised by their Commonwealths for their misgovernment, and of the good and prosperous success that God commonly hath given to the same."

[44] The most illustrious example is, of course, *The Mirror for Magistrates,* publication of which began in 1559 and continued through the remainder of the century and beyond. See *The Mirror for Magistrates,* edited by L. B. Campbell, 1938.

[45] Elyot, *op. cit.,* p. 281.

[46] Plutarch, *The Lives of the Noble Grecians and Romans,* I, xviii. Cf. also Federico Furio Ceriol, *A Very Briefe and Profitable Treatise Declaring Howe Many Counsells, and What Manner of Counsellors a Prince That Will Governe Well Ought to Have* (translated c. 1570), Sig. F, 1 v: "Also he [the counsellor] knoweth the best waye of government, belonging to a commonwealth or kingdome, and how to maintaine the same, and to encrease the power thereof, by reason that he hadde read of so manye common wealthes and kingdomes, and knowne by what meanes they have increased, or decayed."

ticular interest. Similar attitudes on the function of history in relation to the state continued beyond the turn of the century. In *The First Part of the Historie of England,* first printed in 1612, Samuel Daniel writes:

For had we the perticuler occurents of all ages, and all nations, it might more stuffe but not better our understanding. We shall find still the same correspondencies to hold in the actions of men: Virtues and Vices the same, though rising and falling, according to the worth, or weaknesse of Governors: the causes of the ruines and mutations of states to be alike: and the trayne of affaires carried by precedent, in a course of Succession under like colours.[47]

History served, then, as a collection of exempla illustrating, among other political problems, the concept of state basic in sixteenth-century political thinking. It seems evident that what was true in this respect of historical writing in general was true of historical drama. By dramatist and theorist alike, political characters and situations drawn from the past were presented in relation to a preconceived ideal of the purpose and nature of civil society; on the stage, as on the printed page, history revealed the political prosperity which resulted when men acted according to the accepted principles, and the political ruin which resulted when they disregarded them.

In this way drama came to reflect the active contemporary interest in political theory and to embody the concepts and doctrines involved in that interest. History, and the way in which it was read in the Renaissance, turned the attention of playwright and audience alike to these principles. Such treatment of problems of states had been established in the tradition of Tudor drama since Bale's *King Johann* brought the political issues of the Reformation to the stage. *Gorboduc,* to recall to the reader only one of many familiar examples, emphasizes explicitly throughout its action the perils of an undetermined succession and of a divided kingdom.[48] The extensive survey by Dr. Grosse shows clearly how the number and nature of political concepts employed in

[47] Samuel Daniel, *The First Part of the Historie of England,* in *Complete Works,* edited by A. B. Grosart, 1896, IV, 86. (Quoted by L. B. Campbell, "The Use of Historical Patterns in the Reign of Elizabeth," p. 139.)

[48] See S. A. Small, "The Political Import of the Norton Half of 'Gorboduc,'" *PMLA,* XLVI (1931), 641–46.

Renaissance drama reflect current attitudes and interests.[49] That the exposition of such doctrines was considered suitable dramatic material not only by playwrights, but by critics of the drama as well, is indicated in the well-known passage from Heywood's *Apology for Actors* (1612), where education in political theory is used as a point in defense of the drama. Plays, he observes,

are writ with this aim, and carried with this method, to teach . . . subjects true obedience to their king, to show people the untimely ends of such as have moved tumults, commotions and insurrections, to present them with the flourishing estate of such as live in obedience, exhorting them to obedience, dehorting them from all traitorous and felonious stratagems.[50]

And as a modern critic of Renaissance drama concludes:

Denn über die politische-historische Signierung des Stoffes hinaus wurde der Dramatiker Verkünder eines Staatsideales, das im engsten Zusammenhalte mit der zeitgenössischen Theorie in der Staatstätigkeit der Tudors und Stuarts seine Verwirklichung gefunden hatte.[51]

In the light of this fundamental relationship between political theory and history, therefore, plays based on historical subjects, whether Grecian, Roman, or English, would be expected to reveal a deeper purpose and significance than mere theatrical representation of past events.[52] In structure and in development such plays are, indeed, profoundly influenced by a desire on the part of the dramatist to indicate, as did the political theorist, how history demonstrates the truth of political principles which held real and vital interest for Tudor England. Just as Tudor ideas about private ethics and morality are essential to the nature of Elizabethan tragedy and make it the profound philosophical expression it is recognized to be, so Tudor ideas about public ethics and morality, or political conduct, endow historical drama with similar

[49] F. Grosse, "Das englische Renaissancedrama im Spiegel zeitgenössischer Staatstheorien" (1935).
[50] Thomas Heywood, *An Apology for Actors,* 1612. Reprinted in "Shakespeare Society Publications," III (1841), 53.
[51] Grosse, *op. cit.,* p. 95.
[52] The whole problem of the relation of political theory to the history play is an enormous and significant one which has scarcely been touched in these pages. An investigation of the subject suitable to its importance and scope is at present being undertaken by Professor L. B. Campbell.

philosophical significance and are essential to an interpretation and appreciation of the type. Such, I believe, is the source and function of those principles which Sir Mark Hunter has in mind when he writes: "To the study of history for the stage Shakespeare brought—I think there can be no doubt—certain fixed political beliefs and convictions, which can, with no great difficulty, be determined." [53] Such, moreover, is the source and function of the fundamental concept of the state which Professor Charlton finds inherent in the dramatic structures of Shakespeare's "political plays."

[53] Sir Mark Hunter, "Politics and Character in Shakespeare's 'Julius Caesar,'" *Essays by Divers Hands*, X (1931), p. 110.

CHAPTER III

Universal Law and the Origin and Purpose
of Political Society

THEORIES of political society were developed in the Renaissance for the primary purpose of showing how actual states should be organized and maintained. As Thomas Starkey wrote in dedicating his *Dialogue* to Henry VIII:

I perceyue your highnesse now nothing more curith and hath in mynd than the extyrpatyon of all abuses both in custome and law by processe of time growen in here in this your commonwelth, by the reson whereof grete hope I have onys yet to see that veray and true commyn wel whereof I have with myselfe fansied here in your reame to have place.[1]

But in order to make such concepts of the "very and true commonweal" effective as criteria, it was necessary for theorists to ascribe to them some sanction which would give them the force of authority. Writers had to indicate not only how men should organize and conduct themselves in their group life, but also why they were obligated to conform to this pattern of political society. To achieve the latter end, Renaissance-thinkers evolved a comprehensive philosophy of the origin and purpose of civil life and its relation to the laws of God and nature. The political thinking of the day insisted that the pattern of society is a part of a universal plan designed for the highest welfare of man. Because of its place in the divine scheme of things the structure of the state, as generally set forth in sixteenth-century political writing, received a superhuman authority which made it the only acceptable form of social and political organization.

I

In order to understand this authority it is essential to understand the various concepts of law as they were involved in Renaissance think-

[1] Starkey, *A Dialogue between Cardinal Pole and Thomas Lupset*, p. lxxiv, "Early English Text Society," Extra Series, Vol. XXXII (1878).

ing about the nature of political society. Law was generally defined in the sixteenth century, as it had been in the middle ages, as the means whereby an action is directed to a good end. As Hooker expressed it, "A law therefore generally taken, is a directive rule unto goodness of operation." [2] Laws were classified according to the type of action which they affected. Thus laws which direct universal action, including the action of God Himself, were termed the laws eternal; those which direct the action of natural objects were termed the laws natural; those pertaining to the salvation of man's soul were designated the laws divine, and those applying to his civil life, the laws human; those affecting the relationships between societies were called the laws of nations.[3] Except for occasional variations in terminology, these categories, inherited largely from medieval legal terminology, remained fairly constant throughout the century. They receive their clearest expression in the first book of Hooker's *Of the Laws of Ecclesiastical Polity* (1594), but essentially the same principles were expounded as early as 1530 in Christopher Saint German's *The Dialogues in English betweene a Doctor of Divinity and a Student in the Laws of England*. In varying degrees of detail, Bullinger,[4] Musculus,[5] Hayward,[6] Fulbecke [7] and others considered the nature and types of law in the course of the century.

[2] Hooker, *Of the Laws of Ecclesiastical Polity*, I, 177, Everyman's Library (1907).

[3] *Ibid.*, I, 154–55: "Now that law which, as it is laid up in the bosom of God, they call Eternal, receiveth according unto the different kinds of things which are subject unto it different and sundry kinds of names. That part of it which ordereth natural agents we call usually Nature's law; that which Angels do clearly behold and without any swerving observe is a law Celestial and heavenly; the law of Reason that which bindeth creatures reasonable in this world, and with which by reason they may most plainly perceive themselves bound; that which bindeth them, and is not known but by special revelation from God, Divine law; Human law, that which out of the law either of reason or of God men probably gathering to be expedient, they make it a law."

[4] Henry Bullinger, *Fiftie . . . Sermones*, Vol. I, *The Second Decade of Sermons*, "Of Laws, and of the law of Nature, then of the laws of men," edited for the Parker Society.

[5] Wolfgang Musculus, *Commonplaces of Christian Religion*, translated by J. Man (1563). Musculus, born in Lorraine in 1497, was a zealous Protestant theologian often referred to as "the little Luther." He died in Berne in 1563.

[6] John Hayward, *An Answer to the First Part of a Certaine Conference Concerning Succession* (1603).

[7] William Fulbecke, *The Pandectes of the Law of Nations* (1602).

According to these theorists, the supreme law of the universe is the law eternal, which was defined as the will, wisdom, and reason of God. Saint German wrote: "And forasmuch as almighty god is the creator and maker of all creatures, . . . so the reason and the wisdom of God, moving all thinges by wisedome made to a goode ende, obtaineth the name and reason of a law, and that is called the lawe eternall." [8] To this law all things are subject, even, though voluntarily, the Creator Himself, for as Hooker stated: "The rule of divine operations outward, is the definitive appointment of God's own wisdom set down within himself." [9] That is, God establishes His own wisdom as the rule to direct to a good end His actions in establishing and maintaining all things.

When the law eternal manifests itself as the guiding rule in the actions of natural objects, whether animate or inanimate, it is known as the law of nature or, when pertaining particularly to human nature, the law of reason. Hooker makes clear the distinction in the law of nature when he writes:

Wherefore to come to the law of nature: albeit thereby we sometimes mean that manner of working which God hath set for each created thing to keep; yet forasmuch as those things are termed most properly natural agents, which keep the law of their kind unwittingly, as the heavens and elements of the world, which can do no otherwise than they do; and forasmuch as we give unto intellectual natures the name of Voluntary agents, that so we may distinguish them from the other; expedient it will be, that we sever the law of nature observed by the one from that which the other is tied unto.[10]

In either case, however, the law of nature was defined as the natural instinct which guides the actions of created things toward a good end. But it was this law as manifest in human nature, the law of reason, which chiefly interested political thinkers of the Renaissance. Saint German speaks of it in the following terms:

And this law is alway good and righteous, stirring and enclynyng a man to good, and abhorring evil. . . . And it is written in the hart of every man teaching him what is to be done and what is to be fled. And because

---

[8] Saint German, *Dialogues* (edition of 1580), fol. 2 v.
[9] Hooker, *op. cit.*, I, 177.   [10] *Ibid.*, p. 155.

it is written in the hart, therefore it may not be put away, ne it is never chaungeable by no diversitie of place ne time. And therefore agaynst thys lawe, prescriptyon, statute, nor custome may not prevayle. And if any bee brought in agaynst it, they bee no prescriptyones, statutes, nor customes, but thinges voyd and against Iustice. And all other lawes, as well the lawes of God as to the acts of men, as other be grounded thereuppon.[11]

The law of nature or reason, then, was identified with conscience. Bullinger says explicitly that "The law of nature is an instruction of the conscience, and, as it were, a certain direction placed by God himself in the minds and hearts of men, to teach them what they have to do, and what to eschew," [12] and Musculus similarly defines the law as "that light and iudgement of reason, whereby we doe discerne betwixt good and evil." [13] Hayward reveals more clearly the specific injunctions commonly recognized as inherent in natural law. He writes:

God in the creation of man, imprinted certaine rules within his soule, to direct him in all the actions of his life: which rules, because we took them when we took our being, are commonly called the primarie law of nature: of which sort the canon accompt these precepts following. To worship God: to obey parents and governors, and thereby conserve common society: lawful coniunction of men and women: succession of children: education of children: acquisition of things which pertaine to no man: equall libertie of all: to communicate commodities: to repell force: to hurt no man and generally to do another as he would be done unto: which is the sum and substance of the second table of the decalogue.[14]

Hooker agreed with this and wrote that the whole substance of the law of reason could be summed up in the commandments, Love God and love thy neighbor.[15]

When the law eternal is discovered by reason in the actions of men, it is the law natural. But some aspects of the law eternal, especially those pertaining to the injunction that man love God, cannot be so determined. These are made known only through divine revelation, as in the Scriptures, and are known accordingly as the laws divine, or the laws of God. These laws, moreover, direct the actions leading to

[11] Saint German, *op. cit.*, fol. 4 r.
[12] Bullinger, *op. cit.*, I, 194.
[13] Musculus, *op. cit.*, fol. 29 v.
[14] Hayward, *op. cit.*, Sig. A, 4 r.
[15] Hooker, *op. cit.*, I, 183.

the felicity not of this life, but of the life eternal. Saint German makes clear in the following passage how the law of God differs from eternal and natural laws:

And this law of reason differeth from the law of God in two maners. For the lawe of God is given by revelation of God, and this law is geven by a natural light of understanding. And also the law of God ordereth a man of it selfe by a nigh way to the felicity that ever shal endure. And the law of reason ordereth a man to the felicity of this life.[16]

Bullinger similarly distinguished the law of God from other types of law,[17] but again Hooker must be referred to for the clearest definition; he writes:

We see, therefore, that our sovereign good is desired naturally; that God the author of that naturall desire had appointed natural means whereby to fulfill it; that man having utterly disabled his nature unto those means hath had other revealed from God, and hath received from heaven a law to teach him how that which is desired naturally must now supernaturally be attained.[18]

The laws of nature enable man to attain sensual and intellectual felicity, but to attain the highest good, which is spiritual, these laws are not enough and must be supplemented by the law of God, which is revealed to man in the written word of God.

Those elements of the law eternal which, as made manifest in the law of nature, pertain to the injunction that men love their neighbors and establish common society, were variously called by Renaissance theorists the law human, civil or positive, or the law of man. This is the law which, as Hooker says, men "make by composition for multi-

[16] Saint German, *op. cit.*, fol. 4 v.

[17] Bullinger, *op. cit.*, I, 209; "The law of God, openly published and proclaimed by the Lord our God himself, setteth down ordinary rules for us to know what we have to do, and what to leave undone, requiring obedience, and threatening utter destruction to disobedient rebels. This law is divided into the moral, ceremonial, and judicial laws. . . . The moral law is that which teacheth men manners, and layeth down before us the shape of virtue; declaring therewithal how great righteousness, godliness, obedience, and perfectness God looketh for at the hands of us mortal men. The ceremonial laws are they which are given concerning the order of holy and ecclesiastical rites and ceremonies. . . . Last of all the judicial laws give rules concerning matters to be judged of between man and man, for the preservation of public peace, equity, and civil honesty."

[18] Hooker, *op. cit.*, I, 212.

tudes and politic societies of men to be guided by"; [19] that is, the law of man comprises the specific rules which direct the social actions of men in conformity with the general ordinance of nature that men live together in brotherly love. Civil laws, therefore, receive their life and force from the higher universal laws, and must be agreeable to these latter precepts to be valid. As Saint German expresses it:

> The law of man the which sometime is called the lawe positive, is derived by reason as a thing which is necessarily and probably following the lawe of reason and of the lawe of god. . . . And therefore the lawes of princes, the commandements of prelates, the statutes of comminalties, ne yet the ordinance of the Church, is not righteous nor obligatory, but it be consonant to the law of God.[20]

All civil laws, therefore, must be of such a nature that they direct the actions of men in society not only to the sensual and intellectual perfection ordained by the law of nature, but to the spiritual perfection required by the law of God.

Finally, there is the law of nations, which, according to Thomas Floyd in *The Picture of a Perfit Commonwealth* (1600), "no otherwise may be described than of customes, maners, and prescriptions, which is of like condition to all people." [21] These are the elements of the laws eternal and natural which pertain particularly to the actions and relationships of the nations of the earth. Such elements comprise the *jus gentium* or law of peoples, and were defined in the Renaissance as "rules common to the laws of all nations." Generally the law of nations was identified with certain long-established and universally accepted customs, such as the prohibition against human slavery. Thus Hayward defines it as follows:

> Out of these precepts of the law of nature are formed certaine customes, generally observed in all parts of the world: which, because they were not from the beginning, but brought in afterwards, some as a consequence or collection, others as a practice or execution of the first natural precepts, are called the secondarie law of nature, and by manie also the law of nations.[22]

---

[19] *Ibid.*, I, 224.   [20] Saint German, *op. cit.*, fol. 7 r.

[21] Pages 61–62. Cf. also Fulbecke, *The Pandectes of the Law of Nations* (1602). The classic treatment of the subject in the Renaissance is, of course, in Alberico Gentili's *De jure belli libri tres* (1612).

[22] Hayward, *op. cit.*, Sig. A, 4 r.

Hooker's conception of the law of nations is basically the same, but in his definition of it he limits the term to those practices now known more specifically as international law. Thus he writes:

Primary laws of nations are such as concern embassage, such as belong to the courteous entertainment of foreigners and strangers, such as serve for commodious traffick, and the like. Secondary laws in the same kind are such as this present unquiet world is most familiarly acquainted with; I mean laws of arms, which yet are much better known than kept.[23]

In sixteenth-century thought, then, the actions of all things in the universe, including man and his political society, were held to be directed by a highly integrated system of laws. "See we not plainly," writes Hooker, "that obedience of creatures unto the law of nature is the stay of the whole world?" [24] The concept of all-embracing law was frequently expressed by referring to laws as the "sinews" whereby universal action received force and direction.[25] Because the laws of nature, God, man, and nations are merely manifestations of the one supreme law eternal, and because "all other laws do thereon depend," [26] the whole system possesses a unity of purpose. This purpose is to direct all things to the highest good for which they were particularly ordained.

2

Because its origin is directed by the law of nature and its operation is directed by the subsidiary laws of man, the institution of political society possesses an authority founded in the will of God which makes acceptance of it obligatory for all men.[27] The authority of the body politic and the link between human civil life and the universal plan which provides such sanction was demonstrated by Renais-

[23] Hooker, op. cit., I, 199.   [24] Ibid., p. 157.

[25] Cf. for example Sir John Fortesque, A Learned Commendation of the Politique Lawes of England, translated by R. Mulcaster (1567), fol. 31 r: "Furthermore the lawe under the which a multitude of men is made a people, representeth the semblance of synews in ye body natural Because that lyke as by synews the ioynyng of the bodie is made sounde so by the lawe which taketh the name a ligando yt is to witte of byndynge suche a misticall bodie is knytt and preserved together."

[26] Hooker, op. cit., I, 158.

[27] For a full treatment of the relation of the concept of the state to theories of natural law see Otto Gierke, Natural Law and the Theory of Society, 1500–1800, translated by Ernest Baker (1934).

sance theorists in a definite theory concerning the beginnings of social organization.

In describing the origin of civil society a number of sixteenth-century theorists began with a description of man's condition at the creation of the world. They portrayed a Paradise or Golden Age in which perfect order in the communal life of men was established at the time the world began. For Christian theologians this original state of social perfection existed in the Garden of Eden. Thus the *Homilie agaynst Disobedience and Wylful Rebellion* (1571) outlines the divine order in which God ruled man and man ruled the animals in Paradise.[28] Blandy similarly describes the original perfection of man, governed in his private and public life by virtue and reason.[29] Among theorists influenced primarily by classic thought the conception of Paradise was identified with the Golden Age portrayed in pagan literature. The theory, as it found expression in Renaissance political thinking, is clearly set forth by Goslicius, who writes:

That olde worlde (which the Poets called Golden) produced a race of men, of themselves most happy and wise: and truly not unlike, for in that time of man's first age (vertue onely raigning) the misery of vices and wickedness was not known, for they loved an upright, iust and simple life, wherunto vertue and reason consenteth. They were therefore inforced to vertue and honesty, even by the spurre of their owne nature fleeing vice, which because it was to them unknowen, might more easily be eschewed.[30]

But such an ideal state of affairs was not destined to continue. Vice, passion, and other manifestations of evil reduced men from their

[28] *Certaine Sermons or Homilies, Appointed to Be Read in Churches* (1640), p. 275: "For as long as in this first kingedome the subjects continued in due obedience to God their king, so long did God embrace all his subjects with his love, favour, and grace, which to enjoy is perfect felicity, wherby it is evident, that obedience is the principall vertue of all vertues, and indeed the very roote of all vertues, and cause of all felicity."

[29] William Blandy, *The Castle or Picture of Pollicy Shewing Forth Most Lively, the Face, Body, and Partes of a Commonwealth* (1581), fol. 6 v.

[30] Laurentius Grimaldus Goslicius, *The Counsellor* (1598), pp. 56–57. According to Gollancz (*Archiv*, CXLII, 141) the original translation of *The Counsellor* was suppressed because of the work's attitude against absolute monarchy. Gollancz maintains that the book was very popular, however, and that Shakespeare rewrote *Hamlet* for the purpose of ridiculing Goslicius' ideas on counselors. Goslicius (1535–1607) was a Polish writer and cleric who became Bishop of Posen. The product of

angelic perfection to beastly disorder and wickedness. Thus Goslicius proceeds:

But so soone as the sone of trueth declined, and with the clouds of vices began to be darkened, forthwith the minds of men fell into wickednesse, as desirous rather to knowe vice then vertue, delighting in the one and shunning the other. Then every man armed himself against vertue, thinking it lawfull to offend others, to live ungodly, abusing reason, and employing it in evil exercise . . .[31]

This classic conception was also paralleled in Christian literature of the century. The Homily of 1571 charges the Devil with bringing mankind to "utter confusion and utter ruin" in his social life as in his private life,[32] and Blandy describes the overthrow of reason, the prevalence of violence and passion, the "great darkness," "Common myserye," and "universall woefullness" which followed the fall of man from the Garden of Eden.[33]

It was at this point that the majority of sixteenth-century theorists took up the problem of the origin of society and government. They sought for the power or authority which enabled man to forsake his life of vice and conflict for an ordered, virtuous, and peaceful social existence approaching that which prevailed in the Age of Innocence. For all writers agreed with Chelidonius that civil society

grew upon necessitie which did enforce the common people to search out a way and meane by the whiche they might correct the furious and oppresse the violence of the wicked, because that of nature we are prompt and inclined to do evil; and always some are found so far out of order, that by their wickedness they confound and trouble all humain device and pollicie, and spoile (contrarie to all equitie) their neighbors of their goods.[34]

For some writers the utilitarian explanation of social origins was sufficient in itself. Machiavelli, for example, does not recognize any power other than man's will to protect himself against injuries from his

---

his own experience in practical politics, his *De optimo senatore* was published in Venice in 1568. Cf Sleeth, *Revue anglo-américaine*, XIII (1935).

[31] Goslicius, *loc. cit.*   [32] *Certaine Sermons or Homilies* (1640), p. 276.

[33] Blandy, *op. cit.*, fol. 9 v.

[34] Tigurinus Chelidonius, *A Most Excellent Historie, of the Institution and Firste Beginninge of Christian Princes* (1571), p. 27.

neighbors to account for the beginnings of political life.[35] In this connection, then, there is no mention of divine or natural law in his writings. But in England particularly, most theorists sought for some force above and beyond the utilitarian will of man which, in drawing men together into civil bodies, placed the seal of superhuman authority on their social organization.

In explaining such a force, Renaissance theorists accepted the classic argument that the state originated in a natural instinct in men to live socially. Aristotle, it will be recalled, maintained that "man is naturally a political animal," [36] and that "there is then in all persons a natural impetus to associate with each other in this manner." [37] The discovery of the basis of civil life in natural instinct is characteristic of Renaissance political thinking from the very beginning. Starkey, among English writers, argues that men, desiring to follow a life "convenient to their nature and dignity," abandoned their bestial, presocial life and built cities and states.[38] Civil life he elsewhere defines as "a polytyke ordur of a multytude conspyryng togyddur in vertue and honesty, to the wych man by nature is ordeyned." [39] Goslicius, having described the confusion which followed the Golden Age, ascribes the rebirth of society to "the force of nature and reason which remained in a fewe." [40] John Case, in his *Sphaera civitatis* (1588), gives expression to the same concept of social instinct when he answers affirmatively his own question, "An civitas sit a natura?" and "An homo sit animal politicum aut civile a natura?" [41]

By identifying this social instinct with the universal law of nature implanted by God in the hearts of men, Renaissance theorists were able to attribute the origin and authority of the state to eternal law and the will of God. Moreover, they were able to place human political society in the universal scheme of things. Speaking of the inherent human impulse to live socially, Starkey remarks that men "have roted

---

[35] Cf. Allen, *A History of Political Thought in the Sixteenth Century*, p. 453: "For Machiavelli there was no *lex aeterna* and therefore no *lex naturalis*. He never even thought it worth while to refer to that conception."

[36] Aristotle, *The Politics*, p. 4, translated by William Ellis, Everyman's Library (1912).

[37] *Ibid.*   [38] Starkey, *op. cit.*, p. 7.   [39] *Ibid.*, p. 20.

[40] Goslicius, *The Counsellor* (1598), p. 57.   [41] Case, *op. cit.*, p. 19.

in theyr heartes a certayne rule . . . called of phylosopharys and wyse men, the unyversal and true law of nature, wych to all nationys is commyn, no thyng having of the opinion and folysch fansy of man." [42] Ponet, in *A Short Treatise of Politike Power* (1556), demonstrates how the identification of divine will and natural law was applied to the theory of social origins when he writes:

He [God] hath taken upon him the Order and Government of man his chiefe Creature and prescribed him a rule, how he should behave himselfe, what he should do, and what he may not do.

This rule is the law of nature, first planted and grafted onely in the minde of man.[43]

Buchanan takes a similar view in his *De iure regni apud Scotos* (1579). Nature, or the natural social impulse, he defines as "that light infused by God into our minds," [44] and Maitland, with whom Buchanan is conversing in the dialogue, accordingly replies:

You do not then make Utility, but that Divine Law rooted in us from the beginning, to be the cause (indeed the far more worthy and divine of the two) of mens incorporating in political societies.[45]

Hooker, after establishing the identity of the laws eternal and natural, asserts that in directing the political actions of men the latter law enables them to escape the chaos of the presocial era and to live in accordance with the will and wisdom of God. He writes:

Howbeit, the corruption of our nature being presupposed, we may not deny but that the Law of Nature doth now require of necessity some kind of regiment; so that to bring things unto the first course they were in, and utterly to take away all kind of public government in the world, were apparently to overturn the whole world.[46]

In distinguishing between the primary law of nature and the secondary law of nature, or law of nations, Hayward introduced a refinement in the generally accepted theory. But basically his conception of divine and natural sanction is that almost universally recognized in Renaissance thinking about the origin and authority of political society. The primary law of nature, he argues, enjoins men generally to conserve common society; to comply with this injunction certain universal cus-

[42] Starkey, *op. cit.*, p. 14.   [43] 1642 edition, p. 3.   [44] 1689 edition, p. 7.
[45] *Ibid.*, p. 8.   [46] Hooker, *Of the Laws of Ecclesiastical Polity*, I, 191.

toms, known as the secondary law of nature or law of nations, are established by men. These customs prescribe the particular pattern of organization which will best conserve society. As Hayward concludes:

And because government was not from the beginning, but induced as a consequence of the primary precept of nature; to maintaine humane societie, therefore whensoever wee speake of natural government, we are intended to meane the secondary law of nature, which is the received custome, successively of al, and alwaies of most nations in the world.[47]

Thus indirectly, but no less decisively, the social and political structure receives by virtue of its origins the sanction of divine will and natural law.

These conceptions had become by Shakespeare's day a permanent and almost universal fixture in Elizabethan thinking about the authority and beginnings of political society. It should be observed that, as presented here, these theories concern themselves more with the causes of social organization than with the methods. The latter problem was not neglected by writers, however. Some described how men sought out a strong leader in the beginning to save them from their presocial chaos and thus established kingdoms; [48] or, as Blandy puts it, "these wretched wormes crawled unto him, making a scritch and woeful cry. Of whose sutes and lamentable complaintes, when he had taken compassion . . . became unto them at length a lanterne of Justice, a mirror of mildnesse and courtesie." [49] Other writers, such as Bodin and Craig, told in detail how individuals formed themselves into families, families into streets, streets into cities, and cities into states.[50]

---

[47] Hayward, *An Answer to . . . R. Doleman* (1603), Sig. A, 4 v.

[48] Tigurinus Chelidonius, *op. cit.*, p. 24: "Man being guided by Nature, instructed by reason, and lead by divine inspiration, did elect and choose Kings and princes . . . to the ende to lead and continue the state of their lives together wyth greater felicitie, peace, and tranquility."

[49] Blandy, *op. cit.*, fol. 9 r.

[50] Bodin, *Six Bookes of a Commonweale* (1606), Book I, Chapters II–VII; Thomas Craig, *Concerning the Right of Succession to the Kingdom of England* (1703), p. 15: Families "had then no positive laws, to be the measure of their Obedience: 'twas only Nature, that *Divinae Particula Aurae*, which excited them to it. When Families did incorporate into greater Societies . . . , more people still joined themselves to them, knowing that the more numerous they should be, the more safe from danger, and the better stor'd with the Necessaries and Conveniences of Life, yet in such a Con-

For the present, however, it has been less important to consider these methods of organization than to determine the ultimate power which moved and enabled men to form such groups. In the light of the link between the state and universal laws three fundamental problems pertaining to the nature of political society are clarified. In the first place, as has been shown, these circumstances explain the weight and authority attached to the concept of the state generally accepted in the political thinking of Shakespeare's day. In the second place, as we shall now see, only in relation to these laws can the aims and purposes of civil organization be understood. And in the third place, as will be shown in a subsequent chapter, the structure of society itself is determined by principles of order established for all things by the law of nature.

3

Relative to the purpose for which society is ordained, sixteenth-century thinking was consistent and clear. Attitudes on this problem, and the further emphasis which they placed on the sanctity of the social and political order, can be appreciated by the modern reader only when he recalls the very real horror with which Renaissance writers regarded the presocial state of disorder and bestiality. The "nightmare of a world in chaos," which Professor R. W. Chambers believes was visualized by Sir John Cheke and Shakespeare alone,[51] was, in fact, far more widespread among Renaissance theorists than the scholar indicates. This fear has already been suggested in the graphic accounts of post-paradisiac confusion described earlier in the present chapter. Tremendous respect was attached by sixteenth-century thinkers to the social organization which stood between men and such disastrous chaos.

---

course of People contests could not be possibly avoided, the new Citizens could not be without differences among themselves. Wherefore, to preserve the Peace of the Community, one from among themselves, or some one of greater Reputation was brought from a Neighboring City, and set over them, to whom all their Controversies were brought, and who decided them *ex aequo & bono*, i.e., by equity, there being then no positive Statute Laws. If his decisions seemed just, others had their recourse to him, untill by their common consent and choice of that City or Society, he became the common and constant Arbitrator, and they Swore Fidelity to him."

[51] R. W. Chambers, "The Expression of Ideas, Particularly Political Ideas . . . in Shakespeare," *Shakespeare's Hand in the Play of Sir Thomas More*, by A. W. Pollard *et al.* (1923), p. 149.

The state was recognized as a bulwark of order, reason, and virtue against the confusion which had once almost destroyed mankind, and which, because of the elements of passion and wickedness in his nature, was constantly present and threatening to overwhelm him again. As Hooker warned, to take away the natural order is to overturn the whole world, and, for man in particular, to return to the terrors of pre-social existence.[52]

The ends toward which the law of nature directed men in ordaining political fellowship were the same ends of goodness and perfection toward which eternal law directed the actions of all things. According to thinking prevalent throughout the Renaissance, the ultimate purpose of civil society was threefold in nature. As Hooker expressed it, "Man doth seek a triple perfection" which includes

First a sensual, consisting in those things which very life itself requireth either as necessary supplements, or as beauties and ornaments thereof; then an intellectual, consisting in those things which none underneath man is either capable of or acquainted with; lastly a spiritual and divine, consisting in those things whereunto we tend by supernatural means here, but cannot here attain unto them.[53]

The bulk of sixteenth-century writing about the purpose of political society can be classified under these general headings of the material, intellectual, and spiritual welfare of man. The fusion of classic and Christian elements, apparent in Renaissance theories of the origin of the state, is also found in theories of the aims which the structure is designed to serve. It was agreed by representatives of all schools that the one general and principal end of civil society is, to borrow the Aristotelian phrase which they employed, the felicity of man, individually and collectively. It was further agreed that the state is designed to establish, by civil justice, the social tranquility and order, and to provide, by economic justice, the proper distribution of material advantages essential to this felicity. As to the definition of felicity itself, two types of thought appear most frequently in Renaissance

[52] Hooker, *op. cit.*, I, 191.

[53] *Ibid.*, I, 205. Cf. Aristotle, *Politics*, p. 201, Everyman's Library: "As what is good, relative to man, may be divided into three sorts, what is external, what appertains to the body, and what to the soul, it is evident that all these must conspire to make a man happy."

discussion of the problem; one asserts that felicity lies in the life of virtue and intellectual activity described in classic philosophy, the other, that it lies in the exercise of the Christian religion and the salvation of the soul. By the end of the century these theories of the material, intellectual, and spiritual felicity of man were fairly well blended in a unified concept of the purpose which the state is ordained by God and nature to serve.

In order that men may practice virtue and exercise religion they must first enjoy, according to Renaissance thinking, a certain material peace and prosperity. The basic argument is presented by Hooker when he writes:

All men desire to lead in this world a happy life. This life is led most happily wherein all virtue is exercised, without impediment or let. The Apostle, in exhorting men to contentment although they have in this world no more than very bare food and raiment, giveth us thereby to understand that those are even the lowest of things necessary; that if we should be stripped of all those things without which we might possibly be, yet these must be left; that destitution in these is such an impediment, as till it be removed suffereth not the mind of man to admit any other care. . . . Having by this mean whereon to live, the principal actions of their life afterward are noted by the exercise of their religion. . . . But inasmuch as righteous life presupposeth life; inasmuch as to live virtuously it is impossible except we live; therefore the first impediment, which naturally we endeavor to remove, is penury and want of things without which we cannot live.[54]

Political society is designed, therefore, to provide this material welfare upon which the higher activities of men depend. The end of social organization as so envisaged is clearly set forth by Starkey when he writes that civil order is necessary

to the intent that thys multitude of pepul and hole commynalty, so helthy and so welthy, hauyng convenyent abundance of all thyngys necessary for the mayntenance thereof, may wyth dew honor, reverence and love, relygyously worschyppe God, as fountayne of al gudnes, Maker and Gouernower of al thys world; every one also dowyng hys duty to other wyth brotherly love, one lovyng one a nother as membrys and partys of one body.[55]

[54] Hooker, op. cit., I, 188–89.   [55] Starkey, op. cit., p. 51.

Bodin came to a similar conclusion; in the following passage he clarifies the relative values attached by most sixteenth-century writers to the purpose of the state:

The same judgment we are to have of a well-ordered commonwealth; the chief end and felicitie whereof consisteth in the contemplative virtues; albeit that publike and political actions of less worth, be first and forerunners of the same, as the provision of thinges necessarie for the maintenance and preservation of the state and people; all which for all that we account farre inferior unto the morall vertues, as we also they unto the vertues intellectual; the end of which is the divine contemplation of the fairest and most excellent object that can possibly be thought of or imagined.[56]

Material welfare as an end of political society was thought of in terms of two concepts, civil tranquility and economic prosperity. Throughout the century theorists consistently stressed the peace, quietness, and order which social organization effected in the life of mankind. Upon civil harmony all other objectives of the state, material or spiritual, were considered to be dependent. Writers pointed to the fact that only within the structure of political society could man enjoy a life of concord with his fellows. Homily X of the series published in 1547 makes this fundamental purpose of the social organism clear, when it warns:

Take awaye kynges, princes, rulers, magistrates, judges, and such states of Gods order, no man shall ride or go by the high waie unrobbed, no man shall slepe in his owne bed unkilled, no man shall kepe his wife, children and possessions in quietness, all thynges shal be comon, and there must nedes folow al mischief and utter destruction, bothe of the soules, bodies, goodes, and commonwealthes.[57]

Similar concepts of the basic objective of social organization found expression in the majority of treatises dealing with the body politic. Starkey asserted that all affairs in a commonwealth "are ever referryd to this end and purpose, that the whole body of the commynalty may lyue in quyetness and tranquylytye," in order that men may "attayne to theyr natural perfection." [58] Aylmer agreed that "the quiet of

[56] Bodin, *The Six Bookes of a Commonweale*, p. 7.

[57] *Certayne Sermons* (1547), Homily X, Sig. K, i v.

[58] Starkey, *op. cit.*, p. 5.

commonweales is the nurse of religion and bulwark of good and faithful men . . . ," [59] and Musculus, who wrote that the chief end of political society is "the commodious lyfe," defined that life as "that whych is quyet and peaceable, w^tout any sore trouble and toyle." [60] Not only because of its divine and natural sanction, therefore, but because "it hath procured us a meane to live happily in quietnesse and concord with contentation" [61] must the social structure be regarded as blessed and inviolate.

It will be pertinent to point out here that for Machiavelli the security of life and property was the sole end for which the state is ordained. Believing as he did that human nature is essentially bad, the Florentine would of course recognize no spiritual end above and beyond this utilitarian purpose. The state does not exist to maintain religion; rather religion exists merely as a tool to aid the state in achieving its material goal. The solitary aim of the state, according to Machiavelli, is the good of all its subjects, and that general good is merely the good desired by each subject individually—security. To borrow Professor Allen's summary of the Florentine's attitude on this problem, Machiavelli maintained "that men may desire wealth or honor or power, but . . . all men desire security of life and property. That security only the State can give and to make the State secure, methods have to be adopted repugnant to normal sentiment and deeds to be done that are commonly regarded as evil." [62]

To return to the arguments of Renaissance theorists more idealistic than Machiavelli, when social peace and stability have been established by the state, then the material prosperity of all inevitably ensues and in turn the higher moral and spiritual activities are made possible. The economic purposes of political society were stressed by a number of writers. Citing the authority of Aristotle, Starkey wrote that as the highest felicity of individual man requires a moderate element of

[59] John Aylmer, *An Harborowe for Faithfull and Trewe Subiectes agaynst the Late-Blowne Blaste, Concerninge the Government of Wemen* [Knox's *First Blast of the Trumpet*] (1559), "Epistle."

[60] Musculus, *Commonplaces of Christian Religion* (1563), fol. 551 r.

[61] Loys Le Roy, "Preface" to Aristotle's *Politiques,* translated from the French in 1598, Sig. B, i v.

[62] Allen, *op. cit.,* p. 481.

physical health and material riches, so the society of men must "have convenyent abundance of all thynges necessary for the mayntenance thereof." [63] Forset, like Starkey, believed that the state is so designed by God and nature that this necessary wealth is produced when the order established by universal law is followed; after citing the parallel function in the human body, he concludes:

So in a State, when each degree conformeth itself to his owne duties, making in the whole a perfection of love and obedience, then the abundance of riches, multitude of people, the titles of honor, the encrease of power, are both available and commendable.[64]

In the matter of worldly necessities, the pattern of social organization ordained for mankind is a just commonwealth, for it insures the material welfare of all its members according to their merit and worth. On the one hand it prevents the selfish acquisition of wealth in the hands of the few at the expense of the many. Ponet writes that the state so ordained tends to "the wealth and benefit of the whole multitude, and not of the Superior and Governors alone," [65] and Loys Le Roy, praising the study of society and government in the preface to his translation of Aristotle's *Politiques* (1598), exclaims: "And it is the more perfect, in that it procureth the welfare not of some particular persons or companies . . . but also universally of mankind." [66] This was the attitude at the basis of the universal reproach directed at Machiavelli as he was represented by Gentillet, for according to "machiavellism" the ruler is inspired only by a desire for selfish personal aggrandizement in wealth and power at the expense of his subjects.[67]

On the other hand, the commonwealth is not a communistic equalization of material benefits. Such a conception was regarded with horror

[63] Starkey, *op. cit.*, p. 51.

[64] Edward Forset, *A Comparative Discourse of the Bodies Natural and Politique* (1606), p. 41.

[65] Ponet, *op. cit.*, p. 6.   [66] Sig. B, i v.

[67] Innocent Gentillet, *A Discourse upon the Meanes of Wel-Governing and Maintaining in Good Peace a Kingdome . . . Against Nicholas Machiavel, the Florentine*, translated by Simon Patericke (1602), Section III, Maxim 15: "A vertuous Tyrant, to maintaine his tyrannie, ought to maintaine partialities and factions amongst his subjects, and to sley and take away such as love the commonweale."

by Renaissance theorists. Plato and More were berated for permitting such a state of affairs to exist in their ideal republics,[68] and the Anabaptists, who were the sixteenth-century practitioners of communism in government and economy, were the constant objects of reproach.[69] Something of the prevalent attitude toward communism is reflected in the Homilies of 1547, which as has been observed, include the

[68] Cf. Loys Le Roy, *op. cit.*, Sig. C, ii r: "Out of doubt Plato had done better if hee had contented himselfe with the order, elegancie, and gravitie which hee kept in the description of his Commonweale, and not medled with the communitie of goods, wives, and children, nor taken upon him to appoint men and women their severall charges and offices." R. Braithwaite, in *A Strappado for the Devil* (1615) edited by J. W. Ebsworth (1878), p. 231, similarly writes:

> For it would breed confusion in the land
> If people did admit of no command.
> But like a Platoes Commonwealth, should be,
> Subiect to none, but in equalitie.

Cf. also note 5, Chapter II, above.

[69] Cf. Allen, *op. cit.*, Part I, Chapter III, "The Anabaptist Protest," for an account of this movement and its political and social doctrines. Ponet, *op. cit.*, p. 40, attacks the Anabaptists in characteristic fashion when he accuses them of denying the law of God that all things must come by the sweat of the brow. Shakespeare in *The Tempest* makes thrusts at concepts of political and economic equality similar to these made against the ideal commonwealths of Plato, More and the Anabaptists. Gonzalo is made the butt of satirical jests when he exclaims in II, i:

> I' the commonwealth I would by contraries
> Execute all things; for no kind of traffic
> Would I admit; no name of magistrate;
> Letters should not be known; riches, poverty,
> And use of service, none; contract, succession,
> Bourn, bound of land, tilth, vineyard, none;
> No use of metal, corn, or wine, or oil;
> No occupation; all men idle, all;
> And women too, but innocent and pure;
> No sovereignty;—
>   .   .   .   .
> All things in common nature should produce
> Without sweat or endeavour: treason, felony,
> Sword, pike, knife, gun, or need of any engine,
> Would I not have; but nature should bring forth
> Of it own kind, all foison, all abundance,
> To feed my innocent people.

As Chambers points out (*William Shakespeare: A Study*, I, 494) this passage is probably borrowed from the essay "Of the Canibales" in Florio's *Montaigne*, Chapter XXX. Shakespeare's satirical intent in including it in *The Tempest* seems evident, however.

common holding of wealth and property to be, with robbery, murder, rape, and kidnaping, among the evils of the presocial era.[70]

It was rather the purpose of the state, according to Renaissance theorists, to maintain justice, which in its sixteenth-century economic sense "is a constant and perpetuall desire to give unto everie man that which to him belongeth." [71] This concept will be considered more fully in a subsequent chapter, when the theory of degree and vocation in the structure of states is explained.[72] Here it need only be pointed out that as each member of the commonwealth has a prescribed rank and function, so each member is entitled to the material reward conformable to his station and service. According to Renaissance thinking, this just distribution of rewards is the primary purpose served by the state in the sphere of material welfare, for it is only within a social organization that such justice can flourish. As Forset concludes:

> If there bee any not yet persuaded of this different respectiveness to be had of men in the state, according as they differ in esteeme and worthinesse; let him farther bethinke himselfe of his owne bodie: doth hee not adorne some of them with silkes . . . , and yet leaveth others wholly naked, or but homely and coarsely attired? . . . Hereof my inference is, That as in our private, so in our publique bodie, difference of regard maketh difference of advancement, by a distributing justice, which yeeldeth to everie one (though not the same) yet his fit proportion.[73]

In addition to the maintenance of orderly and peaceful community life, then, it is the further purpose of the social and political structure to enable man to possess and enjoy the material necessities rightfully his. For these ends God and nature ordained social order, that in turn the supreme end of the individual, and accordingly the ultimate purpose of the state, the felicity of man, might be accomplished.

Generally speaking, the felicity of man was conceived by sixteenth-century writers to lie in the virtuous Christian life. The classic theory that society is ordained to enable men to live virtuously (Aristotle) and to contemplate intellectually the highest good (Plato) was paralleled in essential meaning by the Christian theory that the state is ordained to allow man to live the Christian life in faith, hope, and

---

[70] *Certayne Sermons* (1547), Homily X, Sig. K, i v.
[71] Goslicius, *The Counsellor* (1598), p. 101.
[72] See Chapter VI, below.　　　　　　[73] Forset, *op. cit.*, p. 47.

charity. For the one, the ultimate end of society is the good and happy life of the mind, for the other, the welfare and salvation of the soul. For both, man can achieve this ultimate purpose only within the structure of organized society.

Renaissance theorists influenced primarily by classic political ideology concluded with Aristotle that "that government must be the best which is so established that every one therein may have it in his power to act virtuously and live happily." [74] The virtuous life they defined as the practice of fortitude, temperance, justice, and prudence. The relationship between moral philosophy and political life is made clear by Sir Thomas More when he writes:

In the institution of that weal public this end is only and chiefly pretended and minded, that what time may possibly be spared from the necessary occupations and affairs of the commonwealth, all that the citizens should withdraw from the bodily service to the free liberty of the mind and garnishing of the same. For herein they suppose the felicity of this life to exist. [75]

Thomas Starkey had a similar conception of the aims of political society; "The end of all polytyke rule," he writes, "is to induce the multytude to virtuous living," [76] and he defines a commonwealth as "a polytyke ordur of a multytude conspyryng togyddur in vertue and honesty, to the wych man by nature ys ordeyned." [77] Later in the century Goslicius argued that however much commonwealths may differ in their forms of government, the "end of every one of them is but one thinge, that is to say, good, or wel being, which consisteth in the felicitie of men and every state doth labor to attaine." [78] And according to Goslicius such felicity is synonymous with the practice of virtue. The similar conclusions reached by Bodin have already been observed. [79]

By another group of theorists, ecclesiastics for the most part, the

---

[74] Aristotle, *Politics*, pp. 203–4, translated by Ellis, Everyman's Library.

[75] Thomas More, *Utopia* (1516), edited by W. D. Armes (1912), p. 108.

[76] Starkey, *op. cit.*, p. 54.

[77] *Ibid.*, p. 20. Cf. also John Case, *Sphaera civitatis* (1588), p. 601. After asking "Utrum optima vita civium magis theorica esset quam practica, magisque in virtutibus mentis quam moris poneretur?" he argues at length to show that the best civil life is that which is concerned with the virtues of the mind rather than with practical affairs.

[78] Goslicius, *op. cit.*, p. 8.   [79] See p. 53, above.

aims of political society were discussed in terms of the religious life. According to these theorists civil society is ordained that man, thereby living in peace and order, and equipped with the requisite material substance of life, may be enabled to conform to the principles of Christian living and thus be prepared spiritually for the life hereafter. There was wide disagreement among writers as to which is the final religious authority in a political society, the state or the church.[80] Catholics and Calvinists defended the supremacy of the church, and held the state to be nothing more than a secular servant. Anglicans on the contrary claimed supremacy for state, to which the church, as merely a spiritual minister, is subservient. But such disagreement, however violent, was primarily on a matter of administration, and did not alter the fundamental unanimity of feeling that political society is ordained for the advancement of religion. Thus the Anglican proponent of secular supremacy in the church, Thomas Bilson, could argue that "as every private man is bound to seeke and serve God above all thinges, so everie societie of men . . . is likewise bound to have speciall and principal care of his service." [81] His contention is identical with the conclusion reached by Parsons, the exponent of ecclesiastical supremacy, when he writes:

We are to suppose that the first, cheefest, and highest end that God and nature appointed to every commonwealth, was not so much the temporal felicity of the body, as the supernatural and everlasting of the soule. . . . And consequently al other things of this transitory life, and of this human commonwealth, subiect to mans eyes, are ordeyned to serve and be subordinate and directed to the other higher end, and that all mans actions in this world, are first of all, and in the highest degree, to be imployed to the recognizing, serving and honoring of this great Lord, that governeth the whole, as the author and end thereof.[82]

According to this theory the chief end of the state becomes the maintenance of the Christian life in the temporal world. Political society not only provides the order and welfare essential to such a life; by its laws

[80] On this most difficult of Tudor problems in political theory see Allen, *op. cit.*, Part II, "England."

[81] Thomas Bilson, *The True Difference betweene Christian Subiection and Unchristian Rebellion* (1585), p. 251.

[82] Parsons, *op. cit.*, p. 204.

it forces man, not naturally so inclined, to prepare his soul for the life eternal.

The foregoing account is obviously not a complete treatment of theories of the origin and purpose of civil society. The restricted intent has been to present here the general conclusions about these problems as they appear consistently in sixteenth-century discussions of the whole nature and structure of political society. The investigation has therefore been limited in material to those fairly uniform and widespread expressions of state-theory embodying the concepts which apparently formed the basis of Shakespeare's political attitudes and of those universal in the thinking of his day. The theories of origin and purpose relative to this idea of the state can be summarized as follows: God, or the will of God as expressed in natural law, draws men together from disorganized to organized social living. The structure so established is designed to serve definite purposes for the welfare of man. It enables him to live in peace and quiet with his fellows and to enjoy his share of the material necessities of life. Through the attainment of these immediate ends, the state enables man to live the happiest life, which consists in the exercise of virtue and the practice of religion. Perhaps the most concise summary of this theory of social origins and purpose, as generally accepted in Renaissance political thinking, is that given by William Alexander, Earl of Stirling, in his *Paraenesis to the Prince,* published in 1604. He writes:

> Then building walles, they barbarous rites disdain'd,
> The sweetness of societie to find,
> And all t' attaine that th' union entertained,
> As peace, religion, and a vertuous mind: . . .[83]

[83] Stanza 3.

CHAPTER IV

The Significance of Analogical Argument

A STRIKING FEATURE common to the three passages which embody most clearly the Shakespearean concept of the state is the use of analogical language and argument. On these occasions when he deals most explicitly with the concept of political society the dramatist consistently expresses his theories in figures drawn from the animal, astronomical, and anatomical worlds. Canterbury presents a picture of human society in terms of the structure and activity of a beehive; Ulysses draws parallels from a variety of natural phenomena, but particularly from the order of the solar system, which, he implies, reveal to mankind the principles of civil organization and conduct; Menenius employs the analogy of the belly and its relationship with other members of the human body to illustrate the relationships desirable in the political body.

Scholarly attempts have been made, with varying degrees of success, to find individual and immediate sources for the figures,[1] but it has not

---

[1] See for example R. W. Bond, editor, *The Complete Works of John Lyly*, II, 44–46; Bond follows Malone in describing Lyly's account of the commonwealth of the bees (*Euphues and His England*, 1580, edited by Arber, pp. 261–64) as the source of Canterbury's comparison between the beehive and the state in Shakespeare's *Henry V*; Churton Collins (*Studies in Shakespeare*, p. 81) traces parallels in thought and style between the *Phoenissae*, 528–85, and Ulysses' speech on order and degree in *Troilus and Cressida*; Gayley (*Shakespeare and the Founders of Liberty in America*, pp. 160 ff.) follows Warburton in suggesting Hooker's *Laws of Ecclesiastical Polity*, Book I, as the source for Ulysses' speech; Case (in the Arden *Coriolanus*) argues that the fable of the belly as told by Menenius Agrippa in Plutarch's *Life of Coriolanus* was amplified by Shakespeare in his play from an extended account of the fable quoted from John of Salisbury's *Policraticus* in Camden's *Remaines* (1605), pp. 198–99: Starnes ("Shakespeare and Elyot's 'Gouernour,'" *University of Texas Studies in English*, VII, 112–32) believes that the analogical passages in *Henry V* and *Troilus and Cressida* are based on the opening chapters of Elyot's work. The present chapter is more concerned with why Shakespeare used these materials than with where he found them.

been generally recognized that these passages possibly have a common general source in the technique of presentation adopted almost universally by Renaissance writers on the theory of the state. The dramatist's use of natural analogies for political philosophizing can be paralleled in political writing throughout the century. It can be shown that figures of this sort were consistently employed by theorists not only to portray the structure and functioning of states, but to suggest the philosophical principles upon which states are founded and the relation of states to the fundamental laws described in the preceding chapter. Essential to any understanding of Shakespeare's concept of the state, therefore, is some appreciation of the full significance of the medium of expression which he employed in common with his contemporaries.

I

The widespread use of analogy in sixteenth-century political expression was not without classical and medieval precedent. Aristotle's *Politics*, with the parallels it draws between the bodies human and political, was the authority most frequently cited by Renaissance writers in this regard. The same analogy was developed at length by Menenius Agrippa in a passage from Plutarch which was familiar to Shakespeare,[2] among other Renaissance writers. Vergil in the *Georgics* finds politically illuminating similarities between the society of bees and the society of men,[3] and abundant materials for use in such analogies were provided in the "unnatural natural history" of Pliny.[4] The device of parallels was widely employed in medieval political discussion. "From John of Salisbury to Nicholas Cusanus, Occam, and Dante, no point of fancied analogy between the parts and members of the body and the various functions of Church and State was left unexploited."[5] According to Gierke, "John of Salisbury made the first attempt to find some member of the natural body which would correspond to each portion of the state."[6] An elaborate comparison of this sort, making

[2] Plutarch, *Life of Caius Martius Coriolanus*, pp. 177–78, in *Lives*, translated by Sir Thomas North, Vol. II.

[3] Vergil, *Georgics*, Book IV.

[4] Caius Plinius Secundus, *The Natural History of Pliny*, Book XI, Chapters IV–XXII.

[5] E. E. Kellett, *Suggestions: Literary Essays* (1923), p. 27.

[6] Otto Gierke, *Political Theories of the Middle Age*, translated by F. W. Maitland

extensive use of medical knowledge, was drawn by Nicholas Cusanus,[7] and Aegidius Colonna, in his *De regimine principum*, begins by saying: "For as we see that the body of an animal consists of connected and co-ordinated members, so every realm and every group (*congregatio*) consists of divers persons connected and co-ordinated for some end." [8] Similarly, Marsilius of Padua wrote that "civitas est velut animata seu animalis natura quaedam," and later carried out his comparison of a well-ordered state to an "animal bene dispositum." [9]

The extensive use of analogy in Renaissance treatises on the state and society represents an unbroken continuation of the medieval tradition. As Kellett observes, in describing the origin of the technique of Tudor political argument, "by some process of permeation or other, such medieval ideas . . . had reached Shakespeare as part and parcel of the general intellectual equipment of his time." [10] Few indeed are the political treatises of the period which, in dealing with the whole nature of the state, fail to present the concept, in some degree at least, in terms of natural parallels. As a result of such universal usage analogy became the standard medium for presenting theories relative to the nature and structure of states. A brief examination of several representative works will reveal how and why these figures came to be inevitably associated with the concept of the state generally accepted in the political thinking of the day.

In the opening chapters of *The Boke Named the Gouernour* (1531), Sir Thomas Elyot, following the classic outline of the "institution," seeks to define and describe the nature of civil society. This he does in

---

(1922), p. 24. John's account, which he claims to base on the apocryphal *Trajani* of Plutarch, is as follows: "Princeps vero capitis in re publica optinet locum uni subjectus Deo et his qui vices illius agunt in terris, quoniam et in corpore humano ab anima vegetatur caput et regitur. Cordis locum senatus optinet, a quo bonorum operum et malorum procedunt initia. Oculorum aurium et linguae officia vendicant sibi judices et praesides provinciarum. Officiales et milites manibus coaptantur. Qui semper adsistunt principi, lateribus assimilantur. Quaestores et commentarienses (non illos dico qui carceribus praesunt, sed comites rerum privatarum) ad ventris et intestinorum refert imaginem. Quae, si immensa aviditate congesserint et congesta tenacius reservaverint, innumerabiles et incurabiles generant morbo, ut vitis eorum totius corporis ruina immineat. Pedibus vero solo jugiter inherentibus agricolae coaptantur." (*Policraticus*, edited by Webb, I, 283, Sec. 540 c.)

[7] Gierke, *op. cit.*, p. 24.   [8] Quoted by Gierke, *op. cit.*, p. 25.
[9] *Ibid.*, p. 26.   [10] Kellett, *op. cit.*, p. 23.

terms of the beehive, which, he says, "is lefte to man by nature, as it semeth, a perpetuall figure of a iuste gouernaunce or rule." [11] He analyzes in detail the structure and functioning of the hive in order to illustrate how the society of men should be organized and maintained. Elyot does not, however, limit himself to the one figure; in the hierarchy of heaven, in the arrangement of the four elements, in the order of the plant and animal worlds, and in the system of the solar universe he finds parallels with the state which confirm the political principles he is seeking to expound. All are described to show the essential nature and structure of human social organization.[12]

For the same purpose Thomas Starkey, among early writers on "the very and true commonweal," draws a detailed analogy between the bodies human and political. He feels such an analysis of political society to be warranted

for thys body hath hys partys, wych resembyl also the partys of the body of man, of the wych the most general to our purpose are thes—the hart, hede, handys, and fete. The hart thereof ys the kyng, prynce, and rular of the state. . . . To the hede, wyth the yes, yerys, and other sensys therein, resemblyd may be ryght wel the under offycers by pryncys appoyntyd, for as much as they schold ever observe and dylygently wayte for the wele of the rest of thys body. To the handys are resemblyd bothe craftysmen and warryarys wych defend the rest of the body from iniury of ennymys utward, and worke and make thyngys necessary to the same. To the fete the plowmen and tyllarys of the ground, bycause they, by theyr labur, susteyne and support the rest of the body.[13]

Later in the *Dialogue* Starkey develops in similar fashion parallels between the state and a ship, in which king and captain, populace and crew, are "semblable." [14] Thus early in the century, and in two important treatises, analogy was prominently associated with the exposition of theories of the state.

Midcentury politico-theological writers, concerned mainly with arguments for or against absolute monarchy and passive obedience, frequently employed familiar analogies to summarize, by way of intro-

---

[11] Elyot, *op. cit.*, p. 9.   [12] *Ibid.*, pp. 3–7, 8–9.

[13] Starkey, *A Dialogue between Cardinal Pole and Thomas Lupset* (c. 1538), p. 48, "Early English Text Society," Extra Series, Vol. XXXII.

[14] *Ibid.*, p. 57.

duction, their concept of the whole nature of the state. Homily X in the collection of 1547 describes the hierarchy of heaven, with its orders of angels and archangels governed by one sovereign God, as a model for the order of human society.[15] The same parallel is suggested at the outset of the *Homilie agaynst Disobedience and Wylful Rebellion* (1571).[16] Opponents of absolutism, meantime, were employing similar analogies for similar purposes. John Knox describes the natural body of man, with its various members and organs governed by one head, as a "mirror or glasse given by God in which we may behold the order appointed and established by God in nature," and hence applicable to the natural society of men.[17] He also uses the figure, familiar in Renaissance literature, of the "monster" which perversion of natural order makes of bodies both human and political.[18]

A variety of figures and analogies are introduced by Tigurinus Chelidonius to support the concept of a state which he sets forth in *A Most Excellent Historie of the Institution and Firste Beginninge of Christian Princes and the Originall of Kingdomes,* translated by James Chillister in 1571. In a dedicatory epistle to Elizabeth, Chillister himself gives a general description of the nature and structure of states. His concept of civil society is embodied in an extended analogy drawn between the body of man and the body of the commonwealth, in which the soul in the body is likened to the prince in the state.[19] In a defense of monarchy as the form of government most desirable in a state Chelidonius employs other familiar figures. Chapter One of the treatise is entitled: "The definition of a King, and what a Kingdome is, and how in many insensible things and also in brute beasts we shall find certain similitudes and figures of Kingdomes and Commonwealthes." These similitudes he discovers in "all things universally, and their parts, beginning even at the heavens, and runne thorow all other elements," in the sun among the stars, in fire among the elements, in Asia among lands, in gold

[15] *Certayne Sermons or Homilies* (1547), Homily X, Sig. K, i r.

[16] *Certaine Sermons or Homilies* (1640), p. 275.

[17] Knox, *The First Blast of the Trumpet against the Monstrous Regiment of Women,* in *Works,* edited by Laing, IV, 390.

[18] *Ibid.,* p. 391: "And no lesse monstruous is the bodie of that Common welth where a Woman beareth empire; for either doth it lack a lawfull heade (as in very dede it doth) or els there is an idol exalted in the place of the true head."

[19] Chelidonius, *op. cit.,* Sig. A, ii r and v.

among metals.[20] The beehive is analyzed in detail for political purposes, and the figure is supplemented with parallels found in other groups of animals.[21] The monstrous body of many heads is employed to illustrate the unnaturalness of democracy as a form of government in states.[22] Few treatises, in fact, illustrate more strikingly the instrumental part played by natural figures and analogies in the exposition of concepts of the state.

No such extended use of analogy was made by Bodin. On several occasions, however, he does make rhetorical use of the anatomical figures, and he defends monarchy on the basis of parallels found not only in the body, but in the solar system and the heavenly kingdom.[23] Bodin's theory of the family as the basic unit in a state possibly accounts for the emphasis among later writers on the parallel between the structure of the family and the structure of states. The order of society and virtue of monarchy, writes Thomas Bilson in 1585, "you may learne by the regiment of every private family, which is both a part and paterne of the commonwealth." [24] The appropriateness of this parallel for political argument is further emphasized by Hayward, who observes, "The whole world is nothinge but a great state; a state is no other than a great familie; and a familie no other than a great bodye." [25] The figures of the family, and particularly the parallels between king and father as governors, remained popular throughout the period.

The emphasis on monarchy and arguments in its defense which characterized state-theories of the last quarter of the century was accompanied by corresponding emphasis on analogies which supported these principles. Thus Buchanan developed a variant of the popular anatomical figure; he described the state as a human body much as his predecessors had done, but presented the king as a physician obliged to maintain the health of the body.[26] Merbury opens his *Briefe Discourse*

[20] Chelidonius, *op. cit.*, pp. 16–17.

[21] *Ibid.*, pp. 18–20.

[22] *Ibid.*, Chapter III: "What the Dignitie Royall is, and how the same cannot be supplied without great trouble and danger: with a declaration of what kinde of government is best for the people to live happily and quietly."

[23] Bodin, *The Six Bookes of a Commonweale* (1606), pp. 8, 701, 718.

[24] Bilson, *The True Difference betweene Christian Subiection and Unchristian Rebellion* (1585), p. 249.

[25] Hayward, *An Answer to . . . R. Doleman* (1603), Sig. B, 4 r.

[26] Buchanan, *De iure regni apud Scotos* (1579), translated, 1689, p. 8.

of Royall Monarchie (1581) with an extended analogy between the sun, which rules in the heavens, and the king, who rules in the state.[27] Blandy not only develops the same figure, but adds the hierarchy of angels and an elaborate analysis of the political lessons discernible in the human body.[28]

The anatomical analogy became the focus of considerable attention in the controversy aroused by Robert Parsons' attack on hereditary unlimited monarchy. Parsons adopted the body-state parallel, but in order to prove his contention that kings can be forcibly removed by subjects, he argued that

the Body Natural, if it had the same ability that when it had an aking or sickly Head, it would cut it off and take another, I doubt not but it would so . . . rather than all the other parts should perish or live in pain and continual torment.[29]

Parsons' curious use of the analogy promptly drew the scorn of his opponents Wentworth and Hayward,[30] and Thomas Craig analyzed the parallel in some detail to show the absurdity of Parsons' application of it.[31] Elsewhere in his defense of hereditary monarchy Craig

[27] Merbury, *A Briefe Discourse of Royall Monarchie* (1581), p. 2.

[28] Blandy, *The Castle, or Picture of Pollicy* (1581), fol. 4, r and v.

[29] Parsons, *A Conference about the Next Succession to the Crowne of England* (1594), p. 38. Parsons was not the first of the advocates of limited monarchy to employ analogy in this fashion. John Ponet, in his *Short Treatise of Politike Power* (1556), 1642 edition, p. 28, wrote: "Commonwealths and realms may live, when the head is cut off, and may put on a new head, that is, make them a new Governour, when they see their old head seek too much his own will, and not the wealth of the whole body, for the which he was onely ordained."

[30] Peter Wentworth, *A Pithie Exhortation to Her Majestie for Establishing Her Successor to the Crowne* (1598), p. 47; Hayward, *op. cit.*, p. 36.

[31] Craig, *Concerning the Right of Succession to the Kingdom of England* (c. 1603), edition of 1703, p. 167: "As for reasons for this Doctrine of his [Parsons'], he brings none, but instead of them he entertains us with one Metaphor, and 'tis this, As the whole Body, says he, is of more Authority than the Head alone, and may cure the Head, if it be out of order, so may the multitude . . . cure or cut off their Heads, lest they infect the rest. A noble Metaphor indeed, which I thus retort upon himself. For seeing without the Head, the Body is only a dead Carcass, and can do nothing of itself without the Head, which is the seat of all the Animal Senses, therefore the Body can do nothing against the Head, seeing without the Body it is dead, neither had it Power over any Member, but with the consent of the Head. Who could endure such a Metaphor, that a Body may cut off its own Head, that it may remain a Body? . . . And I do not see . . . how a commonwealth can deprive their King and Sovereigne

employs most of the figures commonly accepted for political purposes in his day. He finds the sovereignty of a single king paralleled in similar leadership among bees, harts, cattle, cranes, geese, ducks, herons, fish, whales, and salmon, to use his own categories; [32] he likens the king to the father of a family, the shepherd of a flock, the sun in the heavens, the general of an army, the schoolmaster in a school, and the captain of a ship; [33] and he likens the divided kingdoms of England and Scotland to various two-headed monsters which have recently been described to him.[34]

Craig's work, written in 1603, shows that natural analogies as a device in political argument continued to flourish in the first decade of the seventeenth century. Thomas Floyd portrays *The Picture of a Perfit Commonwealth* (1600) in terms of parallels with the human body, and likens a democratic form of government to "the ugly Hydra, whych is sayd no sooner to lose one head, than immediately another groweth." [35] Fulbecke in his *Pandectes of the Law of Nations* (1602) denounces democracy as a monstrous body in which the heels stand in place of the head.[36] Hayward's fourfold parallel between world, state, family and body has already been mentioned.[37] Barnabe Barnes's *Foure Bookes of Offices* (1606) not only makes a minute comparison between

---

Lord who is its Head of this Crown and Kingdom. The safety of the whole Body Politick or Kingdom, and the tranquility of the State, depends on the safety of the Prince, who is its Head."

[32] Craig, *op. cit.*, pp. 12–13.

[33] *Ibid.*, p. 198: "For the King in his own Kingdom is the same, as the Sun is in Heaven, the Father in his Family, the General in his Army, the School-master in his School, or the Captain in his Ship."

[34] *Ibid.*, pp. 414–15: " 'Twould seem that God Almighty intended to represent to our Eyes by this Prodigy the State of Britain, which this Monster did greatly resemble, unless in this, that both those Heads, tho they were at variance sometimes, and did not agree between themselves, yet at other times they consulted together which was never as yet done by the two Heads of Britain; God designed, I say, to upbraid the ill agreement, and the inbred Rage and Fierceness of exercising Cruelties on our selves, and Threaten the severity of his Judgments, unless we, being thus admonished, repent and amend our doings. For such strange Monsters are no where Born, neither do unusual Signs and Wonders appear in the Air, but they foretell the Imminent Judgment of God, and indeed very Grievous ones ready to fall upon a people."

[35] Floyd, *The Picture of a Perfit Commonwealth* (1600), p. 19.

[36] Fulbecke, *The Pandectes of the Law of Nations* (1602), fol. 295.

[37] See above, p. 66.

the structure of states and the structure of various natural organisms,[38] but also develops at length the analogy between the king and the physician.[39]

Renaissance use of analogy in describing the nature and structure of states is perhaps most remarkably exemplified in Edward Forset's *A Comparative Discourse of the Bodies Natural and Politique. Wherein out of the Principles of Nature Is Set Forth the True Forme of a Commonweale, with the Dutie of Subiectes and the Right of the Soveraigne: Together with Many Good Points of Political Learning. . . .*[40] Published in 1606, this work makes analogy not a means to an end, as in the preceding works, but an end in itself. Forset was a minor public official under both Queen Elizabeth and her successor. He died in 1629 or 1630 after a career of political activity which included a prominent role in the examination of those concerned with the Gunpowder Plot. Political actualities apparently aroused in him an interest in theoretical aspects of the problems which he encountered. Beside the *Comparative Discourse* he published, in 1624, *A Defense of the Right of Kings; Wherein the Power of the Papacie over Princes Is Refuted, and the Oath of Allegiance Justified.* As the descriptive titles indicate, both works are expositions of a thoroughgoing absolutism.

The *Comparative Discourse* itself is a convincing demonstration of the very real significance which was generally attached to even the most minute parallels between the state and the natural world around it. From its detailed analysis of the human body there emerges a theory of the nature and structure of states complete in almost every respect. Forset begins by assuming "That in every particular person, there is both the seed and similitude of a state incorporat," [41] "That in the very composure of man, there is manifestly discovered a summary abstract of absolute perfection, by which as by an excellent Idea, or an exact rule, we may examine and exemplifie all other things." [42] He then proceeds to discuss the governing authority in a state as it is exemplified in the

[38] Barnes, *Foure Bookes of Offices* (1606), p. 66.

[39] *Ibid.*, "Epistle to King James." Cf. also, "A Iust King . . . is hyeroglyphically represented by figure of the sun," Sig. ¶, iii, r.

[40] For a discussion of Forset's work and of his political doctrines see J. W. Allen, *English Political Thought, 1603–1660*, I, 76 ff.

[41] Forset, *op. cit.*, "To the Reader," Sig. A, i v.   [42] *Ibid.*, p. 1.

relation of the soul to the body. The powers and activities of a political sovereign are described in terms of the vegetative, sensitive, and intellectual functions of the soul, as those functions were understood in Elizabethan psychology and physiology. The force of law in the state is likened to the force of reason which guides to a good end the actions of the body; the function of advisers to the function of the senses, which convey impressions to the soul; the dangers of evil counselors and flatterers to the dangers of the appetites, which seek to seduce the soul with passion. The component parts of the commonwealth are paralleled with the four elements which comprise the body; the generous nobles are the Fire, the learned scholars, preachers and educators are the Air, the yeomen and tillers of the soil are the Earth, and "trafiquers" or merchants are the Water. As the health of the body is determined by the balance and proportion maintained among the elements, so the health of the state is determined by similar proportion among the classes. Forset then goes into an extended discussion of the diseases which afflict the body and state from corresponding causes, and of the proper means—diet, exercise, medicine, surgery—by which both can be restored to health. With prolonged advice to the "physicians" of the body politic he concludes his *Comparative Discourse*.

In some respects Forset's work appears to be an unintentional *reductio ad absurdum* of the whole analogical approach to theories of the state. This effect is particularly evident when the writer carries his parallels to the lungs, lights, liver, gall, and kidneys, and to the various natural functions of the body.[43] For the most part, however, the com-

---

[43] *Ibid.*, pp. 35–36: "The Soule also hath made choice of some other principall parts of the body, which he needfully useth and employeth in the ministeriall functions of life; which if they once either fayle in their offices, or decay in their essence, the body can neither continue living, nor performe his actions: of which sort may be reckoned, first the lungs and lights, ordeined for the alaying of the heat in the heart, and the necessities of respiration: Then the liver, which beginneth the concoction of our sustenance, and the same so prepared, doth recommend over to the hearts more perfect converting and accommodating: Lastly the milt, the gall, and the kidneys, everie wherof is allotted to some good worke of dissevering the refuse and drossie remnants from the selected and purified nutriment. . . . Only two considerations I have conceived, which mee thinketh may not bee omitted. The first, that as these bee placed so helpfully in the body, with such succeeding each other in their works, as accordeth to an accomplishment of health and perfection in the whole: so there must bee in the publike weale, a wise and political ordering of the good gifts and imployments of the chiefe statesmen, that their endeavors be discreetly sorted to the general good."

parisons are handled skilfully and pointedly. The earnestness and care which characterizes his analysis makes strikingly apparent the genuine respect with which Renaissance theorists regarded this method of political discussion.

By Shakespeare's day, therefore, argument by analogy was definitely established as a device almost inevitably associated with the presentation of the state-concept in political literature. Forset, in a preface to his *Comparative Discourse,* alludes to the widespread use of the analogical method, acknowledges its purely rhetorical value, and summarizes the most popular figures:

The commonweale with all her parts, order, qualities and requisites whatsoever, is (for better understanding and illustration) set forth by sundry fit resemblances, as by the architecture of an house, by the swarming and cohabitation of Bees in a hive, by a ship floating on the sea, and such like; but by none more properly than eyther by the universal masse of the whole world . . . or else by the body of man, being the lesser world, even the diminitive and modell of that wide extending universall.[44]

It would not be far from the truth to assert that no concept of the state was presented in Tudor literature without some reference to such parallels in the world of nature. Conversely, as a result of such general currency, the more popular figures came to stand as symbols suggesting, without need of further elaboration, the concept of state with which they had for so long been associated. And so common did this association become that it is frequently found in records of informal conversation. Queen Elizabeth, in denouncing Condé's rebellion before the French ambassador, adopted the familiar anatomical analogy when she asserted:

There is nothing in the world I hold in greater horror than to see a body moving against its head: and I shall be very careful not to ally myself with such a monster.[45]

Few writers failed to recognize the rhetorical value of analogy and to employ it as a means of presenting in concrete, easily comprehended form their abstract theories concerning the nature, structure and government of human civil society.

[44] *Ibid.*, "To the Reader," Sig. ¶, iii r.
[45] F. Chamberlin, *Sayings of Queen Elizabeth* (1923), p. 182.

2

But figurative analogy was apparently more than a rhetorical device in the minds of sixteenth-century theorists, more than a superficial decoration designed to render political theory more attractive and more comprehensible to the layman. It was a key to the philosophical and religious principles, discussed in the preceding chapter, upon which states are founded. The real value of analogies, according to the thinking of the Renaissance, arises from the fact that God created every department of His universe on the same pattern and subject to the same laws. Thus He surrounded mankind with examples, in microcosm and macrocosm, of the divinely ordained order to be followed by man in his own social and political life. Analogies, therefore, were valid illustrations of desirable political order because they revealed the one universal order established by eternal and natural laws for all created things.

The philosophy as well as the practice of analogical political argument was inherited by the Renaissance from the middle ages. Gierke, writing of the principles which determined the use of parallels in the earlier period, concludes:

But as there must of necessity be connexion between the various groups, and as all of them must be connected with the divinely ordered Universe, we come by the further notion of a divinely instituted Harmony which pervades the Universal Whole and every part thereof. To every Being is assigned its place in that Whole, and to every link between Beings corresponds a divine decree. But since the World is One Organism, animated by One Spirit, fashioned by One Ordinance, the self-same principles that appear in the structure of the World will appear once more in the structure of its every Part. Therefore every particular Being, in so far as it is a Whole, is a diminished copy of the World; it is a *Microcosmus* or *Minor Mundus* in which the *Macrocosmus* is mirrored. In the fullest measure this is true of every human individual; but it holds good also of every human community and of human society in general. Thus the Theory of Human Society must accept the divinely created organization of the Universe as a prototype of the first principles which govern the construction of human communities.[46]

---

[46] Gierke, *Political Theories of the Middle Age*, p. 8. As Professor Gerig points out,

This philosophy, which explains the real significance which analogy held for Renaissance political theorists, is most fully and consistently set forth by Forset in the preface "To the Reader" in his *Comparative Discourse*. Forset, however, was merely giving coherent expression to principles which had been recognized by English political writers since the days of Elyot and Starkey. The theory of analogy which he expounds was that generally accepted in Renaissance thinking about the nature and structure of states.

The theory rests on the conception of universal laws which guide the action of all things to the same end. Because these laws, as expressions of divine will, are essentially the same, all things subject to them exhibit the same organization of elements and purpose of action. Therefore, it was argued, God established one order for the whole universe and all its parts. Elyot briefly recognizes this fundamental principle to be involved in his use of analogy when he asks, "For who can denie but that all thyng in heven and erthe is gouerned by one God, by one perpetuall ordre, by one prouidence?" [47] The Homilies of 1547 argue from the same basic assumption: "All mightie God hath created and appointed all thinges, in heaven, yearth, and waters in a most excellent and perfect order." [48]

Because natural law embodies the will of God, nature itself makes manifest to man the divinely ordained order. Thus Chelidonius argues:

For let us behold with iudgement the universall order of Nature and we shall find that in the creation of all things hee hath used a great and marvellous wisedome. . . .[49]

So conceived, nature exhibits in all its phases and aspects a universal parallelism. Whether in the large, as in the framework of the whole universe or of the solar system, or in the small, as in the framework of the beehive or of the human body, one pattern is manifestly apparent. Thus John Knox described the human body as one of the mirrors of natural order.[50] Bodin recognizes the principle of universal parallelism

a comprehensive Renaissance treatment of this medieval philosophy of analogy is found in Maurice Scève's *Microcosmus* (1562).

[47] Elyot, *op. cit.*, p. 8.

[48] *Certayne Sermons or Homilies* (1547), Homily X, Sig. K, i r.

[49] Chelidonius, *A Most Excellent Historie* (1571), p. 16.

[50] Knox, *The First Blast of the Trumpet against the Monstrous Regiment of Women* (1558), in *Works*, edited by Laing, IV, 390.

when he finds evidence for monarchy "whether that we behold this little world which hath but one bodie and but one head . . . or if we look to this great world which hath but one sovereign God." [51] Accepting the same concept of uniformity in macrocosm and in microcosm, Hayward can assert that the world, the state, the family, and the body, are identical in their essential structure.[52]

Mankind, as a creature of God and subject to the laws of nature, must necessarily follow this same universal order in all his activities, whether individual or social. Because his society comes into being at the behest of natural law, it must follow, in its organization and action, the dictates of that law. His communal life will partake of the order established by divine will for communal life throughout the universe, whether of bees or of angels. His society therefore takes its place in the parallel structure of the universe. By looking at the larger world above the state, or at the smaller world within it, man can see and study the pattern which his own social existence must follow. As Forset points out:

I will . . . from this observation of God's own imitating himselfe in the likenesse of the lesse with the greater, gather and infer that which giveth groundworke unto my purpose: That the incomprehensible wisedome of God in the composing and ordering of his works in nature, hath so dignified them with all perfection, as that they be left unto us as eminent and exemplary patterns, as well, for the consolidating as for the beautifying of that wee worke by arte or pollicie; as well for conioining of all discordances into firmnesses, as also for the applyablenesse of particulars in their many services, for the use and benefit of the whole.[53]

Forset brings out more clearly than any of his predecessors the didactic function of analogies. The parallels upon which they are based instruct man not only concerning the form of his social life, but concerning the divine will which prescribes this form. As there can be no organization better than that established by God in the parts of the beehive, of the solar system or of the human body, Forset concludes that man, in organizing the elements of his own community, can best attain the divine order by careful analysis of these examples:

[51] Bodin, *The Six Bookes of a Commonweale* (1606), p. 718.
[52] Hayward, *An Answer to . . . R. Doleman* (1603), Sig. B, 4 r.
[53] Forset, *op. cit.,* "To the Reader," Sig. ¶, iii v.

It is beyond the compasse of any contradiction that in the morall vertues Christes actions are our instructions, and no lesse may the rule hold, that in the contriving of a prudent government, the impressions and footesteps of God's wisedome (which in thynges naturall wee contemplate by study) bee in poynt of regiment, our directories for imitation. Wherefore, seeing that the uttermost extent of mans understanding, can shape no better forme of ordering the affayres of a state than by marking and matching of the works of the finger of God, eyther in the larger volume of the unyversall, or in the abridgement thereof, the body of man . . . I have made my choyce to pursue only applyances, which from the so skillful workmanship of God in man, may be well apted to the civill government of the assemblies of men.[54]

This whole conception of analogies and their use is agreeable, of course, to the Renaissance theory that man by the use of reason discovers in natural law the ordinances of eternal law which affect his own welfare.

In the sixteenth-century discussions of the state, then, analogy serves several important purposes. In the first place, as a result of long-established association, it provides a reliable preliminary identification of the state-concept generally accepted in Renaissance political thinking. In the second place, as a rhetorical device it affords a concrete and simple medium for the expression of abstract theories of civil society. In the third place, and most significantly, it constitutes an approach to political truth founded in the very nature of God's universe, for it reveals not only the nature and structure of states, but also the philosophical and religious principles which both determine and authorize this structure. The nature of political society, as it was ideally conceived to be in the sixteenth century, can largely be determined, therefore, in terms of these analogies.

[54] *Ibid.*

CHAPTER V

The Structure of Political Society

THERE WERE, as Professor Allen has observed, "certain notions concerning society that were very widespread in the sixteenth century, and not only in England."[1] This statement is made with reference to the fundamental agreement among Renaissance theorists concerning the particular structure of political society which, they believed, was prescribed by God for the welfare of mankind. Marked differences might distinguish their opinions on the scope of royal authority, the right of rebellion, the position of the church, and similar problems within the structure of the state. But as to the component elements of the body politic, and the basic order and arrangement of those elements, there was virtually universal concord. With few exceptions, theorists assumed that the pattern established by God for all nature was the pattern ordained by Him for human political society. The structure so envisaged received its most detailed exposition in those works which belong to the genre of "the very and true commonweal"—works such as those by Starkey, Crowley, Smith and Case. But an outline of essentially the same concept appears in numerous works primarily concerned with some particular problem within the whole structure.

The main features of this framework are embodied in the general definitions of political society which were occasionally essayed by Renaissance theorists. Elyot thus compiled "ane definition out of many":

A publike weale is a body lyuyng, compacte or made of sondry astates and degrees of men, which is disposed by the ordre of equitie and governed by the rule and moderation of reason.[2]

---

[1] Allen, *A History of Political Thought in the Sixteenth Century*, p. 135. See *Ibid.*, Part II, Chapter III for a discussion of some of the problems and writers considered in this chapter.

[2] Elyot, *The Boke Named the Gouernour* (1531), p. 1, Everyman's Library.

Some half-century later John Case offered a basically similar, if more extended definition, when he wrote:

Definitur ergo respub. hoc modo, ut sit ordo civitatis cum aliorum magistratuum, tum eius maxime, cui tradita est summa potestas & arbitrium rerum. Est ordo, quia prudenter disponit; est ordo civitatis, quia non unius opinionem sed civilem consensum sapienter postulat; est ordo aliorum magistratuum, quia inferiores classes gradusq; honoris dignioribus iuste distribuit; est denique ordo summae potestatis, quia quis dominus sit in omni civitatis statu honorifice praescribit.[3]

And at the turn of the century Thomas Floyd, in *The Picture of a Perfit Commonwealth* (1600) reiterated the words of Elyot when he maintained that "A Commonwealth is a living body compact of sundry estates and degrees of men . . . ," that it is "a congregation, or a multitude of inhabitants, beyng as it were, the mother of us all," and that it is "the regiment and estate of a citie, disposed by order of equitie and ruled by moderation of reason." [4]

In these and similar passages political society is pictured as a stratified body in which ascending degrees or classes of men, determined by merit and vocation and surmounted by a sovereign controlling authority, work in concord and harmony for the welfare of the whole organization. The entire purport of analogical argument was to demonstrate that political society, like every other department of universal creation, was so arranged that when each constituent part functions in its proper place and to the best of its ability, the purpose for which God established the whole structure will be achieved, whether that purpose be production of honey in a beehive, physical health in a human body, or material and spiritual felicity in a political body. In its essence this is the concept which, by means of dissemination through sermons, histories, and popular pamphlets, as well as through learned treatises, came to occupy a central and dominating position in Renaissance thinking about the nature and structure of states.

Essential to an understanding of such a theory of political society is an awareness of the tremendous significance which the terms "order" and "degree" held for Renaissance thinkers. Few principles in six-

---

[3] Case, *Sphaera civitatis* (1588), p. 224.
[4] Floyd, *The Picture of a Perfit Commonwealth* (1600), pp. 1–4. These definitions are, of course, merely reworkings of Aristotle's definition of the state.

teenth-century political writing received greater or more general emphasis than the concept of order, which was recognized not only as the foundation of human society, but as the first and most important injunction of divine and natural law. For order could be observed as the very basis of existence throughout the universe. As Elyot concludes:

More over take away ordre from all thynges what shulde then remayne? Certes . . . *Chaos:* which of some is expounde a confuse mixture. Also where there is any lack of ordre nedes must be perpetuall conflicte: and in thynges subiecte to Nature nothyng of hymselfe onely may be norisshed; but whan he hath distroyed that where with he doth participate by the ordre of his creation, he hym selfe of necessitie must then perisshe, whereof en-sueth universall dissolution.[5]

Such order could not exist, theorists argued, without the differences of degree which distinguish the elements in any organization. To quote from Elyot again:

In euery thyng is ordre, and without ordre may be nothing stable or perma-nent; and it may nat be called ordre, excepte it do contayne in it degrees, high and base, accordynge to the merite or estimation of the thyng that is ordred.[6]

In every aspect of divine creation these grades and ranks could be observed, for as Elyot asks, "Hath not [God] set degrees and astates in all his glorious warkes?" In searching for examples to prove his point Elyot leaves few corners of the universal frame unexplored. In heaven he finds "divers degrees called hierarchies," and in the body of man, "the foure elements . . . set in their places called spheris, higher or lower, accordynge to the soveraigntie of theyr natures . . ." A similar order of degrees, "begynnyng at the most inferior or base, and assend-ynge upwarde" he observes also in "every kynde of trees, herbes, birdes, beastis, and fisshes." [7] Homily X of those published in 1547 opens its arguments for obedience to kings with a general statement of the princi-ple of order based on differences of degree; it asserts:

All mightie God hath created and appointed all thinges, in heavē, yearth, and waters, in a most excellent and perfect order. In the heaven he hath appointed distinct order and states of archangelles and Angels. In yearth

---

[5] Elyot, *op. cit.*, p. 3.   [6] *Ibid.*, p. 4.   [7] *Ibid.*, pp. 3–4.

he hath assigned kynges, princes, with other governors under them, all in good and necessary order.[8]

Chelidonius, translated in 1571, makes the same observation when he writes:

We shall finde that in the creation of all thinges hee [God] hath used a marvellous and great wisdom not making therein all thinges to bee equal, but hath made a separation and difference among them, and gyuen a certaine preheminence and notable mark, by whiche they may be discerned the one from the other. . . .[9]

Man, subject to the laws of God and nature, is affected by these universal principles of order and degree no less than other creatures. The concept of political society as a hierarchical organism is based on the assumption that all men are not created equal. This assumption the modern student, reared on doctrines of democratic equality, must understand clearly if he is to appreciate the temper of Renaissance political theory and the character of the Renaissance state. According to sixteenth-century theorists, men are endowed with abilities, powers, and virtues which vary with the individual and determine his rank in the social and political scheme of things. Having observed the inequalities which characterize the degrees in the order of heaven and the natural world, Elyot, in arguments typical of his century, concludes that one should expect to find similar differences in men:

Nowe to retourne to the astate of man kynde . . . , hit semeth that in hym shulde be no lasse providence of god declared than in the inferior creatures, but rather with a more perfect ordre and dissposition. And therfore hit appereth that god gyueth nat to euery man like gyftes of grace, or of nature, but to some more, some lesse, as it liketh his diuine maiestie.[10]

---

[8] *Certayne Sermons or Homilies* (1547), Homily X, Sig. K, i r.

[9] Chelidonius, *A Most Excellent Historie of the Institution and Firste Beginning of Christian Princes, and the Originall of Kingdomes* (translated, 1571), p. 16. In this connection it is interesting to note the argument for order advanced by James I: "Heaven itself is governed by order, and all the good Angels there; nay, Hell itself could not subsist without some order; and the very devils are divided into Legions, and have their chieftans: how can any society upon earth subsist without order and degrees?" (*A Premonition to All Kings of Christendom*, quoted by C. J. Sisson in "King James the First of England as Poet and Political Writer," *Seventeenth Century Studies Presented to Sir Herbert Grierson*, 1938, p. 59.)

[10] Elyot, *op. cit.*, p. 4.

The reprehension with which Renaissance theorists viewed concepts of the equality of men expresses in converse form the principle of natural inequality. "To have all degrees alike, and no inequalities, how inconuenient," remarks the marginal commentator in the Holinshed version of Cheke's *Hurt of Sedicion,* and he adds, "The unconscionable wishing of equalitie, how hurtful." [11] Cheke himself, in redressing the rebels of 1549, accuses them of seeking unnatural equality when they attempt to seize the power and wealth of those superior to them; he urges them to be content with their God-given inferiority when he writes:

And think besides that riches and inheritance be Gods providence, and given to whom of his wisedome he thinketh good . . . Why doe not we then beinge poore beare it wisely, rather than by lust seek riches uniustly; and shew our selves contented with God's ordinaunce, which we must either willingly obey, and then we be wise; or else we must unprofitably strive withall, and then we be mad? [12]

Further support for this point of view, particularly as it applies to political power, was given by Bodin later in the century. There can, by the laws of God and nature, be no equality in the wealth and talents of men, he argues, "And as for the power of command, which popular men would make equal, there is lesse reason then in goods; for discretion and wisdom is not equally given to all men." [13]

To Renaissance thinkers the wisdom and goodness of God was particularly manifest in the existence of these inequalities in men. The needs of mankind are many and varied, they argued; all men must be fed, clothed, protected from enemies domestic and foreign, and instructed in virtue. It would be impossible for each man to do all these things efficiently and perfectly for himself, or for one man to do them for all. God therefore creates each man with a particular talent or ability designed to satisfy a particular requirement not only for himself but for his fellows, who meantime are exercising their special gifts to fill other needs for him. Thus Elyot can assert that the differences among individuals are "distributed in to sondry uses, faculties and of-

[11] In Raphael Holinshed, *Chronicles of England, Scotland, and Ireland* (1807), III, 990.
[12] *Ibid.*   [13] Bodin, *The Six Bookes of a Commonweale* (1606), p. 707.

fices, necesary for the lyuyng and gouernance of mankynde." [14] According to this theory no man, however limited his means, is created without a definite purpose. The principle is made clear to man by the examples in universal nature. For as Forset maintains:

In the bodie there is not any part so weake, so little or so base, which God hath not framed and appointed to some good use, . . . Let us but observe nature, who because she would be sure to make nothing in vain, (thereby teaching us in the order of government, to allowe no needelesse or fruitlesse parts) hath endued and designed some one part unto many uses.[15]

Blandy, in *The Castle, or Picture of Pollicy* (1581), illustrates how, in the sixteenth century, the diversities among men were considered to be divinely adapted to the needs and purposes of society. He exclaims:

When I consider with my selfe how requisite and necessary it is, that men should differ in degree and dignity, and that innumerable artes and sciences have been devised to mayntayne the common society of men, and no man may excell in all, and few at any time may attaine the best: I can no lesse maruayle at, then commend, the deuine decree of nature, whose prouidence hath wrought and appoynted the varyetye of wittes, dispositions, and qualities.[16]

On the basis of these inequalities and the functions to which they are adapted men are divided, according to Renaissance theory, into distinct classes or estates. Such groups constitute the "degrees" which comprise the order of civil society. Each group is a "vocation" in the most literal sense of the word, for it is the position to which the individual or group of individuals has been called by God. The list of vocations which make up the structure of political society was, in a large degree, an inheritance from the "estates" of medieval social philosophy; it remained fairly constant throughout the Renaissance. The principal vocations appearing in sixteenth-century theory are the ruling nobility, the learned scholars and priests, the military forces, the merchants, the craftsmen, and the agricultural workers. Not all the lists agreed in particulars,

---

[14] Elyot, *op. cit.*, p. 5.
[15] Forset, *A Comparative Discourse of the Bodies Natural and Politique* (1606), pp. 54-55.
[16] *Op. cit.*, fol. 27 v.

however. Starkey, in his analogy between the bodies human and political, considered the component elements of society to be rulers, magistrates, craftsmen, soldiers, farmers, and laborers.[17] Robert Crowley, seeking in *The Voyce of the Laste Trumpet* (1549) to impress upon a corrupt England the need for the proper functioning of all its vocational classes, addresses his appeal to beggars, servants, yeomen, priests, scholars, physicians, lawyers, merchants, gentlemen, magistrates, and women—in that order.[18] The homilists similarly define the ranks of political society in economic and sociological terms.[19] Bodin devotes an entire chapter to an account of the classes which comprise a commonwealth—king, clergy, Senate, army, lawyers, doctors, schoolmen, business men, and craftsmen.[20] Numerous treatises written in the sixteenth century deal specifically with the nature and duties of individual classes, and they frequently evolved quite different theories about them.[21] But all such works, and certainly all treatises concerned more generally with the structure of political society, concurred in recognizing such vocational groups as the basic elements of the social system.

Human inequality, which according to sixteenth-century thinking determined the nature of each vocation, determined also the pattern in

[17] Starkey, *A Dialogue between Cardinal Pole and Thomas Lupset*, pp. 48–49, "Early English Text Society," Extra Series, Vol. XXXII.

[18] Crowley, *The Voyce of the Laste Trumpet*, in *Select Works*, p. 57, "Early English Text Society," Extra Series, Vol. XV.

[19] Cf. for example the passage quoted below (p. 84) from *Certayne Sermons or Homilies* (1547).

[20] Bodin, *op. cit.*, Book III, Chapter VIII. To these examples should be added the work attributed to William Stafford, *A Compendious or Briefe Examination of Certain Ordinary Complaints* (1581), in which a Knight, a Merchant, a Doctor, a Capper and a Husbandman, discussing the economic ills of the country, conclude that every degree must act in its vocation if England is to be restored to national health. Thomas Smith in *The Commonwealth of England* (translated, 1589), p. 43, describes the classes which comprise a political society as "The gentlemen, which be divided into two partes, the Baronie, or estate of Lordes conteyning barons and all that be above the degree of baron . . . and those that be no lordes, as knights, Esquires, and simply Gentlemen. The thirde and laste sort of persons is named the yeomanrie." Goslicius, in *The Counsellor* (translated, 1598), p. 19, recognizes six classes of men in a state: husbandmen, artisans, merchants, soldiers, priests, and judges and counselors.

[21] A bibliography of such works, with illustrative material will be found in *Shakespeare's England*, edited by C. T. Onions, 2 vols. (1917), Vol. I, Chapters XI and XII. For a more extensive discussion of the subject see Ephraim Lipson, *The Economic History of England* (1931), Vols. II and III, and Ruth Mohl, *The Three Estates in Medieval and Renaissance Literature* (1933).

which these vocations were organized in a political society. Depending on the value of its contribution to society, each vocation was assigned a rank or degree in the structure of the state, and was expected to maintain that position, performing its ordained function and obeying the degrees superior to it. Generally in Renaissance theory the rank of a vocation depended on its relative content of intellectual understanding and moral virtue. Elyot has the former quality in mind as a criterion for establishing degree when he writes:

Nat withstanding for as moche as understandyng is the most excellent gyfte that man can receive in his creation, wherby he doth approche most nyghe unto the similitude of god; whiche understandynge is the principal parte of the soule: it is therefor congruent, and accordynge that as one excelleth an other in that influence, as therby beinge next to the similitude of his maker, so shulde the astate of his persone be auanced in degree or place where understandynge may profite . . .[22]

Bodin, on the other hand, argues at length to prove that moral virtue is the mark of true nobility and therefore the determining factor in the order of degrees among vocational groups in the commonwealth. Thus he maintains that "painters, image makers, carvers, makers and sellers of womens paintings, minstrels, players, dancers, fencers, tumblers, iesters, and bawds are in mine opinion either to be quite driven out of cities, or else placed in the lowest place of all." [23] Whether intellectual or moral virtue be the criterion, it will be observed that this principle of ranking is in complete conformity with theories of the highest purpose of the state, that the positions of greatest authority and honor are given to those vocations which are most conducive to the spiritual felicity of man.

There is the "very and true commonweal," therefore, where the vocations to which men are naturally adapted are maintained in the proper order of their degrees of merit and contribution. As Elyot concludes, "it is onely a publike weale, where, like as god hath disposed the said influence of understandynge, is also appoynted degrees and places accordynge to the excellencie thereof." [24] A more comprehensive picture of essentially the same structure is that given in the Homily of 1547, which asserts, on the authority of parallels in nature, that

[22] Elyot, *op. cit.*, p. 5.   [23] Bodin, *op. cit.*, p. 402.   [24] Elyot, *op. cit.*, p. 6.

every degre of people, in their vocation, callyng, and offyce, hath appoynted to them, theyr dutie and order. Some are in high degree, some in lowe, some kynges and princes, some inferiors and subiectes, priestes and laimen, masters and servants, fathers and chyldrē, husbandes and wifes, riche and poore, and every one have nede of other; so that in all thinges, is to be lauded and praysed, the goodly order of God, without the whiche, no house, no cite, no commonwealth, can well continue and endure.[25]

John Knox argued that just as in the human body God has appointed the head to guide and control the whole organism and has ordained that "the rest of the members have every one their own place and office appointed," so in the political body each constituent element has its own office, and, conformable to that office, its particular rank in the structure.[26] Perhaps the clearest exposition of the principle of order and degree as it was associated with the concept of vocation in Renaissance thinking about the nature of political society is that given by Blandy in *The Castle, or Picture of Pollicy.* The following passage may be quoted at length not only to indicate the relative values most commonly attached to each vocation, but to reveal the hierarchical arrangement of the degrees generally recognized by theorists of the sixteenth century. Having described rulers as most highly endowed with godly virtue and wisdom, he continues:

Dame Nature therefore the mother of all thinges hath placed in the world principally such in the highest Roomes; of which order are kinges and Princes. Other some she hath not framed in such perfect wyse, for the clearnesse and shining glory of virtue and nobility; yet she hath imparted unto them a most sharp wit and ready capacity, great value and singular providence. Herehence the iusticer and souldiar springeth. . . . On other she hath bestowed a mind and courage that . . . adventure strainge and untried vioges. Herehence ye famous companies of adventuring Marchaunts floweth. . . . Other she hath made more simple of understanding, more cold of courage, and therefore iustly hath appointed unto them, to toyle in servile arts, of which sort are they whom we term artificers, men of oc-

---

[25] *Certayne Sermons or Homilies* (1547), Homily X, Sig. K, i r.

[26] Knox, *The First Blast of the Trumpet against the Monstrous Regiment of Women,* in *Works,* edited by Laing, IV, 390.

cupation, Tillers of the grounde with theyr helpers, poore, simple and laboursome men.[27]

In a political society so constructed it was considered essential that each individual adhere rigorously to the established order. The doctrine of obedience, one of the most fundamental in Renaissance political thinking, extended not only to political authority, but to vocation. Whether his function was to carry the hod or to carry the scepter, each man was expected to remain in his appointed rank and do the job assigned to him. As Professor Allen remarks, "The religious duty of obedience to the Prince was constantly associated with the conception of a similar duty in relation to every recognized form of authority in human society. . . ."[28] Moreover, "It is every man's duty to labour in his vocation and be obedient to his superiors. So he does his duty in that state of life to which it has pleased God to call him."[29] Obedience in this double sense was the principle of action whereby the pattern of social organization was maintained and was enabled to function as God meant it to function.

The revival of classic theory tended to reinforce the doctrine of obedience which the Renaissance had inherited, in a large part, from medieval social and political thinking.[30] Thus Isocrates, in an English translation made in 1580, spoke as follows to the Tudor period:

I require and charge you that euery one of you doe execute that office and function whereunto he is called, both diligently and faithfully . . . be so carefull and diligent in those thinges whiche you take in hand as to perswade your selves that the well doing and ordering of every particular matter, is the only meanes whereby the universall estate of every commonweale doth flourish and prosper, for there must needes bee a most happie Realme where every man perticulerly hath a care to performe his dutie, and to amende himself in ought that is amisse.[31]

These views are identical with those expressed by practically all sixteenth-century theorists. Even those who defended the right of rebellion against rulers asserted without qualification the duty of adherence to vocation and urged obedience to authority except under the most ex-

[27] Blandy, op. cit., fol. 27 v.   [28] Allen, op. cit., p. 135.   [29] Ibid., p. 136.
[30] Cf. Gierke, Political Theories of the Middle Age, p. 26.
[31] Isocrates, A Perfite Looking Glasse for All Estates (1580), fol. 43 r.

traordinary and limited circumstances. Starkey's attitude is fairly representative of the latter group; he writes:

Ther ys the true commyn wele where as al the partys, as membrys of one body, by knyt togyddur in perfayt love and unyte; every one dowyng hys office and duty, aftur such maner that, what so ever state, offyce or degre, any man be of, the duty therto perteynyng wyth all dylygence he besyly fulfyl, and wythout envy or malyce to other accomplysh the same.[32]

Much of the odium attached to ambition in both medieval and Renaissance thinking and writing was derived from the belief that it led men to forsake their vocations and thus upset the social and political order. Robert Crowley makes this association of ideas apparent when he writes in *The Voyce of the Laste Trumpet* (1549):

> Whoso woulde that all thynges were well
> And woulde hymselfe by wyth out blame,
> Let hym geue eare, for I wyll tell
> The waye how to performe the same.
> Fyrste, walke in thy vocation
> And do not seke thy lotte to change,
> For through wycked ambition,
> Many mens fortunes hath bene straynge.[33]

Forset finds support for the concept of obedience in the law of nature, as exemplified in the organization and functioning of the parts of the human body:

Each part is to know and administer his owne proper worke, without entermising or entermeddling in the offices of an other. Shall the foot be permitted to partake in point of preeminence with the head? or were it seemlie for the head, leaving his state, to abuse himselfe to a toyle manibus pedibusq; in the trading business. For each member to take upon him all works, as it hath in nature an impossibilitie, so hath it in governaunce as great an incongruitie. And for any part to neglect the duties properly to it allotted, or to run forth of the circle within the which it is fixed . . . as

---

[32] Starkey, *op. cit.*, p. 55.

[33] Crowley, *op. cit.*, p. 57. Crowley asserts further (*The Way to Wealth*, p. 147) that vocation is binding on successive generations: "And if for youre worthinesse God have called you to offyce so that ye may wyth good conscience take upon you the state that ye be called unto, then se you deal iustly in all poyntes, and folow not fylthy lucre to make your chyldren lordes, but studye to furnish them with al knowledge and godly maners, that they may worthily succeed you."

it agreeth not with that so well parted, yet uniforme frame of Gods work-manship, so is it not to be suffered neither in any well contrived pollicie of the governing wisdome.[34]

Besides the injunctions of divine and natural law there were, theorists argued, very practical reasons for this obedience to duty and authority. In order to understand these reasons it is necessary to realize that in sixteenth-century thinking the welfare of the state was placed before the welfare of the individual. All the activities of men are to be pointed not to their own particular ends, but to the one, common end, the health and prosperity of political society. Ponet, for example, asserts that "Next unto God, men ought to love their country, and the whole Commonwealth before any member of it." [35] And Forset writes:

It is not therefore called a Commonwealth, that all the wealth should be common; but because the whole wealth, wit, power, and goodnesse, what-soever, of every particular person, must be conferred and reduced to the common good: and that in the same sort and semblance as the distinct members of the bodie, being ordained to different uses, do yet concurre in this consonance of intention, as to impart and referre all their helps and indeavors (to the uttermost reach of their abilities) for the procuring and preserving of the comfort and continuance of this one bodie.[36]

This, of course, is in quite unqualified form the concept of state which the twentieth century has learned to call totalitarian. As a modern scholar has concluded with reference to the earlier concept:

In that perfect commonwealth, waste and dishonesty and mere self-seeking disappear and every member of the community works single-mindedly for the common good . . . Society must be thought of as a cooperative association, in which the duty of every member to the whole is primary. That is, above all, what the political thinking of the time insisted upon.[37]

Such a structure, with its gross economic and political inequalities, and with its complete subordination of the individual to the autocratic

[34] Forset, *op. cit.*, pp. 48–49.
[35] Ponet, *A Short Treatise of Politike Power* (1642 edition), p. 28. With this should be compared Goslicius, *op. cit.*, p. 59: "It is . . . the part of a good citizen and good man, entering into magistracy, to preferre the welfare and honour of the commonweale before his private reputation and domesticall commoditie."
[36] Forset, *op. cit.*, p. 48.   [37] Allen, *op. cit.*, p. 137.

authority of the state, was justified in Renaissance theory by the belief that only thereby was the ultimate welfare of the individual to be brought about. In working solely for the common good, the individual was working most efficiently, and in greatest conformity with divine and natural purpose, for his own good. No more striking an expression of this rationalization of the totalitarian state can be found than that given by Starkey in the following excerpt from his *Dialogue:*

> But even as the commyn wele ys in every mannys mouth, so also hyt schold be fyxed in theyr hartys; hyt schold be the end of theyr cogyta-tyones, conseylys, and carys. For even as gud marynerys, when they, by theyr craft and dylygence, bryng theyr schype save out of tempestys into the sure port and haven, dow not only save other beyng in theyr schype but themselfe also, so cytyzens in any cuntrey, cyte or towne, when they, by prudent pollycy, maynteyne cyvyle ordur and gud rule, ever settyng forward the veray and true commyn wele, dow not only save other wych be under the same gouernaunce, and state, but also themselfe.[38]

When men conform to the pattern of political society ordained by God, general health and prosperity are naturally and inevitably produced. Hooker writes: "For we see the whole world and each part thereof so compacted, that as long as each thing performeth only that work which is natural unto it, it thereby preserveth both other things and also itself." [39] As has been suggested, the unequal abilities of individuals are adapted to the various general needs of mankind. So closely integrated is the system of vocational degrees that each class, functioning in its proper place and respecting those above it in authority, makes a contribution essential to the welfare of the whole and hence to the welfare of the individual. Political society, according to this conception, is a delicately geared machine, and if any one cog fail in its individual task, the whole machine, designed for the good of all, is thrown out of commission. Obedience, diligence, love, and honor will keep each man in his vocation and enable the commonwealth to achieve the ends for which it was established; rebellion, ambition, greed, and envy will turn a man from his duty and thus upset the whole order.

Maintenance of the order of degrees was frequently identified with the harmony or proportion essential to the health of any organization

---

[38] Starkey, *op. cit.*, pp. 66–67.
[39] Hooker, *Of the Laws of Ecclesiastical Polity*, I, 185, Everyman's Library.

of dissimilar elements. Such is the "Proportion" which Blandy describes as "that whiche dothe most firmly and strongly ioyne and knitt these parts together," and which he defines as "the just, right and natural measure of thinges, directed to theyr originall and first creation." [40] A similar concept is implicit in Sir John Cheke's injunction to the rebels in 1549; he warns them that

it is plainly impossible that that Countrey shall well stand in government and the people grow to wealth, where order in every state is not fitly observed, and that body cannot be without much griefe, where any least part is out of joint, or not duly set in his own naturall place. Wherefore order must be kept in the Commonwealth like health in the body, and all the drift of pollicie looketh to this end, how this temper may be safely maintained, without any excesse of unmeasureablenesse, either of one side or of the other. [41]

Forset describes the same phenomenon as the "temperature" by which the health of bodies anatomical and political alike is preserved. He argues that the four elements which comprise the human body—Fire, Air, Earth, and Water—are paralleled in the political body by the nobility, the learned, the yeomen, and the merchants. It is essential to the well-being of both bodies that "a concurrence or even mixture" of these four elements be maintained. In either instance, any disproportion among the elements, any change in the natural "temperature," will produce illness and deformity. "Wherefore," he concludes,

right needful it is in any Commonweale, to contrive the true and proportionable mixture of these foure elements, lest when they be put at odds, reverting to the original repugnances of their nature, they do fill the state with hateful strifes, in the steed of blessfull peace. [42]

Starkey draws a vivid picture of that commonwealth in which, through the observation of the principle of obedience, this proportion is maintained:

For when al theys partys thes couplyd togyddur, exercyse wyth dylygence theyr offyce and duty, as the plowmen and laburarys of the ground dylygently tyl the same, for the gettyng of fode and necessary sustenance to the rest of the body; and craftysmen worke al thynges mete for mayn-

---

[40] Blandy, op. cit., fol. 4 r.
[41] Cheke, The Hurt of Sedicion, in Holinshed, Chronicles (1807), III, 1003.
[42] Forset, op. cit., pp. 38–39.

tenance of the same; ye, and they hedys and rularys by just pollycy maynteyne the state stablysched in the cuntrey, ever lokyng to the profyte of they hole body; then that commyn wele must nedys florysch, then that cuntrey must nedys be in the most prosperous state.[43]

In such a state, when the king and his magistrates follow their vocations and administer civil justice, all men enjoy a life of peace and tranquility with their fellows. When soldiers follow their vocation all men live secure in life and property. When merchants and farmers follow their vocations, all men are provided with the material wealth necessary for existence. When scholars and priests follow their vocations, all men are led to practice virtue and to exercise true religion. Thus by the grace of God, who ordained such a structure, all men are enabled to live the happiest life in peace, prosperity, and virtue.

On the contrary, when through "disobedience and wilful rebellion" men leave their degrees and vocations and thereby destroy the natural proportion of the common wealth, then the state is beset by a host of evils. The whole structure is impaired by a flaw in any of its parts, and put in danger of ultimate collapse. Writers constantly warned against the social disruption which would follow failure to maintain the established order of degree and vocation. Sir John Cheke's admonition to the rebels is a graphic account of the miseries which such a disturbance inflicts on the body of society—theft, murder, rapine, plague, famine, idleness, waste, and, in general, "A topsie turvie of all thinges by rebellion." [44] Blandy asserts that Proportion,

when broken and defaced, not only renteth and plucketh in sunder the frame, but tottereth withall and tumbleth down the *Prince*, perverteth iustice, poysoneth and plucketh downe the good and upright minde of the *Souldiar*, robbeth the Marchaunt, ransacketh the *Artificer*, spoyleth utterly the simple and poore laboursome man.[45]

Rebellion by subjects against a ruler was widely condemned in the Renaissance not only because it was an outrage against the appointed representative of God, but because the whole integrated structure of society was thereby affected for the worse. The disastrous results of upsetting the highest degree were felt by degrees all down the line. Thus

[43] Starkey, *op. cit.*, pp. 58–59.   [44] Cheke, *op. cit.*, III, 996.
[45] Blandy, *op. cit.*, fol. 3 v.

the *Homilie agaynst Disobedience and Wylful Rebellion,* issued in 1571, contains a castigation of rebellion in the following terms:

For he that nameth Rebellion nameth not a singular or one onely sinne, as is theft, robbery, murther and such like; but he nameth the whole puddle and sinke of all sinnes against God and man, against his Prince, his Country, his Country-men, his parents, his children, his kinsfolks, his friends, and against all men universally; all sinnes, I say, against God, and all men heaped together nameth he that nameth Rebellion.[46]

This aspect of the sin of rebellion is the keynote of Ralph Birchensha's *Discourse Occasioned upon the Late Defeat, Given to the Arch-rebels, Tyrone and Odonnell* (1602). He exclaims:

> Rebels to Prince, rebels to native home,
> Traitors to Prince, traitors to countries due,
> Supplanters of all rule and government,
> Infringing lawes, the waste of Commonweale:
> The broode of wolves, the elder sonnes of *Cain,*
> The impes of hell, and very markes of shame.[47]

After hurling further epithets against rebels—"Haters of truth, sworn slaves to rape and sporte," "Breakers of Wedlocke," "Lovers of theft," and "Authors of mischief: all on murther set"—he emphasizes the social sin of rebellion by contrasting with the peace and quiet of Ireland before the uprising her confusion and weakness after it; asserting that rebels harm not the ruler alone, but the whole commonwealth, he writes:

> That this is true, view Irelands present state,
> Which whilome sate in faire and rich attire,
> While whilome flow'd in plentie of the earth,
> But now growne naked, feeble, weake, and bare:
> Who lately held sweete peace both neer and farre,
> But now in every place at deadly iarre.
>
> View now their houses wasted as they lie,
> View now their fields all barren round about,
> View now their meadowes overgrowne with weedes,
> View their high waies untrodden as they are:

---

[46] *Certaine Sermons or Homilies* (1640), p. 292.
[47] Birchensha, *Discourse* (1602), Sig. C, i r.

All honest trades are ceased very nie,
And plague on plague you perfectly may spie.[48]

In these few lines, Birchensha makes clear enough the horror at disorder and the enthusiasm for order which led men of his day so to revere the structure of political society. For it was universally felt that if the system of degrees be broken, man will find himself engulfed by the chaos and confusion which characterized his presocial existence. He will be afflicted with all the pestilences which his fellow men and God can devise; he will be deprived of the very necessities of life; fortitude, temperance, justice, and prudence will be supplanted by cowardice, excess, injustice, and recklessness, while faith, hope, and charity will be replaced by irreligion, despair, and malice. In a word, the felicitous life will be made impossible and man's soul as well as his body will perish.

[48] Birchensha, *op. cit.*, Sig. C, i v.

CHAPTER VI

"The Specialty of Rule"

PREËMINENT in the hierarchy of political society, according to Renaissance theory, is that degree whose vocation is rule and government. Because the governor, as the keystone of the state structure, became the central problem in sixteenth-century political thinking, this particular degree among those comprising the body politic requires special consideration. The present chapter, however, must not be mistaken for a complete study of kingship in the Tudor period; the host of existing investigations into the subject, and the requirements of the present purpose, make so comprehensive a study unnecessary here.[1] It will be pertinent, only, to demonstrate the relationship between the governing authority in a state, and the structure and purpose of that state as described in the preceding chapters. To this structural outline will be subordinated the manifold problems involved in the Renaissance conception of kingship.

I

The key passages in Shakespeare suggest the principal points to be examined. In each of the instances previously cited, authority and government are described as an integral part of the pattern ordained by God and nature for the political society of mankind. In Canterbury's analogy the degree of superiority is exemplified by the "king" and

---

[1] For general studies of the problem of kingship in Tudor political theory see J. W. Allen, *A History of Political Thought in the Sixteenth Century*, particularly Part II, Chapters I and X; J. N. Figgis, *The Divine Right of Kings* (1896; 1914); W. A. Dunning, *A History of Political Theories from Luther to Montesquieu* (1921); R. G. Gettell, *History of Political Thought* (1924), Chapters VIII–XI; R. H. Murray, *The Political Consequences of the Reformation* (1926); J. W. Gough, *The Social Contract* (1936); Pierre Mesnard, *L'Essor de la philosophie politique au XVIme siècle* (1937).

"emperor" of the hive; [2] Ulysses finds models for government in the solar system, where "the glorious planet Sol In noble eminence" is "enthron'd and spher'd Amidst the other"; [3] and Menenius, though concerned more especially with the legislative "belly," acknowledges the anatomical authority of "the kingly-crowned head." [4] In each instance, moreover, the vocation of the governing authority is indicated; that is what Ulysses calls "the specialty of rule," the task of maintaining and coördinating the complex structure of degrees and vocations. Finally, there is consistent affirmation of the unitary nature of the governing authority in a state; one bee rules the hive, one sun the solar system, and one head the body. On all these problems of "the specialty of rule" Shakespeare's thought was in fundamental agreement with the prevalent views of his day.

Governing authority, as a general conception, was universally recognized in the sixteenth century as essential to the structure of political society. As Professor Allen has observed, God "has so constructed society . . . that whatsoever section or aspect of it be regarded, we shall find ordained superiors and ordained subjects, the one bound to rule for the welfare of the other, the other loyally to obey." [5] This principle of "the specialty of rule," like the principles of order, degree, and vocation, was considered to be the dictate of divine will and natural law, for it could be remarked that authority, like the complementary concept of obedience, had been ordained in every department of creation. Theorists were not at a loss to provide examples of such superiority from the world of nature. For as Chelidonius concludes, "if we consider all things universally, and their parts, beginning even at the heavens, and runne thorow all the other elements, wee shall finde a sparke of Royaltie and a certaine preeminence to appeare in all thinges." [6] The same principles receive more concrete expression in the anatomical analogy of Forset, who writes that

As in the creation of man God conioined a soul for action, in a body passive: so in his ordinance of mans sociable conversing (to make the union of the body politike) he hath knit together a passive subiection to an active

---

[2] *Henry V*, I, ii, 190, 196.   [3] *Troilus and Cressida*, I, iii, 89–91.

[4] *Coriolanus*, I, i, 119.   [5] Allen, *op. cit.*, p. 135.

[6] Chelidonius, *A Most Excellent Historie of the Institution . . . of Christian Princes* (translated, 1571), p. 17.

superioritie: and as in every man is both a quickening and ruling soule, and a living and ruled bodie; so in every civill state, there is a directing and commanding power, and an obeying and subiected allegiance.[7]

Whatever they thought about its form and scope, theorists invariably asserted that the institution of government is the ordinance of God. Musculus expressed the general conviction when he argued that

No godlye person doubteth, but that the worlde is governed by God, by whome it was also made, wherefore all the powers and governaunces whiche be in the worlde, and whereby mankynde is ruled, must needes come of him whom they doo serve in the governance of the world, that is to say, of God, the creator, comforter, and governor of them all together.[8]

The supporters of elective, limited monarchy asserted no less emphatically than supporters of absolute hereditary monarchy that the society of men must accept sovereignty in some form; as Goslicius, a member of the former group, put it, "Thus beeing made of God his society . . . , it must needs be, that in the government of this world we have from him the authority and rule of commanding." [9] Government, like the order of degrees, was a part of the universal plan established by God to preserve the world from chaos and destruction.

2

The universal emphasis on authority was a conclusion inevitably reached by reasoning founded on the principles of order and degree. As men are not created equal, there must logically be a highest and best degree, supreme above the others in all the political and social virtues with which men are endowed. Moral virtue and intellectual understanding are the criteria by which this degree, like all degrees, is determined. Moreover, the wisdom of God, which has adapted the differences in men to the needs of society, has similarly equipped the highest rank for that vocation which is "the specialty of rule." Generally speaking, the vocation of rule is ordained to achieve the main purposes of political society, which are peace, prosperity, virtue, and

[7] Forset, *A Comparative Discourse of the Bodies Natural and Politique* (1606), pp. 2–3.
[8] Wolfgang Musculus, *Commonplaces of Christian Religion* (1563), fol. 546 v.
[9] Goslicius, *The Counsellor* (1598), p. 3.

wisdom for all men. This philosophy of government as it is related to the whole pattern of the state was set forth early in the century by Elyot. The language as well as the ideas in the following passage are typical of the thinking dominant throughout the Renaissance:

And like as the angels whiche be most feruent in contemplation be highest exalted in glorie . . . , and also the fire whiche is the most pure of elementes, and also doth clarifie the other inferiour elementes, is deputed to the highest sphere or place; so in this worlde, they whiche excelle other in this influence of understandynge, and do imploye it to the detaynyng of other within the boundes of reason, and shewe them howe to prouyde for theyr necessarye lyuyng; suche oughte to be set in a more highe place than the residue where they may se and also be sene; that by the beames of theyr excellent witte, shewed throughe the glasse of auctoritie, other of inferiour understandynge may be directed to the way of vertue and commodious liuynge.[10]

Whether theorists believe that rulers are appointed by God or by the people, they consistently maintained that only certain men are enabled, by virtue of natural gifts and abilities, to bear authority. As Sir John Cheke expressed it, "In countries some must rule, some must obeie, euerie man maie not beare like stroke; for euerie man is not likewise. And they that haue seen most and be best able to bear it, and of iust dealing besides, be most fit to rule." [11] A similar concept is involved in the statement by Musculus that "they be borne to the aucthoritie of governance, and that by the ordinance of God, whom we doe fynd to be more excellent than the rest." [12] The excellence which marks a man for the degree of rule is determined by standards of religious piety, moral virtue, and intellectual wisdom. Thus Goodman argued that although a king is chosen by the people, only that man may be chosen who is designated by his abilities as "a promoter and setter forth of Godd's lawes and glorie, for whiche cause chieflie this office was or-

---

[10] Elyot, *The Boke Named the Gouernour*, p. 5, Everyman's Library.

[11] Cheke, *The Hurt of Sedicion* (1549), in Holinshed, *Chronicles* (1807), III, 989. This concept found further support in Hoby's translation of Castiglione's *Courtier* (1561), p. 275, Everyman's Library: "And some things are borne and so appointed and ordained by nature to command, as some other to obeysance."

[12] Musculus, *op. cit.*, fol. 548 r.

deyned." [13] A more general statement of the same principles is given by Craig, who writes that since nature

has produced some Stupid, some Feeble, and others wise, who is so Blind, as not to perceive some men to excell others, as much as these do Brutes? Some seem to be Born for Empire and Government, who have a Divine Spirit, others Foolish Stupid, Weak and without good Sense or Ingenuity, and yet Nature has endowed them with bodily Strength for drudgery, and executing commands of others. For Nature her self directs dull and unskilfull persons to obey the more wise and prudent, and one who discerns something great in another, which Nature has deenied to himself, naturally loves, esteems, yea and obeys him, for his own advantage, as knowing that the wiser man's foresight and conduct in the management of business, will be for the safety of them both. He readily performs what depends more on bodily strength than judgment, . . . So that from Nature there is such a disparity among men, that some seem born for Governing and other to obey.[14]

The genre of political literature described in a preceding chapter as "the institution of a prince" was chiefly devoted to an enumeration and detailed description of the excellences which should characterize the governing authority in a state. The discussion in these works seldom departed from the traditional pattern, in which the qualities were analyzed in terms of the classic virtues of justice, temperance, fortitude, and prudence, and the Christian virtues of faith, hope, and charity. These points comprise the substance of Elyot's discussion in *The Boke Named the Gouernour,* although the reader is familiar with the details and subdivisions which enrich his discussion. Blandy, in his *Castle, or Picture of Pollicy* (1581), adheres more closely to the four classic virtues, as does Barnabe Barnes in *Foure Bookes of Offices* (1606). Harington, however, in describing the virtues which marked James of Scotland as the logical successor to Elizabeth, follows Elyot in adding verity, magnanimity, liberality, affability, and clemency to the basic scheme.[15] Machiavelli, of course, discarded these idealistic virtues in

[13] Christopher Goodman, *How Superior Powers Oght to be Obeyd* (1558), p. 51, Facsimile Text Society (1931).

[14] Thomas Craig, *Concerning the Right of Succession to the Kingdom of England* (1703), p. 13.

[15] Sir John Harington, *A Tract on the Succession to the Crown* (1602), p. 83.

favor of his own concept, *virtù*, as the one quality which distinguishes sovereign authority. As the Florentine employs the term, *virtù* "never has . . . the Christian sense of goodness; it always means courage and energy for evil as much as for good." [16] In this sense, it retains only so much of Roman *virtus* as is applicable to the will, intelligence and ability of one who has succeeded in his purpose, whatever that purpose may be. But like his more idealistic contemporaries, Machiavelli too recognized the fact that "the specialty of rule" is reserved for those naturally endowed with the peculiar talents which the vocation as he saw it demands.[17]

For, as with all degrees in the hierarchy of political society, the qualities which establish some men in authority above others were considered by Renaissance theorists to be adapted to the requirements of the vocation of government. To the functions and duties involved in "the specialty of rule" sixteenth-century writers devoted innumerable pages in treatises, tracts, sermons, histories, and other media of dissemination both learned and popular. For the most part, however, this vast literature can be reduced to a few essential precepts which will be adequate for the present purpose. Because the vocation of rule is chiefly, among the other degrees, responsible for attaining the ends for which society is ordained, the functions of "the specialty of rule" were generally presented in terms of these ends.

Until the advent of Bodin's *Republic* in 1576, and even, to a large extent, afterwards, the concepts established early in the century by politico-theological writers were employed by theorists in describing the vocation of rule. According to these concepts the principal marks of government were the administration of justice, the maintenance of religion and virtue, and the provision of the material necessities requisite to these higher ends. The general theory is expressed in *The Institution of a Christen Man* (1534), where it is remarked that

[16] R. H. Murray, *The Political Consequences of the Reformation* (1926), p. 14. Cf. E. W. Mayer, *Machiavellis Geschichtsauffassung und sein Begriff virtù* (1912).

[17] Cf. Allen, *op. cit.*, p. 468: "Great as is the part played by accident in human affairs, the Prince according to Machiavelli who can accurately adjust his means to his ends and who pursues those ends with single-minded ruthlessness, is always likely to be successful. What is required for success is just two things: will and intelligence, a ruthless will and an intelligence that sees things as they are."

it apperteyneth unto the office of princis, to se that the ryght religion and
true doctrine of Christe may be mayntained and taught, and that theyr
subiectes may be well ruled and governed by good and iuste lawes, and
to prouyde and care for them, that all thynges necessarie for them may
be plentuouse, and the people and comune weale may encrease and to defend them from oppression and inuasion as well within the realm as without, and to se that iustice be administered unto thē indifferently.[18]

Whether the ruler, like the political society of which he is a part, is
master or servant of the church, was a question heatedly debated in the
Renaissance.[19] But there was fundamental agreement that the chief
responsibility of the vocation of rule was the spiritual welfare of men.
Thus on the one hand the vigorous exponent of secular sovereignty in
ecclesiastical affairs, Thomas Bilson, wrote:

If private men be bound to traine up their families in the feare of God
and love of vertue, much more are princes (the publike fathers of their
countries and exalted to farre greater and higher authority by Gods ordinance than fathers or masters) I say much more are they in conscience
and by calling licenced to frame their subiectes to the true service of God
and right obedience of his law, which be thinges not temporal but spiritual.[20]

On the other hand, the equally vigorous opponent of secular domination of the church, Robert Parsons, argued that as the servant of the
church the first and principal office of the ruler is the maintenance of
religion.[21]

Similar accord characterized Renaissance theory concerning the
administration of justice as the vocation of governors. Thus in the
translation of Isocrates' *To Nicoles* made in 1580 a ruler is admonished
to govern in such a fashion

that due honour may be given unto the godly and well disposed, executing justice in such sort upon the transgressors and breakers of thy laws
that the rest quietly inioying their owne may be the lovinger and obedi-

[18] *The Institution of a Christen Man* (1534), fol. 82 r.

[19] See Allen, *op. cit.*, Part II, Chapters IV, V, VII, and VIII in particular.

[20] Bilson, *The True Difference between Christian Subiection and Unchristian Rebellion* (1585), p. 249.

[21] Parsons, *A Conference about the Next Succession to the Crowne of England*
(1594), p. 204. Cf. Chapter III, p. 59 above.

enter to thee . . . , for this is the first and chiefest point of a well ordered publike weal.[22]

Starkey argued similarly when he wrote: "And thys ys the offyce and duty, brevely to say, of hedys and rularys, aftur thys maner dylygently to se the admynystratyon of justyce to the hole commynalty." [23] Blandy described this requirement of the vocation of government more specifically when he wrote:

The excellencie therefore of iustice, stands of force and vertue: the vertue of iustice resteth in the measure of thinges ordered, according to reasons prescription, which teaches that all men should beare the lyke affection to other, as they would be affected by other. The force of iustice is to make of many one, to unite and knit many partes in one: whiche evidently may appeare, if we call to mind that in the beginning it did so greatly excite and stirre up mens mindes, that for her love they surrendered their goods and possessions into the handes of one especiall man, in whose amiable face this vertue did through flashing flames shewe forth her cleare light of glory.[24]

After the turn of the century the point continued to receive emphasis in treatises of this sort. Thus Barnes writes:

So certainly cannot any Prince be verely good unto himselfe, if he doe not governe his flocke (whiche is the greater part of himselfe) in the feare of God and exercise of Iustice . . . Sanctitie and Iustice therefore . . . by the propagation, corroboration, and aeternization of all crowns and Monarchies, are the two maine pillars of principalitie; . . .[25]

By giving to each man according to his degree his just deserts, whether of reward or of punishment, the ruler administers justice and thereby enables the whole social organization to attain the ends for which it was ordained—peace, prosperity, and virtue. As stated by Bullinger,

The magistracy . . . may be defined to be a divine ordinance or action, whereby the good being defended by the Prince's aid, and the evil sup-

---

[22] Isocrates, *A Perfite Looking Glasse for All Estates* (translated, 1580), fol. 19 v.
[23] Starkey, *A Dialogue between Cardinal Pole and Thomas Lupset* (c. 1538), p. 55, Early English Text Society, Extra Series, Vol. XXXII.
[24] Blandy, *The Castle, or Picture of Pollicy* (1581), fol. 10 r.
[25] Barnes, *Foure Bookes of Offices* (1606). "To . . . James," Sig. A, i v.

pressed by the same authority, godliness, justice, honesty, peace and tranquility, both public and private, are safely preserved.[26]

At about the same time Musculus wrote that "It doth belong unto the Magistrate so to order the lyfe of his subiectes, that they may lyue not onely commodiously and honestly, but godly also and religiously in ye true service of God." [27] The Tudor translation of Isocrates lent classic support to this conception of "the specialty of rule"; it admonishes rulers: "Account the principall token and perfect proofe of good government, to be, to see thy people inriched, as also godly and well instructed, obeying thy laws, and living in unitie and concord together." [28] A sovereign authority administering justice is essential to the successful operation of society, Isocrates argued, because only thereby can the various degrees of worthiness, skill and virtue be appropriately rewarded.[29] By means of justice, which keeps each man in his degree and vocation, the ruler maintains that natural order and proportion in the structure of political society which produces the social, economic, and moral welfare of all its members. To borrow a figure from Forset, the ruler is a physician obligated to keep the body politic functioning in the way and for the purposes which God and nature intended.

These writers of the early and middle parts of the century were concerned primarily with what the governing authority does, rather than with what it is. In 1576 Jean Bodin attempted to formulate a definition of the specialty of rule, or sovereignty. "Maiestie or Sovereigntie," he wrote, "is the most high, absolute and perpetuall power over all Citizens and subiects in a Commonweal . . . , that is to say, the greatest power to command." [30] And the "principall point of sovereigne maiestie and absolute power," he continued, consists "in giving laws unto the subiects in generall, without their consent." [31] That is, the sovereign power in a state, regardless of the form it takes, functions in

---

[26] Bullinger, *Fiftie . . . Sermones, Divided into Five Decades*, edited for the Parker Society, I, 309.

[27] Musculus, *Commonplaces of Christian Religion* (1563), fol. 552 v.

[28] Isocrates, *op. cit.*, fol. 24 v.

[29] *Ibid.*, fol. 20 r. Cf. also Buchanan, *De iure regni apud Scotos* (translated, 1689), p. 9, who defines justice as "that which doth regard every Member and cureth it so as to be kept in its function."

[30] Bodin, *The Six Bookes of a Commonweale* (1606), p. 84.   [31] *Ibid.*, p. 98.

its vocation when by decreeing laws it maintains the order of degrees
and procures the tranquility, wealth, and felicity of all men. Whether
the authority itself was subject or superior to these laws was a matter of
dispute both before and after Bodin's work appeared. But theorists
generally agreed that the good ruler, even if he is not technically bound
to do so, will rule and abide by the laws of his realm. As Bodin remarks:

And certainly there is nothing better, or more beseeming a prince, than by
his deeds and life to confirme those lawes which hee himselfe hath made.
. . . But it is one thing for a man so to doe willingly and of his owne
accord, and another thing to be bound by bond or oath to do it.[32]

The ruling authority of a political society will obey the laws because
they are designed to procure the health of the whole realm. In this way
the governor in his vocation, as every man in his respective degree,
will work not for his own selfish good but for the good of the entire
organization. The political thinking of the time insisted that authority
and obedience alike are justified because "the specialty of rule" is ordained for the benefit not of a privileged few, but of subjects of all
degrees. There is the flourishing commonwealth, said Starkey, where
"they hedys and rularys by just pollycy maynteyne the state stab-
lysshed in the cuntrey, ever lokyng to the profyte of they hole body." [33]
Tyndale held different opinions on the form of authority in a realm,
but he agreed with Starkey on the vocation of government; he wrote in
his *Obedience of a Christen Man:*

Though that the kynge in the temporall regymente be in the rowme of
God, and representeth God himselfe and is without al comparyson better
then his subiectes: yet lette him putte of that and become a brother, doynge
and leuinge undone all thynges in respecte of the commune wealth that
all men maye se that he seketh nothynge but the profyte of his subiectes.[34]

Much later in the century Sir Thomas Smith set forth essentially the
same conception of "the specialty of rule" when he wrote that the good
ruler "doth administer the Commonwealth by the lawes of the same,
and by equitie, and doth seeke the profite of the people as much as his
owne." [35]

[32] Bodin, *op. cit.*, pp. 103–4.   [33] Starkey, *op. cit.*, p. 58.
[34] William Tyndale, *The Obedience of a Christen Man and How Christen Rulers
Ought to Govern* (1528), edition of 1561, fol. 56 r.
[35] Sir Thomas Smith, *The Commonwealth of England* (1589), Chapter VII, p. 6.

In exercising his vocation the ruler is to adopt the attitude of a father toward his family, or of a shepherd toward his flock; sovereign authority is to be tempered with a love and regard for the welfare of all his subjects, regardless of rank. Sir John Cheke, describing the state in terms of a household knit together by brotherly love, concludes that "The kings best kind of government is so to rule his subjects, as a father ordereth his children. . . ." [36] The widespread appearance of this figure in Renaissance descriptions of "the specialty of rule" reveals much of what was expected of the degree and vocation of government in its relation to the whole structure of political society. The autocratic powers with which most sixteenth-century theorists endowed political sovereignty were thus constantly qualified by emphatic assertions that the ruler assumes heavy responsibilities pertaining to the physical and spiritual welfare of his people. The typical attitude toward the vocation of governing is represented in the following passage from Goslicius, who writes that counselors should understand

that the office of a king is not to care or studie so much for his owne private profit, as the common commoditie of his subiectes, to observe his lawes, to preserve the rights and liberty of the people, and to maintaine the authority and reputation of his counsell. . . . A good king ought therefore to have no lesse care of those he governeth, then hath the shepherd of his flock, that is, to make them blessed and happy. . . . Moreover a king ought to governe his people: not as maisters doe their servants, but as a father ruleth his children. . . . So shoulde a Prince behave himselfe towardes his subiectes, as well for the peoples preservation, as the safetie of the commonweale . . . , defending and enlarging the common profit with no lesse care, then a father provideth for the sustenation of his children. [37]

For the highest degree of the political and social hierarchy as for the lowest, there is, therefore, a definite vocation based on the natural differences of men and adapted to the needs and welfare of the whole

[36] Cheke, *The Hurt of Sedicion* (1549) in Holinshed, *Chronicles* (1807), III, 1006.
[37] Goslicius, *The Counsellor* (1598), p. 74. Cf. for example Castiglione, *The Courtier*, p. 284: "And the rule both for the subjects and for the prince shalbe most happie, not Lordly, as the maister over his bondsman, but soft and meeke, as a good father over his good children"; and Buchanan, *op. cit.*, p. 28: "That as Fathers ought to carry toward their children, so in all his life he would behave himself towards his Subjects, whom he ought to account as Children."

structure. As administrator of the whole system, however, this degree, more than any other, must be maintained in its vocation and must conduct itself in accordance with its rank and office.

3

What has been said heretofore regarding "the specialty of rule" held true in sixteenth-century political thinking for government in whatever form it appeared in the state. Whether single or multiple, elective or hereditary, authority was consistently described in these terms of degree and vocation. Concerning one fundamental problem of the form or type of government, however, there was further unanimity among Renaissance theorists. Throughout the century it was generally maintained that "the specialty of rule" was vested in a single individual, that government by one was ordained for the structure of political society. In the language of the day monarchy was held to be superior to either aristocracy, the rule of the few, or democracy, the rule of the many.

These three categories of government, as defined by Aristotle,[38] were accepted with little change in the political thinking of the Renaissance. In using the terms monarchy, aristocracy, and democracy, however, theorists did not distinguish clearly between the form in which sovereignty is exercised, and the source of this sovereignty. They tended to confuse the execution of authority with its origin. Bodin was among the first to recognize the distinction; he wrote that "to judge an estate, the question is not to know who have the magistracies of offices: but onely who they bee which have the sovereigntie and power to place and displace the magistrates and officers, and to give laws unto every man."[39] On this basis he argued that all states, in form of government, are monarchies, in that one individual administers authority for the whole.

---

[38] Cf. Gettell, *History of Political Thought*, Chapter III, Section 4, "Greek Political Thought," for a description of the Aristotelian terminology which dominated subsequent political discussion. The distinctions may be briefly summarized as follows: Sovereign power held by one person, by a few persons, or by all persons is, respectively, monarchy, aristocracy, or polity when exercised for the common welfare. When in each case such power is exercised for selfish interest it becomes, respectively, tyranny, oligarchy, or democracy. Because rule by the many was almost universally condemned as evil and unnatural, the term democracy is more common than polity in Renaissance political discussion. See Note 45 below.

[39] Bodin, *op. cit.*, p. 249.

It is only a true monarchy when that individual is also the original possessor of sovereign power, a true aristocracy when a few men, possessing sovereignty, delegate their authority to one administrator, and a true democracy when all men so transfer the power which they hold in common. The majority of Renaissance theorists did not reason as accurately as did Bodin, however; their discussions of the relative values of the types of government were limited largely to the form in which sovereignty was exercised, by one, by a few, or by many, rather than to its origins.

Throughout the century theorists admitted that there were circumstances under which the vocation of government might take any one of the three forms. Early Reformation writers—notably Calvin and Bullinger—who were primarily concerned with teaching obedience to established civil authority, gave little attention to the form which that authority took, and accepted monarchy, aristocracy, and democracy on equal terms.[40] Later in the period Goslicius and Bodin agreed that government might take any one of the three forms, depending on the requirements of diverse human natures, geography, climate and other external circumstances.[41] Aristocracy and democracy, therefore, did not go unrecognized in sixteenth-century political thinking as admissible forms which "the specialty of rule" could take. But the sentiment was overwhelmingly in favor of monarchy. Political actuality in Renaissance Europe was probably the principal circumstance which led theorists universally to condemn plurality forms of rule and to defend the unitary form.

Aristocracy was rejected by sixteenth-century critical opinion because

[40] John Calvin, *Institution de la religion chrétienne* (1560), edited by Frank Baumgartner, 1888, p. 684. Bullinger, *Decades*, I, 311: "Now touching the excellency of these forms or kinds of government, it maketh not greatly to my purpose to dispute which ought to be preferred before the rest."

[41] Bodin, *op. cit.*, Book V, Chapter I: "What order and course is to be taken to apply the forme of a Commonweale to the diversities of mens humors and the meanes how to discover the nature and dispostion of the people"; Goslicius, *op. cit.*, p. 11: "The diversitie of commonweales doth not proceed from fortune, nor the disposition of the heavens, but every government is framed according to the mindes of men, their wits, and education. Also the varietie not onely of mens inclinations, but also the nature of commonweals is made divers, through the diversities of countries, their climate, and beeing." Both writers, however, as will be noted below (pp. 109–111), argue that after all is considered, monarchy is the preferable form of government for a political society.

of the dissension and resultant misrule which were believed inevitably to accompany it. As Elyot warned, "some, beinge ones in authoritie, be incensed with glorie; some with ambition: others with covetise and desire of treasure or possessions: whereby they fall into contention. . . ." [42] Bodin, discussing the arguments for and against aristocracy in great detail, concludes on a note similar to Elyot's; he too warns against the dangers of tyranny, rebellion, foreign invasion and like political ills attendant upon aristocracy and the factions it engenders.[43] Forset's analogical arguments against plurality forms of government in general have a particular application to rule by the few; he writes:

Let us imagine a bodie so monstrous, as whereunto two heads were at once affixed, shall not that bodie receive much damage by the division and confusion of those two heads and must not the bodie in that case either be divided by alotting of one side to the one, and the other side to the other head? or else be wholly dissevered by a promiscuous and contentious shuffling of the severall sinewes, forces, and operations from each head proceeding? [44]

Such theories, appearing regularly throughout the century, resulted in the general exclusion of aristocracy from those forms of government desirable in a commonwealth.

Even stronger and more widespread was the denunciation of democracy, the rule of the many, which to the Renaissance theorists meant mob rule rather than the orderly election of representatives and executives.[45] Elyot describes the vengeance, stupidity and cruelty which characterize such rule.[46] Floyd, in *The Picture of a Perfit Commonwealth* (1600),

[42] Elyot, *op. cit.*, p. 8.   [43] Bodin, *op. cit.*, p. 711.

[44] Forset, *A Comparative Discourse of the Bodies Natural and Politique* (1606), pp. 57–58.

[45] I fail to find in Renaissance political literature the word "polity" employed in its Aristotelian sense of rule by the many for the common welfare of all. The term "democracy," which Aristotle used to designate the corrupt type of this form of government is consistently found in discussions of popular rule.

[46] Elyot, *op. cit.*, p. 8: "The popular astate, if it any thing do varie from equalitie of substance or estimation, or that the multitude of people haue ouer moche liberte, of necessite one of these inconueniences muste happen: either tiranny . . . , orels in to the rage of a communaltie, whiche of all rules is moste to be feared . . . : and if they ones throwe downe theyr gouernour, they ordre euery thynge without iustice, only with vengeance and crueltie: and with incomparable difficultie and unneth by any wysedome be pacified and brought agayne in to ordre."

develops the same thesis when he attacks democracy "because in a disordinate multitude the fruites of displeasure, as hate, rebellion, sectes, and factions, and other heynous crimes, must needs be nourished, by a confusion of misgovernment, for defect of one sole sovereign." [47] Democracy was considered moreover to be a violation of the universal principle of inequality and an unnatural perversion of the order of degrees based on natural differences among men. Early in the century Elyot had warned against the "rage of communaltie" which democracy produces. [48] Similar convictions regarding the dangers of equality formed the basis of arguments advanced by Bodin and Craig against rule by the multitude. [49] Fulbecke's definition in his *Pandectes of the Law of Nations* (1602), with its picture of the political monster so familiar in Renaissance literature on "the people," summarizes the dominant Tudor attitude toward democracy:

> Democracie I have alwaies taken contrarie to the ãcient division of Monarchie, Aristocracie, &c. to be no forme of a commonweale, if it be properly taken for the equal sway of the people without any superioritie: for the heel can not stand in place of the head, unless the bodie bee destroyed and the anatomie monstrous: it is against the nature of the people to beare rule; for they are as unfitte for regiment, as a mad man to give counsaille . . . [50]

Democracy conceived as mob rule, therefore, was generally rejected by sixteenth-century theorists because it violated the principles of order, degree, and vocation upon which a healthy political society is founded.

Whatever they thought about the ultimate source of sovereignty, theorists generally agreed that only an individual should exercise "the specialty of rule." The term monarchy as it was usually employed in the sixteenth century must not be too strictly interpreted. It was given a general meaning which extended to the rule of emperors, princes, magistrates, dukes, consuls, and presidents, as well as to hereditary kings. Latimer had such a broad definition in mind when he asserted that "It maketh no matter by what name the ruler be named." [51] In

[47] Floyd, *op. cit.*, p. 15.   [48] Elyot, *op. cit.*, p. 8.

[49] Bodin, *op. cit.*, p. 705 *et seq.*; Craig, *Concerning the Right of Succession to the Kingdom of England* (1703), p. 14.

[50] Fulbecke, *op. cit.*, fol. 28 v.

[51] Hugh Latimer, *Seven Sermons before Edward VI, on Each Friday in Lent, 1549*, edited by Edward Arber (1895), p. 29.

describing the executive power of a state Musculus employed the term "magistrate" which, he wrote, "signifieth the Authoritye and office of them whiche dooe either by ryghte of inheritance, governe subiects, peoples, or Citizens, either have the rule appointed them by free election and choyce." [52] And Merbury, while insisting on unitary sovereignty, nevertheless recognizes monarchy by gift, by will of testament, by law and custom, by adoption, by lot, by policy, by conquest, and by election as types of government acceptable in a commonwealth.[53] Emphasis was placed on the unity of authority, rather than on the peculiar form it took or the name given to it.

Arguments for monarchy in this general sense were based on the theory that such government is the ordinance of divine will and the law of nature. The rule of one, theorists maintained, is an integral part of the concept of political society founded on the principles of universal order. Historical examples as well as natural analogies were drawn upon to support the monarchic argument. Elyot devotes a chapter to the belief "That one sovereigne governor ought to be in a publike weal. And what damage hath happened where a multitude hath had equal authorite without any soueraygne." [54] After discussing the weaknesses of aristocracy and democracy, he concludes:

Wherfore undoubtedly the best and most sure governance is by one kynge or prince, which ruleth onely for the weale of his people to hym subiecte: and that maner of governance is beste approud, and hath longest continued, and is moste auncient. For who can denie but that all thynge in heven and erthe is governed by one god, by one perpetuall ordre, by one providence? One Sonne ruleth over the day, and one Moone over the nyghte; and to descende downe to the erthe, in a litell beest. . . . I meane the Bee, is left to man by nature, as it semeth, a perpetuall figure of a iust governance or rule: who hath amonge them one principall Bee for theyr governor, who excelleth all other in greatnes.[55]

Castiglione defends the rule of one "because it is a good government more agreeable to nature, and if it bee lawful to compare small matters with infinite, more like unto God's, which one and alone governeth the universal." He goes on to draw parallels with the human anatomy,

---

[52] Musculus, *op. cit.*, fol. 546 r.
[53] Merbury, *A Briefe Discourse of Royall Monarchie* (1581), pp. 16–19.
[54] Elyot, *op. cit.*, Book I, Chapter II.   [55] *Ibid.*, pp. 8–9.

bees, "Deeres, Cranes, and many other foules," in all of which the principle of single leadership is apparent.[56] To the testimony of history and nature Chelidonius added that of classic and medieval authorities; he writes:

It resteth now to conclude with *Aristotle, Apolonius, S. Jerome, S. Cyprian* and many others, that the *Monarchia* which is the government that is absolute, that is to say, by one onely king or prince, is the most excellent, the best approved, and most receyued of all.[57]

In the translations of Bodin,[58] as well as in original works by Blandy,[59] Merbury,[60] and a host of others,[61] monarchy was defended on similar grounds. In method and purpose Hayward exemplified the prevailing attitude when he wrote:

The whole world is nothinge but a great state; a state is no other then a greate familie; and a familie no other than a great bodye. As one God ruleth the world, one maister the familie, as all the members of one bodye

---

[56] Castiglione, *The Courtier*, p. 274.

[57] Chelidonius, *A Most Excellent Historie of the Institution . . . of a Christian Prince* (translated, 1571), p. 36.

[58] Bodin, *op. cit.*, p. 718: "Although it be not needful to insist much upon this proofe, that a Monarchie is the most sure, seeing that a familie which is the true image of a Commonweale can have but one head, and that all the lawes of nature guide us unto a Monarchie, whether that we behold this little world which hath but one bodie, and but one head for all the members, whereon depends the will, moving, and feeling: or if we look to this great world which hath but one soveraigne God: or if we erect our eyes to heaven, we shall see but one sunne: and even in sociable creatures, we see they cannot admit many kings, nor many lords, how good so ever."

[59] Blandy, *op. cit.*, fol. 27 v.

[60] Merbury, *op. cit.* In a preface "To the Reader" Merbury tells of his studies in "ideal commonwealths" which led him to believe that monarchies were the preferable form.

[61] Cf., for example, Craig, *op. cit.*, p. 6: "We on the contrary contend that Monarchy is of a Divine Original, Ordain'd of God, and that no other form of Government obtain'd among his peculiar People, yea, that no other is so conducive to the safety of any Nation, nor is so agreeable to the Laws of God and Nature. Yea moreover I undertake to prove (with Gods assistance) that it has been receiv'd by the constant practice of all ages, and the perpetual custom of all Nations"; Barnes, *Foure Bookes of Offices* (1606), p. 66: "The first and best forme of government and empire is, where one king moderateth and ruleth all nations under his dominion united, according to the true spirit of virtue, which domination is properly tearmed by the sages of wisedome a monocracie; for it representeth the perfect ordination of nature, by which everie multitude and deformitie submitteth it selfe to some one thing which governeth the same."

receive both sense and motion from one heade, which is the seate and
tower both of understanding and of will; so it seemeth no lesse naturall,
that one state should be governed by one commander.[62]

The foregoing authorities were among those theorists, preponderant
in Renaissance political thinking, who argued in favor of absolute monarchy as represented in actual Tudor government. They held that God
ordains a king not only as the executor of sovereignty, but as the source
of sovereignty in a state. In this they agreed with Bodin, who wrote:

But the chiefe point of a commonweale, which is the right of sovereigntie,
cannot be, nor subsist . . . but in a monarchie: for none can be sovereigne in a commonweale but one alone: if they be two or three, or more,
no one is sovereigne, for that no one of them can give or take a law from
his companion. And although we imagine a bodie of many lords, or of a
whole people to hold the sovereigntie; yet hath it no true ground nor support, if there be not a head with absolute and sovereigne power, to unite
them together.[63]

A smaller, but by no means negligible group of theorists insisted just as
strongly that government is the institution of God and that monarchy is
the most acceptable form which it can take. Unlike the former group,
however, they argued that the source of authority and the exercise of
authority resided in two different parts of political society, and not in
one unlimited monarch. According to these thinkers the administration
of sovereignty lay with the king, but the power itself came originally
from the people and could be revoked by them at will. The ruler held
an authority delegate and not an authority absolute. This in substance
was the argument advanced by Knox, Goodman, Ponet, Buchanan, and
Parsons, the last of whom summarizes their point of view when he
writes:

"Be you subject of every human creature, for God's cause, whether it be
to a king, as the most excellent, or to a Duke sent by God for the punishment of evil men and praise of the good." [1 Peter. 3] Out of which
wordes some do note two pointes, first that as on the one side the Apostle
doth plainly teach that the magistrates authority is from God, by his first
institution, in that he sayeth, we must be subiect to them for God's cause,
so on the other side he calleth it a humane creature or a thing created by

---

[62] Hayward, *An Answer to . . . R. Doleman* (1603), Sig. B, 4 r.
[63] Bodin, *op. cit.*, p. 715.

man, for that by man's free choice this particular forme of government (as al other also) is appoynted in every commonwealth . . . and that by man's election and consent the same is layed uppon some particular man or woman, accordyng to the laws of every country. . . .[64]

Parsons, however, devotes an entire chapter to prove that monarchy is the best form which such delegated sovereignty can take, and his arguments, drawing on natural analogies, scriptural and classical authority, and historical precedent, closely parallel those of his Protestant opponents in method and purpose.[65] Similarly, Goslicius asserts that a monarchy in which a king governs by law is the best form of government, although he maintains that kings should be elected by the people.[66]

For theorists of all schools, therefore, the concept of civil society, as it involved "the specialty of rule," was fundamentally the same. The hierarchy of degrees which comprises the structure is surmounted by a highest and best degree which is unitary in nature and whose vocation is the exercise of rule and government. Upon the ruler's adherence to his vocation, as upon the similar adherence of every class in the structure, depends the welfare of the whole organization.

[64] Parsons, *op. cit.*, p. 17. [65] *Ibid.*, Chapter II.
[66] Goslicius, *op. cit.*, pp. 10, 15.

CHAPTER VII

Social Corruption in *Troilus and Cressida* and *Timon of Athens*

I N THE FOREGOING CHAPTERS we have attempted to describe with some accuracy a pattern of thought which was basic in almost all Tudor discussions of the nature and structure of political societies. As has been indicated, the pattern was by no means limited to obscure treatises or to the arguments of an isolated group of speculative theorists. In popular pamphlets, sermons, histories, and general literature the principles and terminology of the concept were made familiar to the rank and file of the Elizabethans as well as to the more learned element in the population. Indeed, the doctrines embodied in this concept of the state seem clearly to have been part and parcel of the political thinking of the day. The analogical references and such terms as order, degree, vocation, and rule were as significant to the layman in the sixteenth century as the terms freedom, equality, and individualism to the layman in the twentieth century. A Tudor writer dealing with problems of states would almost certainly think and express himself in the language of the universally accepted concept.

That Shakespeare was such a writer is a fact made clear in his five Greek and Roman plays. Those "fixed political beliefs and convictions" which, according to Sir Mark Hunter, Shakespeare brought to his study of history for the stage, and which, according to Professor Charlton, are the "fundamental principles conditioning the form of life he is displaying" in his "political plays," are essentially those principles of social and political order accepted by the majority of his contemporaries. Thus in the camp action in *Troilus and Cressida* and in *Timon of Athens* the political atmosphere of the drama is that of a society corrupted in purpose and function because vocation has been neglected in the upper degrees of the hierarchical structure. In *Coriolanus* the violation of degree by both ruler and ruled in the Roman commonwealth brings the state to the verge of disaster. In *Julius Caesar* and *Antony and Cleopatra* a political society which forsakes monarchic government returns painfully but inevitably to that form of rule ordained by the laws of nature. In no case can this political theme be considered the primary source of dramatic interest; but in every case it must be regarded as an integral part of the structure and movement of the play and accordingly essential to a complete understanding of Shakespeare's thought and purpose.

I

Of all the problems which beset readers of Shakespeare's *Troilus and Cressida* certainly one of the most perplexing has been the strange presentation of Homer's heroic account of the Greek forces at the siege of Troy.[1] Petty, quarrelsome, and degenerate warriors are exhibited in an action characterized by cowardice, boasting, and scheming, all of which seems to end in nothing. Shakespeare elected to portray the besieging army as almost completely demoralized, and to present it at a moment in its history when total disintegration threatened to wreck the campaign against Troy. Beyond this brief segment of the epic story the dramatist does not go. There is no conclusive indication of regeneration on the part of the Greeks, and no clear hint of the ultimate triumph which Homer celebrated. The atmosphere in the Greek camp is as essentially unhealthy at the close of the play as it is at the beginning. Such distortion of the heroic legend shares with a similar debasement of the love story responsibility for the coarse, bitter spirit which students of the play have sought to explain in a variety of ways.

It has been fairly well established by this time that the presentation of the camp action, like that of the love story, is the result not of deliberate vulgarization by Shakespeare, but of the influence of characteristic Renaissance attitudes toward the Troy legend. "Shakespeare," writes

---

[1] In this study I am chiefly indebted, as will be readily apparent, to Professor O. J. Campbell's *Comicall Satyre and Shakespeare's Troilus and Cressida* (1938). Although Professor Campbell discusses the political concept present in the military action of the play, further elaboration of the point seems justified here, if only to make complete and consistent the present study of Shakespeare's use of the pattern in his Greek and Roman plays.

Professor Lawrence, "was fully under the influence of medieval rather than classical conceptions of the tale of Troy." [2] The dramatist's treatment of his material was primarily determined not by the Homeric original, but by the vastly different medieval version of the story as represented, in the later stages of its development, in Benoît de Sainte-Maure's *Le Roman de Troie,* in Caxton's *Recueil of the Histories of Troy* and in Lydgate's *Troy Book.*[3] Such works, retellings many times removed from Homer's account, debased the legend in all respects. Few opportunities were lost to present the characters as arrogant, treacherous, cowardly bullies. The Greeks, Homer's heroes, suffered particularly in this respect. A conscious effort was made by medieval writers to belittle them. Lawrence, among others, suggests that the shift in sympathy was induced by the widespread belief in medieval and Renaissance Europe that western nations were descended from the Trojans through Aeneas and Ascanius.[4] But the Trojans themselves did not always escape abuse in these versions of the story.[5] Caxton especially has little good to say of them. Perhaps, as Professor Campbell argues, the individualism and self-glorification which mark the character and conduct of Homer's heroes appeared only as treacherous selfishness to medieval writers animated by the ideals of chivalry.[6] But whatever the cause, the history of the Troy story in the middle ages is a history of degeneration and debasement in which the Greek forces are the principal victims. And until the appearance of Chapman's Homer, it was this tradition which principally determined Renaissance attitudes toward the siege of Troy. To summarize the situation in Professor Campbell's words:

In short, by Shakespeare's time these Homeric heroes, no longer a band of youths fighting joyously in the sunlight on the plains of Troy, appeared

---

[2] W. W. Lawrence, *Shakespeare's Problem Comedies* (1931), p. 157.

[3] This argument has been most convincingly presented by J. S. P. Tatlock in "The Siege of Troy in Elizabethan Literature, Especially in Shakespeare and Heywood," *PMLA,* XXX (1915), 760, and in "The Chief Problem in Shakespeare," *Sewanee Review,* XXIV (1916), 129. Further development of the thesis will be found in Hyder Rollins' "The Troilus-Cressida Story from Chaucer to Shakespeare," *PMLA,* XXXII (1917), 428.

[4] Lawrence, *op. cit.,* p. 154; O. J. Campbell, *op. cit.,* p. 189.

[5] Boas, *Shakspere and His Predecessors* (1902), p. 574.

[6] O. J. Campbell, *op. cit.,* p. 195.

as a group of undisciplined individuals acting at cross purposes. They were often driven to action by evil passion, and frequently revealed conduct that would seem base to all those gentlemen of the time who still retained some of the generous impulses of chivalry.[7]

It seems clear that Shakespeare so regarded the materials of the Troy story, whether he took the materials themselves from Chapman's Homer, or, as seems more probable, from some representative of the medieval tradition.[8]

What mood or idea directed Shakespeare to recreate dramatically this picture of demoralization in the military society of the ancient Greeks? Many critics, in explanation of his choice of materials and the bitter spirit of his treatment, postulate a period of personal disillusionment and pessimism.[9] So eminent an authority as Sir Edmund Chambers similarly advances a subjective interpretation of the play and concludes that "in *Troilus and Cressida* a disillusioned Shakespeare turns back upon his own former ideals and the world's ancient ideals of heroism and romance, and questions them." [10] Other critics suggest that Shakespeare chose the story for purposes of satire.[11] Few of these scholars are willing to admit anything more definite than a satirical temper in the play, but Professor Campbell has recently demonstrated with great plausibility that not only the tone, but the structure itself is that of a "comicall satyre," a dramatic form developed by Jonson and Marston after the suppression of formal literary satire in 1599. It was Shakespeare's purpose in the camp action, this scholar argues, to show, in terms of the Troy story as he found it, the folly and futility of war as

[7] O. J. Campbell, *op. cit.*, p. 195.

[8] See Tatlock, *PMLA*, XXX, 738 *et seq.*, on the possible sources of Homeric materials in Shakespeare's play. Professor Tatlock argues that these came not from Chapman but from a lost source play which was used by both Shakespeare and Heywood (*The Iron Age*, Part I).

[9] Cf. Georg Brandes, *William Shakespeare: a Critical Study*, translated by William Archer *et al.* (1935), p. 528: "How plainly is one of the sources betrayed here [III, iii, 145–179] of the black waters of bitterness which bubble up in *Troilus and Cressida*, a bitterness which spares neither man nor woman, war nor love, hero nor lover, and which springs in part from woman's guile, in part from the undoubted stupidity of the English public." Professor Tatlock (*Sewanee Review*, XXIV, 132, note 1) enumerates other exponents of this argument.

[10] E. K. Chambers, *Shakespeare: A Survey* (1925), p. 193; quoted in Campbell, *op. cit.*, p. 188.

[11] Cf. for example Boas, *op. cit.*, p. 384.

conducted by a disorganized military society, just as in the love story it was his purpose to show the folly and futility of lust. "The tale of Troy," writes Professor Campbell, "had become a story well suited to serve as a picture of social disintegration, which Shakespeare decided to paint in dark colors." [12]

But whether his ultimate purpose was satirical or otherwise, Shakespeare was clearly not willing to present the demoralized Greek camp without analysis and explanation of the conditions which he found therein. That he considered the enervating confusion to be the result of violation of those principles of social and political organization which he held in common with the majority of his contemporaries seems to be the evident purport not only of Ulysses' celebrated discourse on order and degree, but also of the entire camp action which follows. Specifically, Shakespeare shows that when any one degree in a social hierarchy, and particularly the degree of rule, fails in the performance of its appointed function, the whole highly integrated machine breaks down and is unable to achieve the purpose for which it was ordained by the laws of God and nature. Professor Campbell recognized this thesis when he wrote that Shakespeare

presents anew the philosophy that animates many of the chronicle history plays—namely, that when a prince ceases to command the customary allegiance of his subjects, each as required by his degree, the authority of all other social duties is destroyed at its source. The inevitable result is confusion, in which every sort of co-operative effort is rendered futile and abortive. [13]

In his desire to stress the satirical nature of the play, however, the critic neglects to show how closely Shakespeare's analysis of the situation follows the political thinking of the dramatist's day.

It will be recalled that according to majority opinion in Tudor England subordination of the individual to the common cause was a fundamental principle of social conduct. [14] Selfish, ambitious action and the dissension which it creates were recognized as disastrous to social enterprise. Such an explanation of Greek disintegration had been suggested long before Shakespeare took up the theme. There is a hint of it in Homer's epic itself, when Ulysses, in Book II of the *Iliad*, tells those

[12] O. J. Campbell, *op. cit.*, p. 195.   [13] *Ibid.*, p. 226.
[14] See above, Chapter V.

who would revolt against Agamemnon, "We must not all be kings. The rule is most irregular Where many rule." [15] Medieval writers, however, not only develop this theme more specifically but enlarge upon the social disorder which results from Greek violation of the principle. Concerning the dissension of Palamides against Agamemnon and its consequences to the morale of the Greek forces Lydgate writes:

> Lo, what meschef lyth in variaunce
> Amonge lordis, whan þei nat accorde
> For to drawe fully by a corde:
> Envie is cause of swiche division,
> And covetyse of dominacioun,
> Þat eueryche wolde surmounte his felow.
> Þis cursid vise ofte hath withdrawe
> Hop & grace in many regioun:
> For whan discord & false discencioun
> Allied ben in hertis for to strive
> Among lordis, þat kyndam may not þryve
> Til þei reformed ben ageyn to pes
> Amonge hem self—pleinly þis no les. [16]

There was, then, in the medieval tradition, not only the representation of disintegration among the Greeks, but also an indication of the philosophical principles which controlled this condition in several instances. Unless a lost source play intervened, however, it seems clear that Shakespeare, if he received the idea at all from this tradition, developed the suggested principle fully and consistently in terms of the thinking of his own day. The details of language and the philosophical implications in Ulysses' speech are precisely those employed by Renaissance proponents of degree, vocation, and government in organized societies.

That Shakespeare should select Ulysses to present the true analysis of the situation in the Greek camp seems perfectly logical. There is no reason to accept Fripp's conclusion that the general is merely "a wiseacre, full of maxims and wiles." [17] Ulysses certainly suffered along

[15] Book II, l. 172 (*Works of George Chapman: Homer's Illiad and Odessy*, edited by R. H. Shepherd, 1875, p. 31).

[16] John Lydgate, *Troy Book*, Book III, ll. 2343 *et seq.*, Early English Text Society, Extra Series, Vol. CIII, pp. 461–62.

[17] E. I. Fripp, *Shakespeare, Man and Artist* (1938), II, 580.

with the rest of the Greeks in the medieval debasement of the Troy legend, but he retains at least some of the dignity and wisdom with which Homer invested him, and it is this aspect of the portrait which Shakespeare seems to have developed.[18] Richard Grant White went so far as to say that "Ulysses is the real hero of the play; the chief, or at least, the great purpose of which is the utterance of the Ulyssean view of life and in this play Shakespeare is Ulysses, or Ulysses Shakespeare." [19] Boas, praising the "sane, equitable worldly wisdom of Ulysses," maintains that he "plays the reverse role to Pandarus." [20] Ulysses it is who sees not only the folly and error of the Greek conduct, but also the true characters of Troilus and Cressida.[21] Thus he fills a role much like that taken by Menenius in *Coriolanus*. He is the spokesman for a moral and social order, the violation of which by the other figures in the play constitutes the principal action of the drama.

"In his great speech on degree," writes Professor Campbell, Ulysses "enunciates the ethical and political standards by which the anarchistic folly of the Greek warriors is judged and found ridiculous and socially destructive." [22] There is no discrepancy in the fact that we find the sagacious general critically applying to a military organization those principles of order which Renaissance theorists applied primarily to political societies. Ulysses makes clear, as did Shakespeare's contemporaries, that degree, vocation, and government are decreed by the universal law of nature and are ordained, accordingly, not only for all forms of human organization, but also for the world in macrocosm and in microcosm.[23] His whole argument relies for its authority on the universality of the principles which it sets forth. The laws which should govern the conduct of the Greeks are those, he points out, which govern the community of bees, the community of planets and stars, and the communities of men in families, schools, cities, and states. Moreover, he points out, failure to observe these laws bears the same fruits of dis-

[18] Thus Tatlock (*PMLA*, XXX, 753) argues that Ulysses maintains his stately dignity in Shakespeare's play and Heywood's *The Iron Age*, Part I, although the quality is more heightened in the former. Both plays, Professor Tatlock maintains, are based on the medieval tradition.

[19] Quoted in *Troilus and Cressida*, p. xxv, edited by K. Deighton, The Arden Shakespeare (1922).

[20] Boas, *op. cit.*, p. 380.   [21] Cf. *Troilus and Cressida*, IV, v, 54–63; 96–112.

[22] O. J. Campbell, *op. cit.*, p. 197.   [23] Cf. Chapter VI, above.

order and frustration in all these social groups. The purposes of societies differ according to the ends for which nature established and equipped them, but the principles of structure and conduct are the same for all. The standards by which Shakespeare judges the Greek army can therefore quite justifiably, in fact, must necessarily, be those of contemporary Tudor political thinkers who were primarily concerned with states and commonwealths.

The basic concept in Ulysses' analysis of the situation is briefly this: no community can successfully attain the ends for which it was established if one of its members, forsaking the degree and vocation to which he is naturally ordained, acts for self-interest rather than for the interests of the whole body. It will be recalled that according to Renaissance theory, degrees in a social organization are determined by those natural differences in men which are adapted to the various needs of the whole community. Some vocations are of more, some of less importance to the group, and the rank of the individual is fixed accordingly. Upon the preservation of this hierarchy of vocations and of the authority of superior degrees over inferior depends the welfare of the whole body and of every individual in it. Ulysses insists upon the necessity for recognizing these natural differences: "Degree being vizarded, The unworthiest shows as fairly in the mask." [24] He finds the principle operating macrocosmically in the structure of the solar system:

> The heavens themselves, the planets, and this centre
> Observe degree, priority, and place,
> Insisture, course, proportion, season, form
> Office, and custom, in all line of order: . . .[25]

Turning to the human plane he asks,

> How could communities,
> Degrees in schools, and brotherhoods in cities,
> Peaceful commerce from dividable shores,
> The primogenitive and due of birth,
> Prerogative of age, crowns, sceptres, laurels,
> But by degree stand in authentic place? [26]

Violation of this order restores that primordial chaos which existed before God gave law to the universe:

[24] I, iii, 83–84.　　[25] I, iii, 85–88.　　[26] I, iii, 103–8.

But when the planets
In evil mixture to disorder wander,
What plagues and what portents! what mutiny!
What raging of the sea! shaking of earth!
Commotion in the winds! Frights, changes, horrors,
Divert and crack, rend and deracinate
The unity and married calm of states
Quite from their fixture! . . .

. . . .

Take but degree away, untune that string,
And, hark, what discord follows! Each thing meets
In mere oppugnancy. The bounded waters
Should lift their bosoms higher than the shores,
And make a sop of all this solid globe.
Strength should be lord of imbecility,
And the rude son should strike his father dead.[27]

In the realm of human social organization similar confusion follows
neglect of the principles of order and degree; tranquility, virtue, and
justice give way to the violence, the wrongs, and the injustice which
characterized the presocial existence of men.

O, when degree is shak'd,
Which is the ladder to all high designs,
The enterprise is sick! . . .

. . . .

Force should be right; or rather, right and wrong,
Between whose endless jar justice resides,
Should lose their names, and so should justice too.
Then everything includes itself in power,
Power into will, will into appetite;
And appetite, an universal wolf,
So doubly seconded with will and power,
Must make perforce an universal prey,
And last eat up himself.[28]

Ulysses implies that an army in which there is disregard for these laws
of order will similarly fail to achieve its purpose, which is the successful
conduct of war, and will ultimately destroy itself.

[27] I, iii, 94–101; 109–15.   [28] I, iii, 101–3; 116–24.

But all this is merely philosophical groundwork for the main point which the general is trying to make in his speech. In the hierarchy of superiors and inferiors which constitutes a human social organization there is naturally and logically a highest degree to which all others are subservient. To the paramount degree is assigned the vocation of rule and government of the whole body. In the Greek camp the highest office is held by Agamemnon, the "head and general" to whose "topless deputation" Ulysses himself refers in the course of his speech.[29] But high in the structure of the hierarchy stands Achilles, "whom opinion crowns The sinew and the forehand of our host." [30] He it is who, disregarding his vocation by refusing to fight and disparaging the authority of his natural superior by mocking the person and government of Agamemnon, destroys the social order and spreads the infection of disobedience and inaction through the entire system. "The specialty of rule hath been neglected" by Achilles, and, in consequence,

> Look, how many Grecian tents do stand
> Hollow upon this plain, so many hollow factions.
> When that the general is not like the hive
> To whom the foragers shall all repair,
> What honey is expected? [31]

Ulysses later shows specifically how the individualistic and antisocial conduct of Achilles has disrupted the whole complex structure and rendered it completely ineffective:

> Great Agamemnon,
> This chaos, when degree is suffocate,
> Follows the choking.
> And this neglection of degree is it
> That by a pace goes backward, in a purpose
> It hath to climb. The general's disdain'd
> By him one step below, he by the next,
> That next by him beneath; so every step,
> Exampled by the first pace that is sick
> Of his superior, grows to an envious fever
> Of pale and bloodless emulation;
> And 'tis this fever that keeps Troy on foot,
> Not her own sinews.[32]

---

[29] I, iii, 222, 152.   [30] I, iii, 142–43.   [31] I, iii, 79–83.   [32] I, iii, 124–36.

Nestor cites the case of Ajax to confirm the argument made by Ulysses and to illustrate how in imitation of Achilles "many are infect." [33] As Ulysses himself concludes in a statement explaining the scheme which he is about to propose:

> The seeded pride
> That hath to this maturity blown up
> In rank Achilles must or now be cropp'd
> Or, shedding, breed a nursery of like evil
> To overbulk us all.[34]

If the Greek cause is to be saved, Achilles must be brought back to his natural and proper vocation and degree in the military society.

Achilles' antisocial conduct is the result of flaws in character which are explicitly revealed by Ulysses and illustrated throughout the camp action of the play. Sir Sidney Lee writes that "Shakespeare's portrait interpreted the selfish, unreasoning, and exorbitant pride with which the warrior was credited by Homer's medieval expositors." [35] Achilles violates the universal laws of order because he substitutes personal and selfish action for social action. He acts for himself rather than for the body of which he is a member. Wounded vanity and excessive pride lead him, on the one hand, to forsake his true function as a soldier, and, on the other hand, to disregard and ridicule the function of the degree superior to him. His conduct in the latter respect is clearly analyzed by Ulysses when he says of Achilles and those whom the recalcitrant soldier has infected:

[33] I, iii, 185–96:

NESTOR. And in the imitation of these twain—
  Who, as Ulysses says, opinion crowns
  With an imperial voice—many are infect.
  Ajax is grown self-will'd, and bears his head
  In such a rein, in full as proud a place
  As broad Achilles; keeps his tent like him;
  Makes factious feasts; rails on our state of war,
  Bold as an oracle, and sets Thersites,
  A slave whose gall coins slanders like a mint,
  To match us in comparisons with dirt,
  To weaken and discredit our exposure,
  How rank soever rounded in with danger.

[34] I, iii, 316–20.

[35] Sir Sidney Lee, *A Life of William Shakespeare* (1922), p. 372.

They tax our policy, and call it cowardice,
Count wisdom as no member of the war,
Forestall prescience, and esteem no act
But that of hand. The still and mental parts,
That do contrive how many hands shall strike
When fitness calls them on, and know by measure
Of their observant toil the enemies' weight—
Why, this hath not a finger's dignity.
They call this bed-work, mappery, closet-war;
So that the ram that batters down the wall,
For the great swing and rudeness of his poise,
They place before his hand that made the engine,
Or those that with the fineness of their souls
By reason guide his execution.[36]

In the blindness of his personal passion Achilles cannot see that each part of the body has a function without which action by the whole is impossible. He cannot see, as did Shakespeare's politically thinking contemporaries, that a body without a head, a body unguided by reason, is, regardless of its physical prowess, a monster running to its own destruction. He cannot see, as he dawdles lasciviously in his tent, that action by the body, no matter how rationally planned, is impossible without the sword which only his arm can wield.

If the disintegrated Greek military machine is to be repaired, then, "the chief architect of the chaos" must be purged of the humor which has led him to his disruptive social misconduct. The so-called "camp-action" is the story of Ulysses' attempt to accomplish this purpose and to restore the normal functioning of degrees and vocations. First he causes Ajax to be selected instead of Achilles for the honor of meeting the Trojan Hector in single combat. This act, and the parade of contemptuous Greeks before his tent, make Achilles acutely aware that his much-treasured reputation rests on his acting in his vocation, not on his indulging in antisocial pride. Ulysses enhances the effect which he has thus achieved by delivering a sermon at this point on the nature of reputation. He stresses the fact that a man must use his natural abilities, and use them constantly, if he is to expect a justifiable fame for them. His words are shrewdly pointed:

[36] I, iii, 197–210.

> . . . no man is the lord of anything
> (Though in and of him there is much consisting,)
> Till he communicate his parts to others;
>
> .   .   .   .
>
> O heavens, what some men do,
> While some men leave to do!
> How some men creep in skittish Fortune's hall,
> Whiles others play the idiots in her eyes!
> How one man eats into another's pride,
> While pride is fasting in his wantonness!
>
> .   .   .   .
>
> The present eye praises the present object.
> Then marvel not, thou great and complete man,
> That all the Greeks begin to worship Ajax;
> Since things in motion sooner catch the eye
> Than what not stirs. The cry went once on thee,
> And still it might, and yet it may again,
> If thou wouldst not entomb thyself alive
> And case thy reputation in thy tent;
> Whose glorious deeds, but in these fields of late,
> Made emulous missions 'mongst the gods themselves,
> And drave great Mars to faction.[37]

Ulysses is attempting here to turn Achilles' concern for his reputation from selfish to socially coöperative ends. The argument, therefore, is a cleverly contrived expression of political reason. But it is of little avail against the passion of Achilles. The warrior's infatuation for Priam's daughter turns him once again from his vocation. It is only when Patroclus, his favorite, is slain, that he rises from his lethargy and takes up arms. Then it is scarcely an action directed by the rational planning of his superiors, but a deed rising from self-centered passion.[38] Agamemnon, however, accepts it as a sign that the natural order can perhaps be restored in the Greek camp and the purpose of the organization forwarded once more:

> March patiently along; let one be sent
> To pray Achilles see us at our tent.

---

[37] III, iii, 115–17; 132–37; 180–90.   [38] Cf. O. J. Campbell, *op. cit.*, p. 201.

If in his death the gods have us befriended,
Great Troy is ours, and our sharp wars are ended.[39]

But as Professor Campbell observes, Ulysses' scheme to make
Achilles conscious of his social obligations, the backbone of the camp
action, is frustrated. The thread of the military plot, like that of the
love story, remains in the end untied. The theory that another hand
than Shakespeare's was responsible for this seeming lapse in dramatic
construction has generally been rejected in favor of the belief that the
ending is a part of the poet's original design.[40] The latter contention has
been most extensively developed by Professor Campbell, who holds
that the conclusion is characteristic of the "comicall satyre," the type of
play, as this critic argues, which Shakespeare was writing in *Troilus and
Cressida*. He asserts that "the unusual ending of *Troilus and Cressida*
serves to dismiss the derided characters in a way that was conventional
to satire and leaves the audience in a mocking attitude toward them that
is demanded by the type." [41] Of the camp action in particular he writes:
"so failure overtakes Ulysses' nicely devised plan to induce this Olym-
pian school-boy to obey the dictates of self-interest as rationalized and
implemented by a social idea. The outcome, as in the case of all the
other efforts of the characters, whether reasonable or irrational, is futility, and was meant to awaken scornful laughter." [42]

It is not inharmonious with this plausible argument to suggest that,
insofar as the camp sequences embody Shakespeare's exposure and analysis of a chaotic and destructive social condition, Ulysses' scheme and
its outcome is ideally adapted to the purpose. In the Troy legend as it
came to him in its medieval garb Shakespeare found a degenerate and
demoralized Greek camp; his purpose in treating this phase of the story
dramatically was to show the causes of the condition, not to extricate the
Greeks from their difficulties and glorify them in defiance of the prevalent condemnatory attitude of his day. Viewed as a problem in applied
political theory, the action has as its main point the presentation of a
social organism infected in its every part and rendered useless because

---

[39] V, ix, 7–10.
[40] Cf. E. K. Chambers, *William Shakespeare: A Study of Facts and Problems*
(1930), I, 445–47, for a summary review of these claims.
[41] O. J. Campbell, *op. cit.*, p. 225.   [42] *Ibid.*, p. 201.

of corruption spread from one of its topmost degrees. In the language of Thersites in Act V:

The policy of those crafty swearing rascals, that stale old mouse-eaten dry cheese, Nestor, and that same dog-fox, Ulysses, is not prov'd worth a blackberry. They set me up, in policy, that mongrel cur, Ajax, against that dog of as bad a kind, Achilles; and now is the cur Ajax prouder than the cur Achilles, and will not arm today; whereupon the Grecians begin to proclaim barbarism, and policy grows into an ill opinion.

As Boas summarizes the problem in relation to the love story, "Exaggerated self-love is as fatal to the success of the common enterprise as exaggerated idealization of the bond between the sexes." [43] In the great speech given to Ulysses, Shakespeare set forth the theory behind his explanation of the situation; then he devised the plot, intended by Ulysses to cure the condition but serving actually to illustrate in action the violation of these principles. The consequences emphasize Shakespeare's insistence on the futility and folly of such conduct. Consistently to the end the drama reveals the results of the frustration of political reason by selfish passion. The attempt by Ulysses to shame Achilles out of self-centered idleness into social action, the tenor of Ulysses' discourse on reputation, and the violently emotional and individualistic act which rewards his efforts—all display the fundamental clash between a rationally organized society and an individual motivated by passion. It is this clash, according to Shakespeare, which lies at the heart of the problem. Agamemnon's final comment is a hopeful suggestion that order will be restored, but scarcely indicates that the problem has been conclusively solved. At the end of the play, as at the beginning, "The Greek chieftains, with all the right on their side, with the shrewdest policy of their wisest leaders to guide them, are powerless, just like Troilus, before egotism, selfishness and lust." [44]

2

In *Timon of Athens* Shakespeare returns to the problem of a diseased society. And again the dramatist brings to his study of an unhealthy state those standards of political organization and conduct generally accepted in the thinking of his own day. The nature of the corruption

[43] Boas, *op. cit.*, p. 380.   [44] Lawrence, *op. cit.*, p. 165.

portrayed here differs from that analyzed in *Troilus and Cressida,* and its effects are studied in greater detail, but the fundamental principle is the same. Misconduct in the higher ranks of the society contaminates every degree in the hierarchical structure and prevents the community from functioning for the purposes for which God ordained it. These results of political infection are examined particularly as they bear on two individual members of the commonwealth, Timon and Alcibiades. The career of the former is, of course, the central theme of the play, but to consider Timon's tragedy apart from this political structure is to deprive it of much of its philosophic and dramatic significance.

In their concern with the problems of text and authorship which *Timon of Athens* presents, scholars for the most part have failed to emphasize sufficiently the importance of its political concepts to the structure and meaning of the play.[45] In seeking for some structural link between the respective fortunes of Timon and Alcibiades, however, several critics—Deighton, Wright, Parrott, and Wecter among them [46] —have called attention to the ungrateful state which is the common enemy of the two men, motivating the misanthropy exhibited by the one and the vengeance taken by the other. But because they fail to find enough evidence to support anything more than conjectural con-

[45] For a convenient summary of the complex problems of text and authorship in this play see E. K. Chambers, *William Shakespeare: A Study of Facts and Problems* (1930), I, 480. The present study, not primarily concerned with authorship, is based on the text of the play as presented in the Cambridge Shakespeare, edited by W. A. Neilson. Footnote reference will be made in those instances where the political material seems to support Deighton, Boas, and Chambers in accepting the whole play as substantially Shakespeare's.

[46] *Timon of Athens,* "Introduction," edited by K. Deighton, The Arden Shakespeare (1905); E. H. Wright, *The Authorship of Timon of Athens* (1910); T. M. Parrott, *The Problem of Timon of Athens,* Shakespeare Association Bulletin, No. 10 (1923); Dixon Wecter, "Shakespere's Purpose in Timon of Athens," *PMLA,* XLIII (1928), 701 *et seq.* The general attitude of these critics may be summarized in the following words of Professor Wright: "Critics have held that Timon's troubles were domestic matters; that he suffered little or nothing from the state; and that the downfall of the state is therefore no revenge for him. But even if it were, it is but incidental to the revenge of Alcibiades; and so hardly natural and certainly unsatisfactory. It is hardly natural because we can see no great reason why Alcibiades should avenge Timon. It is certainly unsatisfactory because in the first place the revenge falls rather on the state which has done Timon little wrong than on the private friends who have played him utterly false; and in the second place because even his avengement of the hero, instead of being Alcibiades' chief motive, is only subsidiary to his revenge for himself" (p. 72).

clusions, these writers tend to minimize the significance of their suggestion. A reëxamination of the play in the light of Renaissance political
thinking reveals the fact that there is perhaps more reason for developing this thesis than these scholars suspect.

It is true that Shakespeare in *Timon of Athens* devotes little time to a
discussion of the structural features of political society. There is no
concrete expression of the concept of the state such as is found in *Troilus
and Cressida* and *Coriolanus*. But there are indications that Shakespeare
had such a concept in mind in analyzing the Athenian commonwealth.
The date of *Timon* is conjectural, but it is generally grouped with
Coriolanus in the period 1607–1608.[47] That *Timon* appears in conjunc-
tion with a play which contains one of the dramatist's clearest expressions of his theory of the state is a significant fact in itself. Possible
echoes of this expression are found on two occasions in *Timon*. Addressing the senators in Act V, the title figure directs his diatribe against
Athens "in the sequence of degree, From high to low throughout." [48]
And in an earlier outburst against Athenian society, at the mock banquet
in Act III, he refers to "the senators of Athens, together with the common legge of people" as the objects of his wrath.[49] Professor Wright,
following most editors, considers "legge" a textual corruption and reads
"tag" in its place.[50] But in its context the Folio reading seems rather
clearly to be an analogical allusion familiar in sixteenth-century parallels drawn between the bodies human and political. It is comparable
to Menenius' "You, the great toe of this assembly" as a reference to the
lowest members of the political body. But whatever the interpretation
of "legge," the passage in which it occurs, and that which appears in
Act V, suggest that Timon thought of Athenian society much as Shakespeare's contemporaries thought of society, as a hierarchy embracing all
classes and culminating in "the specialty of rule."

In *Timon*, however, Shakespeare is more interested in the moral
degeneration of such a society; his discussion is couched not so much in
terms of its structure, as in terms of the ends and purposes for which

[47] For a summary of the problems of dating *Timon of Athens* see Chambers, *William
Shakespeare: A Study*, I, 480.
[48] *Timon of Athens*, V, i, 211–12.
[49] III, vi, 90. This is the reading of the First Folio.
[50] Wright, *op. cit.*, p. 73; cf. also Deighton's edition of the play. The Cambridge
editor, following Rowe, reads "lag."

political societies are established by the laws of God and nature. It will be recalled that according to the political thinking of the Renaissance, states are ordained that men may enjoy social tranquility, the material necessities of existence, and above all, a life of moral and intellectual virtue.[51] Because they administer justice—that is, because they reward virtue, punish vice, and give unto every man his due— the rulers of states are chiefly responsible for the attainment of these ends. When justice is perverted and these ends, virtue in particular among them, are ignored, the society disintegrates and its individuals are in danger of returning to the bestial existence of the presocial era. This in substance is what happens to the political society of Athens in *Timon.* Shakespeare portrays a commonwealth which has placed material welfare before virtue as its activating purpose; accordingly it has degenerated into a state of social corruption in which, among other evils, the perversion of justice has brought harm, rather than reward, to the truly virtuous members of society.

As in *Troilus and Cressida,* so in *Timon* the infection which demoralizes the social organism flows down from the head. According to the political ideology of the Renaissance, as has been shown in Chapter VI, above, the temper of a whole society is largely determined by the temper of the ruler, whose vocation is to coördinate the complex machine of state. This conception, frequently reiterated in the literature of the sixteenth century, is clearly expressed by Goslicius when he writes:

And as the commonweale is many times infected and corrupted, by the vices and wickednes of Magistrates: so is the same corrected and repaired by their virtues: Neyther is the mischiefe of their faultes so great, as that many others will imitate those evill examples. Such are the people of every state, as are the manners of those that governe; and what mutation of manners the prince useth, the same is by the subiectes followed.[52]

Something of this same opinion is expressed in the closing scene of the play. The senators beseech Alcibiades, in his triumph over Athens, to destroy only those responsible for the general corruption, to "Approach the fold and cull the infected forth, But kill not all together." [53] He himself recognizes the fact that the correction of the Athenian state does

[51] See Chapter III, above.
[52] Goslicius, *The Counsellor* (translated, 1598), p. 65. [53] V, iv, 43–44.

not necessitate its destruction, but only the purging of those of its leaders who have corrupted the whole organization.

In Act III, scene v, the causes and nature of the infection in the governing head of the state are explicitly described by Alcibiades. And significantly enough these causes are identical, as will be shown, with those to which Timon later in the play attributes the corruption of the whole Athenian social order. According to Alcibiades it is lust for gold, a disproportionate emphasis on material welfare, which has turned the Senate from its appointed vocation of government. It will be remembered that in Renaissance political thinking a government which ruled for its own selfish purposes, for the increase of its own wealth at the expense of others, was considered nothing short of a tyranny. As Goslicius expressed it, "To excell in riches is proper to Tyrants, but a kings chief desire is honour." [54] In distinguishing a just governor from a tyrant Merbury wrote: "The one hath his minde, and all his care upon the health, and wealth of his subiectes: th' other estemeth his own pleasure more than their profit, his owne wealth, more than their good willes." [55] And Floyd asserted that a tyrant "esteemth it better to have his own palace costly furnished, and the commonweale poore, than his palace poore, and the commonweale rich." [56] In the same vein numerous sermons were preached to kings and rulers on the text, "He shall not multiply unto himself too much gold and silver." [57] In the scene under consideration Alicibiades makes it clear that the corruption of the Senate can be accounted for in similar terms. Some preparation for his charges is found in the first scene of Act II, where the avarice which has enervated the head of the Athenian political body is exemplified in the greedy anxiety of a single senator. The senator foresees Timon's imminent financial collapse; "It cannot hold," he says of Timon's bounty; "for, I do fear,"

> When every feather sticks in his own wing,
> Lord Timon will be left a naked gull,
> Which flashes now a phoenix.[58]

---

[54] Goslicius, *op. cit.*, p. 75.

[55] Merbury, *A Briefe Discourse of Royall Monarchie* (1581), p. 13.

[56] Floyd, *The Picture of a Perfit Commonwealth* (1600), p. 47.

[57] Cf. Latimer, *Seven Sermons Before Edward VI* (1549), edited by Edward Arber (1895), p. 26.

[58] II, i, 29–32.

Regardless of the consequences to Timon, therefore, he hastens to save his own investments:

> My uses cry to me, I must serve my turn
> Out of mine own. His days and times are past,
> And my reliances on his fracted dates
> Have smit my credit. I love and honour him,
> But must not break my back to heal his finger.[59]

Paramount in the senator's mind are his selfish "uses"; in Act III the theme of Alcibiades' charges against the Senate is this same usury. Even before he openly denounces the corruption of the Senate, Alcibiades hints at the causes of it; he is willing to stake his reputation on his unnamed friend, "for," he says, "I know your reverend ages love Security." [60] The sentence of banishment soon causes Alcibiades to drop his simulated respect, however, and in plain language to tell exactly why "the specialty of rule hath been neglected" in Athens. "Banish your dotage;" he cries, "banish usury, That makes the Senate ugly." [61] After the senators have left the chamber he continues his tirade in the same vein:

> Now the gods keep you old enough; that you may live
> Only in bone, that none may look on you!
> I'm worse than mad. I have kept back their foes,
> While they have told their money and let out
> Their coin upon large interest, I myself
> Rich only in large hurts. All those for this?
> Is this the balsam that the usuring Senate
> Pours into captains' wounds? Banishment! [62]

In the climactic outburst of this scene, therefore, Alcibiades goes beyond the immediate effects, injustice to his friend and banishment for himself, to suggest the ultimate causes. He shows the Athenian Senate to be a governing head which has placed its own selfish greed before justice, mercy, and the welfare of the whole state.

---

[59] II, i, 20–24.   [60] III, v, 80.   [61] III, v, 99.

[62] III, v, 104–11. Draper, "The Theme of 'Timon of Athens,'" *Modern Language Review*, XXIX (1934), 20–31, suggests that condemnation of usury is the theme of the play. The discussion is a cursory one, however; it makes no mention either of the political corruption in Athens or of the injury to Alcibiades, both of which usury produces.

Elsewhere as well as in this scene Alcibiades shows specifically the effects of avarice on the political function of the Senate. Again his charges leave little doubt that the government of Athens had degenerated into a form of tyranny widely recognized in the Renaissance. According to the political literature of Shakespeare's day the governing authority in a state has as its vocation the administration of justice according to the laws of the realm; that is, a good governor rewards virtue and punishes vice as those qualities are determined by the laws of God, of nature, and of men.[63] A tyrant, on the other hand, is described as a ruler who governs not by law, but by his own selfish will. Merbury writes that the good ruler "embraceth equitie and iustice" while the tyrant "treadeth both Gods lawe and mans lawe under his feete." [64] Floyd echoes these words when he remarks that "A Tyrant is a superior Governor that ruleth as he listeth," who "will not live within the precincts and under the rights of lawe and iustice," but governs as his own selfish instinct inclines him.[65] Alcibiades evidently thinks of the Senate of Athens as a tyranny in this sense. As the senators appear on the walls to witness his victorious approach he shouts:

> Till now you have gone on and fill'd the time
> With all licentious measure, making your wills
> The scope of justice; . . .[66]

And after he has overthrown the tyranny, he promises that in its place he will establish true justice according to law:

> Not a man
> Shall pass his quarter, or offend the stream
> Of regular justice in your city's bounds,
> But shall be render'd to your public laws
> At heaviest answer.[67]

The tyranny of the Athenian Senate, however, arises not so much from the fact that it supplants law with selfish will as from the fact that it abuses established law. For according to Renaissance theorists, the governor who rules by law but without equity and mercy is as great a tyrant as he who rules entirely without law. The former makes law an

[63] See Chapter VI, above. [64] Merbury, *op. cit.*, p. 13.
[65] Floyd, *op. cit.*, p. 46. [66] V, iv, 3-5. [67] V, iv, 59-63.

instrument not of public justice, but of his own selfish greed and ambition. Thus Floyd describes as a tyrant a ruler who "persisteth in extremes," for "too much extremetie and overmuch lenitie should not bee used, because extreme law sometimes is thought to bee extreame wrong, and overmuch lenitie breedeth illicentiousnesse and sundrie vices in all sortes." [68] Theorists insisted that only by observing "equitie" could the ruler rightly administer justice according to law. The principle established by Saint German in 1530 was reiterated with little change by political writers throughout the century:

Equitie is a right wisenes that considereth al perticuler circumstances of the deede, the which also is tempered w^t the sweetnes of mercy. And such an equity must alway be observed in every law of man and in every general rule thereof.[69]

Failure to heed this principle is the political crime committed by the Athenian Senate. They disregard the "circumstances of the deed," the plea of self-defense and the obligation of the state to the heroic acts of the unknown soldier. "We are for law," they assert, but it is a law untempered by equity which spurns Alcibiades' repeated petition for mercy and pity. Alcibiades seeks true justice, which will weigh the good with the bad, for his client is "a man, setting his fate aside, Of comely virtues." [70] But the Senate can see only one side of the picture, and they proceed to judge by an "eye for an eye" brand of justice; "He forfeits his own blood that spills another." [71] Accordingly the Senate shows itself to be the tyranny against which Alcibiades warns the governors at the outset of his plea: "For pity is the virtue of the law, And none but tyrants use it cruelly." [72] It is when he becomes aware that the senators are such tyrants that he turns on them with the charges of avarice and corruption.

The avarice which has perverted the function of the Athenian government is contagious. The play makes clear the fact that the same lust for gold which has contaminated the head contaminates in turn the body of the political society. Greed for gold is consistently linked with the com-

[68] Floyd, *op. cit.*, p. 57.
[69] Saint German, *The Dialogues in English between a Doctor of Divinity and a Student in the Laws of England* (1580), fol. 27 r.
[70] III, v, 14. [71] III, v, 88. [72] III, v, 8-9.

plete disruption of the social order in Athens. The evil social effects of
the metal are frequently cited by Timon; thus in Act IV when he
discovers gold instead of roots he exclaims:

> Thus much of this will make black white, foul fair,
> Wrong right, base noble, old young, coward valiant.
> Ha, you gods! why this? What this, you gods? Why, this
> Will lug your priests and servants from your sides,
> Pluck stout men's pillows from below their heads.
> This yellow slave
> Will knit and break religions, bless the accurs'd,
> Make the hoar leprosy ador'd, place thieves
> And give them title, knee, and approbation
> With senators on the bench . . .
>
>   .   .   .   .
>
>   Come, damn'd earth,
> Thou common whore of mankind, that puts odds
> Among the rout of nations, I will make thee
> Do thy right nature.[73]

From his own bitter experience Timon can understand how the lust
for gold can turn topsy-turvy the naturally established order of society,
can cast the virtuous from the top of the hierarchy to the bottom, and
elevate the vicious, can turn men from their true vocations, the priest
from his ministrations and the judge from the execution of true justice.
It is gold which "Settlest admired reverence in a slave." [74] Even worse,
it destroys that natural obedience between king and subject, father and
son, master and servant, husband and wife, superior and inferior in the
whole range of degrees, which holds the social structure together. In
a word, it destroys "the specialty of rule." As Timon cries:

> O thou sweet king-killer, and dear divorce
> 'Twixt natural son and sire! thou bright defiler
> Of Hymen's purest bed! thou valiant Mars! [75]

Much of Timon's tirade can be explained, of course, as variations on
the universal theme that money is the root of all evil. But the consistent
appearance, in these passages and others, of terms and concepts familiar
in Renaissance discussions of political society, suggests that Timon's

---

[73] IV, iii, 28–44.   [74] V, i, 54.   [75] IV, iii, 382–84.

outbursts contain more specifically political implications. His expression is more vehement than theirs, but his meaning is the same as that of political writers from More to Hooker; avarice and greed are diseases which weaken and eventually destroy the body politic.

When a political society becomes impaired for any reason it fails to provide those qualities which distinguish the life of man from the life of beasts—tranquility, security, justice, virtue, and religion. The higher ends for which man peculiarly is ordained are made impossible of attainment; turmoil takes the place of peace, famine of plenty, disorder of order, vice of virtue, and impiety and damnation of religion and salvation. To repeat the warning of the Homily of 1547:

Take awaye . . . such states of Gods order no man shal ride or go by the high waie unrobbed, no man shall slepe in his owne bed unkilled, no man shall kepe his wife, children and possessions in quietness, all thynges shal be comon, and there must nedes folow al mischief and utter destruction, bothe of soules, bodies, goodes, and commonwealthes.[76]

For, as Hooker expressed the broader principle involved in this warning, "the Law of Nature doth now require of necessity some kind of regiment; so that to bring things unto the first course they were in, and utterly to take away all kind of public government in the world, were apparently to overturn the whole world." [77]

Timon describes the corrupt commonwealth of Athens in terms strikingly similar to these. His curse on Athens in Act IV is a negative statement of what the Renaissance expected from a healthy society. So important is this passage as a key to the political structure of the play that it may well be quoted at length:

> Let me look back upon thee. O thou wall,
> That girdles in those wolves, dive in the earth,
> And fence not Athens! Matrons, turn incontinent!
> Obedience fail in children! Slaves and fools,
> Pluck the grave wrinkled Senate from the bench,
> And minister in their steads! To general filths
> Convert o' the instant, green virginity!
> Do 't in your parents' eyes! Bankrupts, hold fast;
> Rather than render back, out with your knives,

---

[76] *Certayne Sermons or Homilies* (1547), Homily X, Sig. K, i v.

[77] Hooker, *Of the Laws of Ecclesiastical Polity*, p. 191, Everyman's Library.

And cut your trusters' throats! Bound servants, steal!
Large-handed robbers your grave masters are,
And pill by law. Maid, to thy master's bed;
Thy mistress is o' the brothel! Son of sixteen,
Pluck the lin'd crutch from thy old limping sire;
With it beat out his brains! [78]

Thus far Timon has portrayed corruption in the private relationships
of men living together in society. Now he turns to the public qualities
upon which healthy political societies are founded:

Piety, and fear,
Religion to the gods, peace, justice, truth,
Domestic awe, night-rest, and neighbourhood,
Instruction, manners, mysteries, and trades,
Degrees, observances, customs, and laws,
Decline to your confounding contraries,
And let confusion live! [79]

He calls down upon Athens those evils which were certain to beset a
state whose divinely ordained structure is impaired or corrupted in any
of its parts. In language as well as in thought his tirades clearly embody
the Renaissance conception of an infected political society.

In this respect the constant reference to the bestiality of Athenian
life is significant. The use of the term "beasts" in Renaissance political
and social writing will be recalled from Chapter III. It was the epithet
commonly employed to describe men either in the chaos of the presocial era or in a commonwealth which for one reason or another had
disrupted the natural civil order. Goslicius writes that before states were
established men, "who then lived as brutish beasts," were every one
"armed . . . against virtue, thinking it was lawfull to offend others,
to live ungodly, abusing reason, and employing it in evill exercises." [80]
Sir John Cheke, describing a society made corrupt by rebellion, denounces the inhabitants of such a state as "worthy to be ordered like
beasts." [81] The frequent appearance of the term in *Timon* is a further
suggestion that Shakespeare was thinking of social disintegration much

[78] IV, i, 1–15.
[79] IV, i, 15–21. The terminology here should be compared with that in the opening
lines of Ulysses' discourse in Act I of *Troilus and Cressida*.
[80] Goslicius, *op. cit.*, pp. 56, 57.
[81] Cheke, *The Hurt of Sedicion* (1549), in Holinshed, *Chronicles* (1807), III, 993.

as his contemporaries thought of it. For as Apemantus says in describing the Athenian state, "The commonwealth of Athens is become a forest of beasts." [82] The full development of this theme is reserved for Timon himself, however. Much of his invective is expressed in terms which suggest the bestiality of Athenian society, and certainly much of it requires no political explanation to make its meaning clear. Of such sort is the string of epithets which he hurls at his guests at the conclusion of the mock banquet. But elsewhere he employs the term "beast" as if to designate more specifically the members of a corrupt society. In his great outburst at the opening of Act IV he bids farewell to the wall of Athens "That girdlest in those wolves"; he will forsake human society and seek the woods, "where he shall find the unkindest beast more kinder than mankind." [83] In scene iii of the same act he hails Alcibiades as one like himself and all men, "A beast." Later in this scene he exclaims that nature has produced "the black toad and adder blue, The gilded newt and eyeless venom'd worm," but no beast worse than man. [84] Still later in the scene Timon asks Apemantus, "Wouldst thou have thyself fall in the confusion of men, and remain a beast with the beasts?" [85] Thereupon he discourses at length upon the wrongs committed by man against man in terms of animal life.

Throughout the play, then, in a variety of ways, Shakespeare builds up a vivid picture of social chaos brought about by corruption in the governing head of the state. Throughout the hierarchy the individual works not for the good of the whole body, but for his own selfish interests. When the fundamental laws of political society are violated, the social conduct of men begins to resemble the rapacious conduct of the presocial era. "Peace, religion and a vertuous mind" are impossible of attainment. Instead, true virtue and nobility go unrecognized and unrewarded, while vice flourishes unpunished. Such is the politico-social scheme in relation to which the drama of Timon and Alcibiades is developed.

In Plutarch's *Life of Marcus Antonius,* Shakespeare's main source for *Timon,* there is a hint that both Timon and Alcibiades believe their real enemy to be not an individual or a particular group of individuals, but the degenerate society of Athens. According to Plutarch, Ape-

[82] IV, iii, 352.

[84] IV, iii, 180 *et seq.*

[83] IV, i, 2, 35–36.

[85] IV, iii, 325.

mantus wondered at Timon's friendship for Alcibiades; "Timon answered him, 'I do it,' he said, 'because I know that one day he shall do great mischief unto the Athenians.' Which words many times he told to Alcibiades himself." [86] The implication is that one link between the two men is their common grievance against Athenians in general, and their common desire to avenge themselves against the state. The implication becomes explicit in Shakespeare's play. It is a striking fact, not hitherto pointed out, I believe, that not once after his flight to the forest does Timon direct his wrath against the particular individuals who caused his downfall. Without exception the great misanthropic outbursts which characterize the last two acts of the drama are directed against Athenian society as a whole. Even when directly addressing the senators in the first scene of Act V he does not once allude to their particular wrongs against him, but pours the full stream of his bitterness and hate against the corrupt society which they represent. Alcibiades' grievance in the play is more specifically against the Senate itself, but he makes clear, as has been shown, that he regards the Senate as the source of Athenian demoralization. Timon's cry is against an evil society; Alcibiades' cry is against the political rulers who have caused that evil. From the sixteenth-century point of view, however, the enemy of the two men is the same.

The tragic victim of these political and social circumstances is the title figure himself. Timon's prudence can be questioned, but certainly not his essential nobility. The principal qualifications of true nobility, according to the standards of the Renaissance, are birth, wealth, heroic deeds, and virtue. Erasmus maintained that

There are three kinds of nobility: the first is derived from virtue and good actions; the second comes from acquaintance with the best of training; and the third from an array of family portraits and the genealogy or wealth.[87]

And Elyot wrote:

[86] Quoted in *Timon of Athens*, "Introduction," p. xxvi, edited by K. Deighton, The Arden Shakespeare. In North's version the passage is as follows: "Timon aunswered him, I do it sayd he, bicause I know that one day he shall do greate mischiefe unto the Athenians." (Vol. VI, p. 382.)

[87] Erasmus, *The Education of a Christian Prince*, translated by L. K. Born (1936), p. 151.

It wold be more over declared that where vertue ioyned with great possessions or dignitie hath longe continued in the bloode or house of a gentilman, as it were an inheritaunce, there nobilitie is mooste shewed, and these noble men be most to be honored.[88]

There can be nobility without birth, or wealth, or deeds, but not without virtue; for as Elyot elsewhere remarks, "thus I conclude that nobilitie is nat after the vulgare opinion of men, but is only the prayse and surname of vertue." [89] The greatest nobility, however, is found when all these qualities are combined in a man. Throughout the first three acts of Shakespeare's play there are indications that Timon is to be considered a man of such dignity and merit. Evidence of his high birth is found in references to him by friends and flatterers alike as "lord Timon," as well as in the description of him in the *dramatis personae* as "a noble Athenian." That he had had great possessions is evident. Frequently in the play reference is made to his heroic deeds in the service of his country. Timon himself alludes to his activities "to the state's best health," [90] and Alcibiades speaks of his "great deeds" against enemy states.[91] But the principal element in Timon's nobility is his virtue. This quality of his nature is clearly attested by the objective and unprejudiced observation of the first stranger in the second scene of Act III. "For mine own part," he remarks,

> I never tasted Timon in my life,
> Nor came any of his bounties over me
> To mark me for his friend; yet, I protest,
> For his right noble mind, illustrious virtue,
> And honourable carriage,
> Had his necessity made use of me
> I would have put my wealth into donation, . . .[92]

In a healthy political society the virtue of a man of Timon's nobility would be recognized and honored. Timon, of course, is by no means blameless; his orgy of spending must have its consequences. But his one weakness does not justify the society in flagrantly disregarding the essential nobility of his character. That his better qualities should be taken into consideration by Athens is indicated frequently in the play.

[88] Elyot, *The Boke Named the Gouernour*, p. 127, Everyman's Library.
[89] *Ibid.*, p. 130.   [90] II, ii, 206.   [91] IV, iii, 94.   [92] III, ii, 84–90.

Timon himself expects recognition of his services from the Senate.[93] The obligations of the state to Timon are implied in Alcibiades' charges against "cursed Athens," which he brands as mindless of Timon's true worth.[94] The Senate itself, speaking for Athenian society, eventually admits that Timon's virtue and nobility have gone unrewarded:

FIRST SENATOR.   O, forget
    What we are sorry for ourselves in thee.
    The senators with one consent of love
    Entreat thee back to Athens; who have thought
    On special dignities, which vacant lie
    For thy best use and wearing.
SECOND SENATOR.   They confess
    Toward thee forgetfulness too general, gross;

                    .   .   .   .

    And send forth us, to make their sorrowed render,
    Together with a recompense more fruitful
    Than their offence can weigh down by the dram;
    Ay, even such heaps and sums of love and wealth
    As shall to thee blot out what wrongs were theirs,
    And write in thee the figures of their love,
    Even to read them thine.[95]

The Senate even adopts the Renaissance attitude that those highest in virtue should be placed highest in authority and honor in the hierarchy of degrees in a commonwealth:

        Therefore, so please thee to return with us,
        And of our Athens, thine and ours, to take
        The captainship, thou shalt be met with thanks,
        Allowed with absolute power, and thy good name
        Live with authority; . . .[96]

---

[93] Cf. II, ii, 204.   [94] Cf. IV, iii, 93.   [95] V, i, 141–47; 152–58.

[96] V, i, 162–66. Cf. Goslicius, *op. cit.*, p. 78: "They therefore that excell others in riches or birth, are not to be preferred, neyther are they to be equally esteemed who are equall in liberty, but those that excell others in vertue, are to be accounted both superiors and equalls: that is, in respect of law or number (as the *Arithmetrician* call it) they are equall, but in dignitie they are superior, because in the bestowing of honours, vertue is chiefly respected.

"For whoso is most vertuous deserveth most honor and glory. . . ."

Such an offer is not merely an empty expression of an abstract principle of political theory; it is a real admission that leadership by a man of Timon's virtue and ability is essential to the welfare of a state.

The political society which determines the action in *Timon of Athens*, however, is not healthy but diseased. The only nobility it can recognize or reward is not that determined by virtue, by deeds, or even by birth, but by wealth alone. At the end of the first scene, one lord exclaims of Timon, "The noblest mind he carries That ever govern'd man." But he obviously means nobility by the gold standard, for his remark is a commentary on the preceding speech on Timon's generosity with money:

> He pours it out: Plutus, the god of gold,
> Is but his steward. No meed, but he repays
> Sevenfold above itself; no gift to him,
> But breeds the giver a return exceeding
> All use of quittance.[97]

And it is at once followed by the salute, "Long may he live in fortunes!" In denying financial aid to Timon in Act II the Senate likewise speaks of Timon's "noble nature," but their attitude toward that nobility is clearly a product of their avarice. The conduct of the Athenian commonwealth, head and body alike, is ironically summarized by the observant stranger when he remarks,

> But, I perceive,
> Men must learn now with pity to dispense,
> For policy sits above conscience.[98]

In the same bitter vein Timon himself epitomizes the situation when he beseeches the gods to "Make the meat be beloved more than the man that gives it." [99] This is his prayer for "our society," this his prayer for "the senators of Athens, together with the common legge of people." Such evidence suggests that at least one cause of Timon's disillusionment is the treatment he suffers at the hands of the Athenian state.

It would be wrong to infer that the dramatic interest in the first three acts of Timon arises from the conflict between an individual and a society and from nothing else. Certainly the play derives much of its

[97] I, i, 287–91.   [98] III, ii, 92–94.   [99] III, vi, 84–85.

power from the exposition of universal human weaknesses such as flattery, avarice, faithlessness, and ingratitude. With characteristic insight, Shakespeare portrays these frailties in all their ugliness. But these evils are in each case consistently treated as products of social corruption. The development of Timon's misanthropy in the last two acts of the play continues in terms of this relationship. Although his hatred comes to embrace mankind universally, and thence derives much of its passionate intensity, Timon makes it clear that the cause of his more comprehensive bitterness is the feeling against the particular community of men which brought about his downfall. He himself, in the first of his misanthropic outbursts, acknowledges this to be the history of his passion:

> The gods confound—hear me, you good gods all,—
> The Athenians both within and out that wall!
> And grant, as Timon grows, his hate may grow
> To the whole race of mankind, high and low! [100]

It is the Athenian state which he viciously denounces in the outburst immediately preceding these lines. It is in terms of the organized society of men that he describes the corrupting influence of gold in Act IV. It is for the destruction of Athens that he gives gold to Alcibiades. It is for the further demoralization of Athenian society that he gives gold to Phrynia and Timandra, and later, for the same purpose, to the bandits. And it is Athens—"in the sequence of degree, from high to low throughout"—that is the object of his wrath in the interview with the senators in Act V.

It is the same degenerate society which motivates the whole action centering around Alcibiades. Here again a state corrupted by avarice fails to deal justly with one of its truly noble citizens, the Athenian general. Critics have been so much concerned with trying to explain the bad verse and the unknown soldier in the fifth scene of Act III that they have failed duly to stress the real importance of this disputed scene to the dramatic structure of the play.[101] At this point Alcibiades

---

[100] IV, i, 37–40.

[101] Following Boas (*op. cit.*, p. 502), Deighton (*op. cit.*, p. xix), and Chambers (*op. cit.*, I, 482), I am accepting this scene as substantially Shakespearean. Fleay ("On the Authorship of *Timon of Athens*," *Transactions of the New Shakspere Society*, Series 1, Nos. 1–2 (1874), 130, 242) and Wright (*op. cit.*, p. 44) reject the scene. If

comes into conflict with the tyranny of the Senate, and he suffers much as Timon suffers. He seeks for himself and for others the justice which it is the vocation of the Senate to administer. The rulers, however, fail to temper law with equity by refusing to recognize or take into account the "comely virtues" of the soldier or the services which he has rendered to the state. A similar failure to recognize and reward the nobility of virtue and deeds results in the completely unjust banishment of Alcibiades, although he specifically reminds the senators of their obligation to him—"Call me to your remembrances . . . I cannot think but your age has forgot me . . . My wounds ache at you"—but all to no avail.

But two additional circumstances indicate that the real cause of his rebellion is the larger political and social evil responsible for these incidents. In the first place, it is immediately upon hearing the sentence of banishment that he denounces the avaricious cause of the injustice which he experiences. In the second place, when in triumph he confronts the senators in the last scene, though referring to his personal grievances, he does not emphasize them as the main reason for his action against the state. It is rather, he tells the senators, because "Till now you have gone on and fill'd the time With all licentious measure, making your wills The scope of justice" [102] that he will reëstablish "regular justice in your city's bounds." [103] Such evidence seems to leave little doubt that exactly the same conditions which Timon blames for his downfall motivate the attitude and action of Alcibiades.

It has frequently been pointed out that the contrast in the reaction of the two men to the same situation is a typically Shakespearean feature of the play's construction. As Evans says of Alcibiades, "It cannot be doubted that he is intended to form a contrast to Timon, and point the moral of his fall." [104] And Boas, citing the parallel situation be-

---

I am correct in arguing that an avaricious political society is the common enemy of the two men, there is additional evidence for believing that this scene, in which Alcibiades is brought into conflict with the state, is an integral part of Shakespeare's original dramatic concept and creation. The scene has in common with the rest of the play the idea of a commonwealth which has placed material gain before virtue and justice as its motivating purpose. Certainly, without reference to such a theme, Alcibiades' invective against the Senate's usury bears little relation either to the injustice which he has just experienced or to the revenge which he vows at this time to take.

[102] V, iv, 3.   [103] V, iv, 61.

[104] In *Timon of Athens*, p. 12, The Henry Irving Shakespeare, Vol. VII.

tween Hamlet and Fortinbras, argues that Shakespeare "represents Alcibiades (who recalls the historical figure in nothing but name) as undergoing an experience akin to that of Timon, and meeting it in a diametrically opposite way." [105] As has been demonstrated, the two men suffer in the same way for the same reason, but Alcibiades is moved to corrective action by the injury against which Timon can do no more than rant.

In a way Timon is as much a "slave of passion" as Miss Campbell has shown Hamlet, Lear, Othello, and Macbeth to be.[106] The tragic flaw in Timon's nature is the excess of feeling which renders him incapable of reasonable action. He is clearly aware of the corruption responsible for his tragedy, but passion prevents him from acting against it as a more rational being would act. The distraught condition responsible for his ineffective outbursts is recognized by those about him. "O my lord," cries Flavius at the very birth of Timon's misanthropy, "You only speak from your distracted soul." [107] The same state of mind is described by Alcibiades when he excuses Timon to Timandra because "his wits Are drown'd and lost in his calamities." [108] And Apemantus accurately diagnoses Timon's condition as "A poor unmanly melancholy sprung From change of fortune." [109] Although on a less magnificent scale, Timon is nevertheless essentially like the other great tragic heroes created by Shakespeare. In his conflict with the chief antagonist of the drama his response is emotional rather than rational. It is this circumstance which gives him vitality as a dramatic figure, but it is also this circumstance which must inevitably bring him to a tragic end. He is the noble victim of an evil force, yet because he cannot act against that force, he must perish.

But although it claims its heroic victim, the evil power is in none of the great Shakespearean tragedies allowed to emerge triumphant at the end of the play. Claudius is killed and Fortinbras restores order to the kingdom of Denmark; Malcolm is restored to his rightful throne and civil peace returns to Scotland at the death of Macbeth; Goneril and Regan fall with Cordelia and Lear; and Iago is carried away to his just deserts. So in *Timon of Athens* the social and political corruption

[105] Boas, *op. cit.*, p. 501.
[106] L. B. Campbell, *Shakespeare's Tragic Heroes* (1930).
[107] III, iv, 114–15.   [108] IV, iii, 88–89.   [109] IV, iii, 203.

is wiped out before the end of the play. Alcibiades' function in the drama is the achievement of this reformation. The injustice from which he and Timon alike suffer arouses his "spleen and fury," but not to the extent of enervating his ability to act. He becomes, as Boas phrases it, "the soldier-statesman using the 'olive' with the sword, and inaugurating a new and sounder era in the Athenian commonwealth." [110] This dramatic link between the two leading characters in the play is frequently made explicit.[111] Timon identifies his cause with that of Alcibiades when he gives the soldier gold, to enable him to march on Athens and

> Be as a planetary plague, when Jove
> Will o'er some high-vic'd city hang his poison
> In the sick air.[112]

The messenger in the second scene of Act V links the cause of Timon with that of Alcibiades when he tells the senators of a courier who

> was riding
> From Alcibiades to Timon's cave
> With letters of entreaty, which imported
> His fellowship i' the cause against your city,
> In part for his sake mov'd.[113]

The senators themselves acknowledge Alcibiades' quarrel with them to be as much for Timon's sake as for his own, for they seek to assuage the soldier's ire by dwelling upon their attempts to make amends to Timon:

[110] Boas, *op. cit.*, p. 503.

[111] Professor Wright (*op. cit.*, p. 95) agrees that "Shakespeare meant Timon for a public benefactor who should suffer from the senate's cruelty; and that he therefore planned the ruin of the state as a great part of the revenge of Timon." But the critic can find no link between this action and that involving Alcibiades. He says further (p. 95) that Shakespeare "made Alcibiades the closest friend that Timon has, and left the way open for some peculiar tie between the two; but he did not see that he must make him fight for Timon." Perhaps the concept of a corrupt political society which I believe to be basic in the structure of the play provides the link which Professor Wright seeks. Deighton (*op. cit.*, p. xix) suggests such a solution to the problem when he writes that the disputed fifth scene in Act III is "absolutely necessary as leading up to the concluding events of the play, as contrasting the character of the two chief actors, and as showing the Senators to be equally ungrateful to both, hard-hearted, unpatriotic, and richly deserving the lofty contempt with which Timon receives their refusal to help him."

[112] IV, iii, 108-10. [113] V, ii, 9-13.

> So did we woo
> Transformed Timon to our city's love
> By humble message and by promis'd means.[114]

This passage immediately follows that in which they describe their similar attempts to make amends to Alcibiades for their injustice and ingratitude. Finally, the general makes it clear that he considers the wrongs done to both Timon and himself to have been caused by the infection which he is about to destroy at its source; he orders the senators to

> Descend, and open your uncharged ports.
> Those enemies of Timon's and mine own,
> Whom you yourselves shall set out for reproof
> Fall and no more; . . .[115]

---

[114] V, iv, 18–20.   [115] V, iv, 55–58.

CHAPTER VIII

Violation of Order and Degree in *Coriolanus*

THE LEGENDARY HISTORY of Coriolanus presents the Roman state in the process of a democratic experiment. The consular government which had supplanted the earlier monarchy underwent further modification in the direction of popular rule when economic unrest forced the Senate to grant political representation to citizens of Rome. One result of this concession was conflict between the democratic and aristocratic elements within the republic.[1]

In the turbulent history of Rome in this period Tudor theorists who argued in defense of monarchy and the hierarchy of degrees found a convincing demonstration of the dangers of democratic government. Hayward, attacking Parsons' arguments in favor of monarchy limited by popular will, wrote:

Lastly, you adde, that the Romans did expell their kings, and erect Consuls in their stead: but you suppresse that which followed, which I hold for a common consequence of ye like disorder. First, that for this cause, they were presently almost overwhelmed with warres: secondly, that in this state, they never enjoyed long time free from sedition; lastly, that as Tacitus saith, there was no meanes to appease these tumults, but by returning to a monarchie again.[2]

The legend of Coriolanus was itself on at least one occasion employed by a Tudor political writer to reinforce his argument against democratic political organization. William Fulbecke, in his *Pandectes*, cites the "history" of Coriolanus to confirm his contention that the people is a "beast of many heads," a "bundle of thornes, which will beare up a great man, but will pricke him if he leane or lie upon it." He argues from his historical evidence that a democracy is contrary to natural law, and hence to God's will,

[1] J. Wells, *A Short History of Rome* (1896), Chapters III and IV.
[2] Hayward, *An Answer to . . . R. Doleman* (1603), Sig. F, 3 v.

for the heele cannot stand in place of the head, unlesse the bodie be destroyed and the anatomie monstrous; it is against the nature of the people to beare rule; for they are as unfitte for regiment, as a mad man to give counsaile.[3]

Thus he concludes that "whosoever shall but ground his owne estate, much lesse the estate of the commonweale upon the peoples fantasies, *domum ex luto facit,* and findeth nothing more certain then uncertain accidents." [4]

Shakespeare approached this segment of Roman history in essentially the same spirit, if far more critically and with deeper insight into the underlying political and social principles involved. In *Coriolanus* he examines a democratic state and, by the standards of civil organization which he seems consistently to have adopted, finds it wanting. The play, in so far as its political content is concerned, is a dramatic picture of a state beset by those "uncertain accidents" which result when men forsake the pattern ordained by God and nature for political societies.

Criticism of *Coriolanus* has suffered from attempts to read the play as a special plea for one party or class.[5] Many critics have maintained that the primary political message of the play is a denunciation of the common people. But expressions of contempt for the plebeians are qualified by a sympathetic presentation of the grievances of the people and of their justified resentment against Coriolanus. Such evidence of sympathy and justification has led other critics to describe the political theme of the play as a condemnation of tyrannical dictatorship. A third group of critics, unable to resolve these apparent inconsistencies in attitude, follow Coleridge in admiring the impartiality of Shakespeare's political views.

This very impartiality suggests, however, that Shakespeare's main political interest is not in the privileges of a special class, but in the welfare of the whole state. As early as 1823 Horn pointed out that "In *Coriolanus* almost every character taking part is in the wrong, the hero himself and his opposer, Aufidius, Menenius and the Tribunes, the Volscians, as well as the Roman Senate, but the Idea of

---

[3] Fulbecke, *The Pandectes of the Law of Nations* (1602), fol. 31 v.

[4] *Ibid.,* fol. 29 v.

[5] See Chapter I, above, for a more detailed discussion of scholarship on this play.

State and Country stands forth predominant." [6] Almost a century later MacCallum revived this interpretation when he wrote, "The Idea of Rome! . . . This, then, is the background against which are grouped with more or less prominence, as their importance requires, Coriolanus' family, his associates, his rival, round the central figure of the hero himself." [7] The democratic activities of the people, the ineffectiveness of the Senate, and the tyrannical conduct of the hero, are consistently presented in terms of their effect on the welfare of the Roman body politic. In the legendary history of Coriolanus Shakespeare discovered and held up to view the disastrous consequences of violation of those principles by which a healthy political society is maintained.

But apparently Shakespeare did not feel that the story of Coriolanus as it came to him in Plutarch was sufficiently pointed for his purposes. Roman violation of order and degree was suggested in his original, but as Professor O. J. Campbell has said in an unpublished lecture on the play, "To convert Plutarch's story of Coriolanus into an urgent warning against disruption of the one divinely ordained social pattern, Shakespeare had to modify the facts that he found in his source." [8] These changes have been analyzed in detail by MacCallum and will require no extended discussion here. [9] It will be sufficient to suggest that they tend consistently to emphasize the conflict between the classes which imperils the state. Thus the nobility of Coriolanus himself is heightened, but at the same time the elements of pride, arrogance, and lack of concern for the people's welfare—all of which disqualify him as a governor according to Renaissance standards—are intensified in the play. Such changes add excuse to the action of the plebeians. But by presenting the tribunes as far more debased in character and motive than they are in Plutarch, Shakespeare emphasizes the evil of an attempt at democratic redress of popular grievances. Finally, out of a

[6] F. Horn, *Shakespeare's Schauspiele Erläutert* (1826), IV, 35 (quoted in *Coriolanus*, p. 669, edited by H. H. Furness, Jr., The New Variorum Shakespeare).

[7] M. W. MacCallum, *Shakespeare's Roman Plays and Their Background* (1925), p. 547.

[8] Cf. also Kreyssig in *Coriolanus*, edited by Furness, p. 669: "Thus it is no longer difficult to prove that Shakespeare departed, too, from his muddy source wherever possible and wherever is reflected the truly pure antique, but unknown to the monarchial-aristocratic life of the State of the 16th century."

[9] MacCallum, *op. cit.*, "Coriolanus," Chapter II.

mere name and fable in Plutarch he creates the character and philosophy of Menenius, whose constant appeal for moderation and compromise brings out by contrast the extremes of social and political conflict which exist in Rome.[10]

According to Shakespeare, and to the majority of his contemporaries, a state can prosper only when it conforms to that pattern of degrees, vocations, and authority ordained by the laws of God and nature. In *Coriolanus* Menenius Agrippa is the spokesman for this order. Dr. Johnson called Menenius a buffoon,[11] and Sir Edmund Chambers agrees that the Roman nobleman is "foolish and ineffective." [12] But as MacCallum has observed, Menenius' half-jocular, half-serious irony and wit, which have full play only when no harm can be done, should not be allowed to obscure the political wisdom and insight which he alone among the characters possesses.[13] It is he who constantly urges on all sides restraint and reason, justice and peace, for the welfare and preservation of Rome. It is he who seeks to advise Coriolanus of his obligations as a potential ruler, and the people of their duties as governed subjects. It is he who most severely upbraids the tribunes for their attempt to subvert the natural order of society by transferring authority from the head to the feet of the political body. The sincerity and unselfishness of his patriotic purpose are acknowledged by all parties in the play; to the citizens he is "Worthy Menenius Agrippa, one that hath always lov'd the people"; [14] to the nobles he is an honored adviser; even the tribunes respect him as "Noble Menenius" when he intervenes to restore order

---

[10] A. H. Tolman, "The Structure of . . . *Coriolanus*," *Modern Language Notes*, XXXVII (1922), 450, complains that Menenius' fable in Shakespeare, "because it is not made causative in any way, super-excellent as it is in itself, is good for nothing." He bases his argument on the fact that in Plutarch Menenius' fable is able to quell the people only when they are granted tribunes at the same time, while in Shakespeare one group is appeased by Menenius and another by the political concession. This seems to me, however, to be another change strictly in accord with Shakespeare's purpose in the play. Civil order is restored when the people conform to the natural pattern described by Menenius; civil turmoil follows when the people, as represented by the off-stage group, attempt to secure the right of participation in government. Thus the justice of Menenius' argument receives new emphasis in the play.

[11] Quoted in MacCallum, *op. cit.*, p. 564.

[12] Quoted in *Coriolanus*, "Introduction," p. xxi, edited by W. J. Craig and R. H. Case, The Arden Shakespeare, 1922.

[13] MacCallum, *op. cit.*, p. 565.   [14] *Coriolanus*, I, i, 52.

in the first crisis of Act III. Menenius consistently adopts the characteristic Renaissance point of view that the good of the individual depends upon the good of the state, and accordingly he places the common welfare and the means of attaining it before the selfish interests of party and class.

In the familiar belly passage in Act I, Menenius outlines the principles of organization and conduct which govern the well-being of a political society. His thinking closely follows that of Ulysses and the Archbishop of Canterbury, and of the proponents of established order among Tudor political theorists. Degree, vocation, and authority are the basic concepts involved in this argument, and as the analogical language indicates, the hierarchical structure which he describes is that ordained by the laws of God and nature for organization and government in all departments of the universe. Majority opinion in the Renaissance, therefore, would consider the state as portrayed by Menenius to be that sanctioned by cosmic law.

In his fable Menenius implies that a political body, like a natural body, is composed of degrees marked off by their relative importance to the whole organism. The Roman plebeians, apparently familiar with analogical political analysis, amplify his remarks by naming the various degrees more explicitly; there are

> The kingly-crowned head, the vigilant eye,
> The counsellor heart, the arm our soldier,
> Our steed the leg, the tongue our trumpeter,
> With other muniments and petty helps
> In this our fabric, . . .[15]

As the attributive adjectives indicate, each degree has a task to perform, a vocation, which is essential to the existence and well-being of the whole political body. In terms of Menenius' fable they

> Did see and hear, devise, instruct, walk, feel,
> And, mutually participate, did minister
> Unto the appetite and affection common
> Of the whole body.[16]

Paramount among these degrees is that which is ordained by nature to govern the whole body and to which, because it is best fitted to

---

[15] I, i, 119–23.   [16] I, i, 105–8.

guide and support the others, all degrees owe allegiance and obedience. In Menenius' fable this "specialty of rule" is aristocratic in form rather than monarchic. The latter type was preferred by the majority of Renaissance theorists, but as has been shown, the former was recognized by them as acceptable under certain conditions. It should be observed that the Senate, according to Menenius, is not a body representing the will of a sovereign people, but a sovereign body in itself. Defending the Senate against the democratic ambitions of the people, he says,

> You shall find
> No public benefit which you receive
> But it proceeds or comes from them to you
> And no way from yourselves.[17]

He would have Rome an aristocracy in the strictest political sense of the term, that is, a state governed by those few best equipped by nature, birth and education. Hence the Senate and consuls assume in Rome those powers and responsibilities which in monarchic states are assigned to a king. The belly, which holds this rank in Menenius' fable, is made to speak as follows:

> "True is it, my incorporate friends," quoth he,
> "That I receive the general food at first
> Which you do live upon; and fit it is,
> Because I am the store-house and the shop
> Of the whole body. But, if you do remember,
> I send it through the rivers of your blood,
> Even to the court, the heart, to the seat o' the brain;
> And, through the cranks and offices of man,
> The strongest nerves and small inferior veins
> From me receive that natural competency
> Whereby they live.[18]

Thus the Renaissance principle of authority and the vocation of government remains unaltered in its essential character.[19]

[17] I, i, 155–58.   [18] I, i, 134–44.

[19] Although Menenius must of necessity defend the established aristocratic order in Rome, the form of government is by no means represented in the play as perfect. The nature of the people's grievances against the Senate (I, i, 81, for example) and the weakness of the senators in handling the popular uprising (III, i, 90 et seq.) suggest the faults which Renaissance theorists regarded as characteristic of divided authority.

But it seems clear that in *Coriolanus* Shakespeare was not so much concerned with the relative merits of monarchy and aristocracy as with the evils which follow disruption of the general structure of degrees and vocations. Menenius argues that when any degree in the social and political order fails to perform its allotted function, or seeks to alter its position in the hierarchy, the whole organism will suffer accordingly. Menenius particularly emphasizes this interdependence of degrees; he describes them as "incorporate friends" because they "mutually participate" for the common welfare. As in the fable the belly performs a function without which the other members of the body could not exist, so in the Roman state, the Senate fulfills a need essential to the welfare of the other members of the political body. Menenius is trying to make his fellow countrymen see that in disturbing the natural order of political society they are threatening themselves with destruction. This is the message of Menenius throughout the play. Had his words been heeded, as in spirit they were in Plutarch, where a greater element of compromise prevailed, the state would have been sounder but the drama and its political lesson perhaps less effective.

The chief offenders against the commonwealth of Rome are the plebeians, whose democratic activities constitute a violation of the natural pattern of the state. Much has been written of Shakespeare's attitude toward the unwashed masses. This attitude has often been described as one of almost unqualified contempt and abhorrence for their fickleness, stupidity and filth.[20] But a distinction has been made, and must be made, in the dramatist's treatment of the common man. It is not the plebeian as he lives and acts in his own degree, but the plebeian spurred by political ambitions, attempting to rise out of his degree, whom Shakespeare ridicules and condemns.[21] The number of lovable

---

According to Shakespeare and to the majority of his contemporaries, however, aristocracy, with all of its weaknesses, is a more natural and desirable form of government than democracy.

[20] Cf. for example Paul Stapfer, *Shakespeare and Classical Antiquity*, translated by E. J. Carey (1880), p. 461: "The dominant features of Shakespeare's plebeians, as of all his sons of the people, are stupidity, inconstancy, and cowardliness. They are always blundering, always incapable of any political idea, and impressionable as wax in the hands of their demagogues."

[21] Cf. for example MacCallum, *op. cit.*, p. 470: "That is, the populace as a whole is stupid, disunited, fickle. . . . He therefore with perfect consistency regards them

and sympathetically presented members of the lower classes in Shakespearean drama makes unwarranted the assumption that his scorn of
the common man was unqualified. But when a commoner, alone or in
a mob, seeks to meddle in politics and government, he becomes the
object of some of the dramatist's fiercest scorn. Towards the common
people acting in their appointed vocations Shakespeare shows tolerance
and sympathy; if he is not their champion, he is certainly aware of
their rights. Out of their degree and vocation, and threatening to dis-
rupt the natural order of political society, they find him an unsparing
and contemptuous foe.

Both sides of this attitude are present in the treatment of the plebeians in *Coriolanus*. The justice of their grievances is recognized, the
course which they take to redress their wrongs is denounced. As members of the corporate body they have a right to expect their just share
of the benefits which political society is ordained to secure for all. But
they are starving while the governing classes enjoy a superabundance
of the material necessities of life. As the Second Citizen says of the
governors who should care for the people as fathers for children:

Care for us! True, indeed! They ne'er car'd for us yet: suffer us to
famish, and their store-houses cramm'd with grain; make edicts for usury,
to support usurers; repeal daily any wholesome act established against the
rich, and provide more piercing statutes daily, to chain up and restrain the
poor. If the wars eat us not up, they will; and there's all the love they
bear us.[22]

They have a right to expect fatherly care and guidance from their governors. But the consul whom they are asked to accept in this position
offers them nothing but contempt, abuse, and the promise of trials
worse than those which they are already enduring.

Such grievances, however, are not sufficient justification for the people to upset the normal order by taking matters of government into
their own hands. Throughout the play it is made strikingly clear that
whatever rights the people have to a tranquil and abundant life, they

---

as quite unfit for rule, and when they have it or aspire to it, they cover themselves with
ridicule or involve themselves in crime. But this is by no means to hate them. On the
contrary, he is kindly enough to individual representatives, and he certainly believes in
the sacred obligation of governing them for their good."
[22] I, i, 81–89.

are not qualified by nature or by God to interfere with "the specialty of rule." The chief implication of Menenius' fable, and of his reference to one citizen as the "great toe of this assembly," [23] is that as the feet cannot supplant the head in the government of the natural body, no more can the commoners supplant the aristocrats in the government of the political body.

The frequent references to the mob as the "many-headed monster" are further indication that the attitude taken toward the plebeians in *Coriolanus* is essentially that taken in the characteristic political thinking of Shakespeare's day. The epithet was employed by a host of Renaissance theorists to suggest the fickleness, irrationality and violence of the people when they sought to act in a political capacity. In 1600 Thomas Floyd wrote:

Wherefore there can no greater daunger ensue, or happen to a Commonwealth, then to tollerate the rude, and common sort to rule, who (as their propertie is) are always noted to be unconstant and wavering, tossed with every sudden blast, and carried with everie light chaffe; . . . Wherefore they are rightly accounted to resemble the ugly Hydra, which is sayd, no sooner to lose one head, then immediately another groweth.[24]

Even Goslicius, a staunch defender of popular rights, nevertheless asserted that the people are unqualified to participate actively in government; "The multitude have alwaies had the desire, but not the iudgement to bestow dignities, for theyr voyces are wonne by flattery, not gained by desert," he writes in a passage peculiarly applicable to the circumstances in *Coriolanus*.[25] In exactly these same terms the common people in Shakespeare's drama are presented as unfit to assume the vocation of government. It is not only in the outbursts of Coriolanus himself that they are described as "the many-headed multitude," "Hydra," and "The beast with many heads." The clearest description of this nature of the mob is given by one of their own number, the Third Citizen in Act II, scene iii. He cautions his fellows against showing ingratitude toward Coriolanus, for "Ingratitude is monstrous; and for the multitude to be ingrateful, were to make a monster of the multitude." [26] Later he candidly explains why the

[23] I, i, 159.
[24] Floyd, *The Picture of a Perfit Commonwealth* (1600), pp. 18–19.
[25] Goslicius, *The Counsellor* (translated, 1598), p. 67.   [26] II, iii, 9–12.

plebeians are unqualified by nature to exercise political power; com-
menting on the epithet, "many-headed multitude," he observes:

We have been called so of many; not that our heads are some brown,
some black, some auburn, some bald, but that our wits are so diversely
colour'd; and truly I think if all our wits were to issue out of one skull,
they would fly east, west, north, south, and their consent of one direct
way should be at once to all the points o' the compass.[27]

The conduct of the populace throughout the play confirms this criticism.

The tribunes in *Coriolanus* are a damning portrait of the type of
governor which the people, when allowed, will choose for themselves.
It must be remembered that in the political action of *Coriolanus* the
tribunes represent an innovation in the structure of the Roman state.
They are a concession granted to the people during the corn riots.
Menenius, upon hearing of the successful petition of the plebeians for
representation, says in the first scene of the play: "This is strange."
Coriolanus agrees, and adds, "It will in time win upon power and
throw forth greater themes For insurrection's arguing." In heighten-
ing the already unflattering portraits of Sicinius and Junius which he
found in Plutarch, Shakespeare suggests further condemnation of the
political institution which they represent. The voices of the multitude
Sicinius and Junius have in fact "wonne by flattery, not gained by
desert." Their motives and actions throughout the play confirm
Menenius' description of these democratic representatives. To this
acute political observer they are "a brace of unmeriting, proud, violent, testy magistrates, alias fools, as any in Rome." [28] They are lack-
ing both the ability and nobility which naturally determine the governors of a state.

You are ambitious for poor knaves' caps and legs. You wear out a good
wholesome forenoon in hearing a cause between an orange-wife and a
faucet-seller; and then rejourn the controversy of three-pence to a second day of audience. When you are hearing a matter between party and
party, if you chance to be pinch'd with the colic, you make faces like
mummers; set up the bloody flag against all patience; and, in roaring for
a chamber-pot, dismiss the controversy bleeding, the more entangled by

---

[27] II, iii, 19–26.   [28] II, i, 46–48.

your hearing. All the peace you make in their cause is calling both the parties knaves. You are a pair of strange ones.[29]

Their action against Coriolanus is motivated not by a desire for the welfare of the state or their constituents, but by selfish fear for their own positions, lest "our office may, during his power, go sleep." [30] To forestall such a possibility they turn the instability and susceptibility of the mob to their own purposes, cynically aware that any official, consul or tribune, who relies for authority on the voice of the people *domum ex luto facit.* The conduct of the tribunes and their relationship to the plebeians in *Coriolanus* might almost be a dramatic exemplification of Goslicius's warning that "the commonweale is many times infected and corrupted, by the vices and wickedness of Magistrates." [31] Directly responsible for the near-ruin of the Roman state are the unworthy tribunes, but indirectly and more fundamentally to blame are those principles of democracy, subversive in the eyes of sixteenth-century theorists, which allow the unqualified masses to act in a political capacity of any sort.

The manner in which these democratic forces impair the health of a political body is most clearly analyzed by Coriolanus himself, though as will be shown, he is totally unaware of his own responsibility in the matter. The purport of the hero's great tirade in the first scene of Act III is that when the people have a voice in government natural political order is inverted, the structure of society ordained by natural law is destroyed, and the ends which states are designed to secure are made impossible of achievement. Like a good Renaissance political theorist he draws on the examples of history to prove his point:

> Sometime in Greece . . .
> Though there the people had more absolute power,
> I say, they nourish'd disobedience, fed
> The ruin of the state.[32]

For Coriolanus believes, as did the majority of Shakespeare's contemporaries, that "the ruin of the state" is inevitable when the natural differences among men are disregarded and when natural authority, determined by nobility, wisdom and virtue, is destroyed. There can

---

[29] II, i, 76–89.
[31] Goslicius, *op. cit.*, p. 65.

[30] II, i, 238.
[32] III, i, 115–18.

be no healthy political society, Coriolanus argues, "where gentry, title, wisdom, Cannot conclude but by the yea and no Of general ignorance." [33] The Senate, in granting political power to the people, has violated universal law and brought in "The crows to peck the eagles." Why, he asks the senators,

> Have you thus
> Given Hydra here to choose an officer,
> That with his peremptory "shall," being but
> The horn and noise o' the monster's, wants not spirit
> To say he'll turn your current in a ditch,
> And make your channel his? [34]

As nature decrees one head for the human body, so it decrees one authority for the political body. When the people participate in government, authority is divided and the political body becomes an unnatural monster, running unguided to its own destruction. As Coriolanus exclaims:

> By Jove himself!
> It makes the consuls base; and my soul aches
> To know, when two authorities are up,
> Neither supreme, how soon confusion
> May enter 'twixt the gap of both and take
> The one by the other. [35]

Its structure thus distorted by the inversion of the hierarchy of degrees, the state is unable to attain those ends for which a political society is ordained, the welfare of the whole organism in general and of each individual in particular. For

> It must omit
> Real necessities, and give way the while
> To unstable slightness; purpose so barr'd, it follows
> Nothing is done to purpose. [36]

Therefore, concludes Coriolanus, it is necessary that the Senate reassert its authority in the Roman state and

> At once pluck out
> The multitudinous tongue; let them not lick

---

[33] III, i, 144–46.   [34] III, i, 92–97.
[35] III, i, 107–12.   [36] III, i, 146–49.

The sweet which is their poison. Your dishonour
Mangles true judgement, and bereaves the state
Of that integrity which should become 't,
Not having the power to do the good it would,
For the ill which doth control 't.[37]

On the one hand, then, the politically ambitious people constitute a menace to the political and social stability of Rome. But they are not wholly to blame for the disasters which threaten to destroy the state. According to the concept presented in Menenius' fable, the health of the civil body depends also on the proper functioning of the governing head in its degree and vocation. In this respect Coriolanus, as a potential ruler, is as responsible as the people for the chaos that envelops Rome. For he is almost totally unaware of the responsibilities of the office he seeks or of its relationship to the whole state. According to Renaissance standards he is unqualified by nature and by training to exercise "the specialty of rule."

Renaissance theorists granted unusual power to the governors of a state, but they also burdened them heavily with duties and obligations.[38] They insisted particularly, as has been pointed out, that governors minister to the welfare of the whole state, and not to the achievement of their own selfish ends. Equal emphasis was placed on the attitude which rulers should take towards their subjects. In describing this attitude as that of a father towards his children or of a shepherd towards his flock, theorists sought to indicate that although the rulers correct and punish wrong-doers when necessary, they act only out of love and care for their subjects, and in their best interests. Governors are to be aware of the needs and rights of all. They are to hold not even the lowest of their subjects in contempt, but to display equal justice and affection to all.[39]

[37] III, i, 155–61.   [38] See Chapter VI, above.

[39] Cf. for example Latimer, *Seven Sermons before Edward VI* (1549), p. 73, edited by Edward Arber (1895): "Heare pore mens causes. And you proud Iudges herken what God sayeth in his holye boke . . . Heare theym sayeth he, the small as well as the greate, the pore as well as the ryche. Regarde no person, feare no man . . . The iudgement is Goddes." Cf. also Musculus, *Commonplaces of Christian Religion* (translated, 1563), fol. 551 v: "The iuste and lawfull magistrate wyl do iudgement and iustice and wyl punish the reprobate of iudgement, according unto the lawes and qualytyes of the offences. Here wyll defende good folke, not because yt they bee rich, but bycause their quarrel is good, whether they be rich or poore; he will punish ye

On neither score—motive or attitude—can Coriolanus qualify for the vocation of governor. It cannot be charged that he acts selfishly for his own advancement and gain. As the Second Citizen observes in the opening scene of the play, "You must in no way say he is covetous." The First Citizen must assent to this, though grudgingly: "If I must not, I need not be barren of accusations." [40] It can be charged, however, that he acts not for the common wealth but to satisfy his own pride, the first of the seven deadly sins. Discussing Coriolanus' service to the state, the First Citizen remarks:

I say unto you, what he hath done famously, he did it to that end. Though soft-conscienc'd men can be content to say it was for his country, he did it to please his mother, and to be partly proud; which he is, even to the altitude of his virtue.[41]

The Second Citizen, whose tendency is to defend Coriolanus, is forced to agree that this is indeed "in his nature." It can be charged, moreover, that he acts not for the welfare of the whole state, but for that of his own class alone. Much has been written of Coriolanus' patriotism and love of country. But loyalty to one class must be distinguished from that concern for all degrees which should characterize the actions of a governor. Little is said specifically of Coriolanus' selfish class interest, but it is the logical implication of his notorious contempt for the common people. And in an aristocratic form of government, political action for the benefit of the privileged few is tantamount to political action for the selfish interests of the ruler. For an aristocracy by definition is a state governed by the privileged few. Accordingly, where Coriolanus is involved, the potential situation reduces itself to a type of tyranny widely recognized and condemned in Renaissance political thinking.

Coriolanus' characteristic attitude toward the plebeians, his prin-

---

evill not because they be pore, and may be easely overtrodden, but bicause they be naughty and mischyevous lyvers, having no respecte whether they bee poore or riche. . . ."

[40] I, i, 43–45.

[41] I, i, 36–41. Cf. Case (*Coriolanus*, "Introduction," p. xix, The Arden Shakespeare, 1922): "Pride, the first of the seven deadly sins, is the more overmastering in Coriolanus from his freedom from the rest, unless wrath be excepted."

cipal disqualification as a potential governor, has been extensively
analyzed by other critics and requires little further treatment here.[42]
It is necessary, however, to place this attitude in the political scheme
of the whole play. From the Renaissance point of view Coriolanus'
condemnation of the people for their political activity is thoroughly
justified. It is his general contempt for the people and for their rights
and position in the social structure that renders him unfit to exercise
"the specialty of rule." This fundamental lack in his political equipment is recognized by all parties in the play, and is generally mentioned in reference to his aspirations to the consulship. The plebeians
consider him "a very dog to the commonalty." [43] Even when they are
elated by his military achievements they do not lose sight of this weakness in him as a governor. As the Third Citizen remarks, "I say, if he
would incline to the people, there was never a worthier man." [44]
Later the Fourth Citizen summarizes exactly the case for and against
Coriolanus as a ruler: "You have been a scourge to her enemies, you
have been a rod to her friends; you have not indeed loved the common people." [45] A change in attitude on the part of Coriolanus is
practically implied as the condition upon which the people eventually
give him their voices; "We hope to find you our friend; and therefore give you our voices heartily," [46] they cry, and again, "the gods
give him joy, and make him good friend to the people!" [47] But there
is little hope that a quality so deeply ingrained in his nature can be
readily transformed. According to the First Officer in Act II Coriolanus is "vengeance proud, and loves not the common people." [48]
The Second Officer blames the people's ingratitude and praises Coriolanus' "noble carelessness" and lack of affectation and flattery, but he
cannot admit the presence of any fatherly affection in the would-be
consul.[49] The tribunes, however base their motives, are skilful enough
as politicians to recognize the essential weakness of Coriolanus as a
candidate for an office of authority, and to plan their attack on him
accordingly. As Junius Brutus says,

[42] Cf. especially MacCallum, *op. cit.*, "Coriolanus"; Edward Dowden, *Shakspere: a
Critical Study of his Mind and Art* (1880), p. 328; Stopford Brooke, *On Ten Plays
of Shakespeare* (1905), p. 226.

[43] I, i, 28.   [44] II, iii, 42.   [45] II, iii, 97.   [46] II, iii, 111.
[47] II, iii, 141.   [48] II, ii, 6.   [49] II, ii, 8 *et seq.*

> We must suggest the people in what hatred
> He still hath held them; that to 's power he would
> Have made them mules, silenc'd their pleaders and
> Dispropertied their freedoms, holding them,
> In human action and capacity,
> Of no more soul nor fitness for the world
> Than camels in the war, who have their provand
> Only for bearing burdens, and sore blows
> For sinking under them.[50]

In spite of his affection for Coriolanus, Menenius himself is aware of this flaw in the hero's political character. Paramount in the old statesman's mind, as always, is the welfare of the Roman commonwealth, which he realizes is threatened by Coriolanus' attitude. Therefore, he seeks to persuade Coriolanus at least to simulate some regard for the commoners. He strengthens his appeal by adopting for the time Coriolanus' contempt for such regard, but his main point, the safety of Rome, emerges forcefully enough. He claims that

> Before he should thus stoop to the herd, but that
> The violent fit o' the time craves it as physic
> For the whole state, I would put mine armour on,
> Which I can scarcely bear.[51]

This plea for tolerance and moderation in the name of the commonwealth is the burden of his urgent advice to Coriolanus in the political crisis which follows; it is "answer mildly . . . Ay, but mildly . . . , Calmly, I do beseech you . . . , Nay, temperately, your promise." [52] But such admonitions are of no avail with a man unsuited in character and temperament to function as a governor.

It should be noted that the true function of Coriolanus in the political and social structure of Rome is clearly indicated in the course of the play. He is "the arm our soldier." There is no evidence, in the source or in the play itself, that his celebrated service to Rome was ever of anything but a military nature. The first to admit that his calling is that of a soldier, not a ruler, is Coriolanus himself. After the victory at Corioli, his ambitious mother exclaims,

> I have lived
> To see inherited my very wishes

---

[50] II, i, 261–69.   [51] III, ii, 32–35.   [52] III, iii, *passim*.

And the buildings of my fancy; only
There's one thing wanting, which I doubt not but
Our Rome will cast upon thee.[53]

Coriolanus, grasping her meaning at once, disclaims any wish to alter his degree and vocation:

Know, good mother,
I had rather be their servant in my way
Than sway with them in theirs.[54]

He never elsewhere expresses any desire for political power, and his wrath when the people reject him is much more credibly explained in terms of wounded personal pride than of frustrated political ambition. Menenius, on two separate occasions, seeks to excuse Coriolanus' chief political failing on the grounds of his military calling. He says to the tribunes after the first clash over the consulship:

Consider this: he has been bred i' the wars
Since 'a could draw a sword, and is ill school'd
In bolted language; meal and bran together
He throws without distinction.[55]

And before their second encounter with Coriolanus Menenius seeks to prepare the people by telling them:

Consider further,
That when he speaks not like a citizen
You find him like a soldier. Do not take
His rougher accents for malicious sounds,
But, as I say, such as become a soldier
Rather than envy you.[56]

No better summary of the case against Coriolanus as a potential governor can be found than that given by Aufidius in the fourth act of the play. Reviewing the career of the hero he says:

First he was
A noble servant to them, but he could not
Carry his honours even. Whether 'twas pride,
Which out of daily fortune ever taints
The happy man; whether defect of judgement,
To fail in the disposing of those chances

[53] II, i, 214–18.   [54] II, i, 218–20.   [55] III, i, 320–23.   [56] III, iii, 52–57.

Which he was lord of; or whether nature,
Not to be other than one thing, not moving
From the casque to the cushion, but commanding peace
Even with the same austerity and garb
As he controll'd the war; but one of these,—
As he hath spices of them all—not all,—
For I dare so far free him,—made him fear'd;
So, hated; and so, banish'd: . . .[57]

Here Aufidius touches the main points which make of Coriolanus' political ambitions a violation of natural civic order. There is pride, which throughout the play has been associated with the hero's contempt for the common people, and which symbolizes his lack of respect for the general welfare of Rome. There is "defect in judgement," the failure to realize the demands and responsibilities of the position which opportunity has offered him. Finally there is the ability or vocation for which Coriolanus is naturally equipped, and Aufidius emphasizes again, in conclusion, that the hero's calling is not that of "the kingly-crowned head," but of "the arm our soldier."

From the lowest to the highest ranks of its hierarchy of degrees, therefore, the republican political society of Rome fails to conform to the principles set forth by Menenius at the opening of the play. Its plebeians, on the one hand, in seeking to exercise political authority, forsake their appointed rank and function. On the other hand, its governors, and one in particular, neglect the obligations which their position carries with it. In the language of Menenius' fable, the great toe has taken the place of the stomach because the latter has failed in its task as "the store-house and the shop of the whole body." Accordingly the order and proportion upon which the health of all bodies, natural or political, depends, is destroyed. Such bodies are monstrous; they cannot achieve the purposes for which they were created, but must soon sicken and die. Having described the monstrous state of Rome, Shakespeare now turns to portray the consequences which bring it to the verge of destruction.

As has been shown in a previous chapter, Renaissance theorists argued that the natural order of states is the bulwark against the chaos of the presocial era. Two outstanding characteristics of this earlier

[57] IV, vii, 35–48.

existence were described as the absence of civil tranquility and the presence of danger of attack from foreign enemies, each of which made impossible the material and spiritual prosperity which organized societies were designed to secure. The effects of Roman disruption of the state-structure are presented in terms of these same two afflictions, internal strife and foreign invasion. In each instance the threat is indicated to be the direct result of the unnatural political order, and is emphasized in its relationship to the whole commonwealth. Thus Shakespeare completes the political lesson which he draws from the history of Coriolanus.

The first fruits of Roman violation of natural law are the vividly presented scenes of civil disorder which mark the beginning of Act III. The political ambitions of the plebeians and the tribunes, and Coriolanus' scorn of the people, are here brought into play against each other for the first time. The unwarranted claims to political power and authority made by the people heighten the contempt of Coriolanus, the "peremptory shall" of Hydra provoking Coriolanus' great denunciatory outburst beginning at line 90. This manifestation of antipathy by a governor toward subjects in turn incites the people to further acts of political violence. Soon civil peace and order have vanished completely. As Menenius expresses the situation, "What is about to be?—I am out of breath; Confusion's near; . . ." [58] The whole political structure has collapsed and men in all degrees have returned to the bestial strife of the presocial era.

In an analysis of this scene for its relationship to the political scheme of the play, the comments of Menenius, and to a lesser extent, those of Cominius, are reliable guides. For to Cominius, as to Menenius, the safety of the commonwealth should be the first consideration of all classes. Cominius expresses this attitude when he says,

> I do love
> My country's good with a respect more tender,
> More holy and profound, than mine own life,
> My dear wife's estimate, her womb's increase
> And treasure of my loins; . . .[59]

The whole purport of Menenius' exhortation to the people and their representatives, as it is later the burden of his appeal to Coriolanus, is

[58] III, i, 189.   [59] III, iii, 111–15.

that all parties must act temperately and in conformity with their respective degrees if the state is to survive. He does not argue that the people have no grievance or right, or that Coriolanus has no cause for contempt; but he pleads that these immediate and individual differences be set aside in favor of the greater allegiance of all to the welfare of the whole civic structure. Thus his first cry is, "On both sides more respect." [60] A little later he appeals to Brutus to

> Be that you seem, truly your country's friend,
> And temperately proceed to what you would
> Thus violently redress. [61]

Still later he depicts a Rome brought to ruin by civil turmoil within itself unless normal order is restored:

>   Proceed by process,
> Lest parties, as he is belov'd, break out,
> And sack great Rome with Romans. [62]

For as Cominius has said earlier in the crisis:

> That is the way to lay the city flat,
> To bring the roof to the foundation
> And bury all, which yet distinctly ranges,
> In heaps and piles of ruin. [63]

In the following scene Menenius uses exactly the same argument in an attempt to persuade Coriolanus to recognize the responsibilities of the office which he seeks. Expediency demands that he adapt his attitude to the mood of Coriolanus and disparage the necessity of stooping to the herd. In this respect he takes his cue from Volumnia. But Volumnia urges compromise that personal ambition might be fulfilled: "I would dissemble with my nature, where My fortunes and my friends at stake requir'd I should do so in honour." [64] For Menenius the primary motive remains the welfare of the state: ". . . the violent fit o' the time craves it as physic For the whole state."

In this first crisis Menenius' arguments prevail with both Coriolanus and the people. He persuades the latter to relinquish justice from their own hands into the hands of naturally qualified and established authority. He persuades Coriolanus at least to simulate the political

[60] III, i, 181.   [61] III, i, 218–20.   [62] III, i, 314–16.
[63] III, i, 204–7.   [64] III, ii, 62–64.

quality which he most sorely lacks. And thus for the moment order is restored and Rome is saved from self-destruction.

But it is only for a brief moment. The passions of resentment in the people, political ambition in the tribunes, and intolerant contempt in Coriolanus soon sweep aside the political reason of Menenius. The action of scene iii duplicates that of scene i, and once again Rome is brought to the edge of disaster. In the earlier scene destruction threatened from within; in the later episode, with the banishment of Coriolanus, the way is left open for destruction from without. Not only has the Roman body politic lost its "arm our soldier," but that defensive member has been turned against its own body. Civil turmoil has weakened the resistance of the political body and rendered it an easy victim to an invader. Thus the Volsce in scene iii of Act IV, upon learning from the Roman he meets on the highway that "There hath been in Rome strange insurrections; the people against the senators, patricians, and nobles," responds: "Hath been! Is it ended, then? Our state thinks not so. They are in a most warlike preparation, and hope to come upon them in the heat of their division." [65] It is additional good news to the Volscians to learn that Coriolanus, their chief terror, is banished. But even thinking Coriolanus still in Rome, they had considered the general strife there sufficient justification for launching an attack at this time.

The cause-and-effect relationship between the perversion of natural order in Rome and the threatened annihilation of the state is ironically pointed in scene vi of the fourth act. Unaware of impending disaster, the tribunes point with pride to the social tranquility which they suppose their democratic order and activities to have effected. Sicinius observes that the "present peace And quietness of the people"

> do make his friends
> Blush that the world goes well, who rather had,
> Though they themselves did suffer by 't, behold
> Dissentious numbers pest'ring streets than see
> Our tradesmen singing in their shops and going
> About their functions friendly.[66]

Even Menenius must admit that "All's well; and might have been much better, if He could have temporized." At the very moment when

---

[65] IV, iii, 16–19.   [66] IV, vi, 4–9.

the Aedile is to enter with tidings of the invasion, Junius remarks with
satisfaction that Rome "Sits safe and still without" Coriolanus.[67]

During the time that Rome is expecting inevitable destruction, the
comments of Menenius and Cominius are again illuminating in showing the relationship between this episode and the political scheme of
the whole play. The two observers clearly regard the impending invasion as the logical consequence of the perverted civil order in Rome.
The tribunes, who have led the people into subversive democratic
activities, must bear the blame. As Cominius exclaims:

> You have holp to ravish your own daughters and
> To melt the city leads upon your pates,
> To see your wives dishonour'd to your noses,—
>
> .   .   .   .
>
>   You have brought
> A trembling upon Rome, such as was 'never
> So incapable of help.[68]

Menenius is particularly scathing in his remarks on these fruits of
democracy; to the tribunes he exclaims:

>   You have made good work,
> You and your apron-men; you that stood so much
> Upon the voice of occupation and
> The breath of garlic-eaters! [69]

And to the citizens he says: "You have made Good work, you and
your cry!" [70] He blames not only those members of the body politic
who have rebelled against natural authority, but also the weakness in
that authority itself which permitted such impairing of the structure
entrusted to its care. He remarks upon the banishment of Coriolanus,
the one political act of the plebeians immediately responsible for the
present crisis:

> How! Was 't we? We lov'd him; but, like beasts
> And cowardly nobles, gave way unto your clusters,
> Who did hoot him out o' the city.[71]

In his comment on the prayer of Sicinius, "The gods be good unto
us!," Menenius suggests something of the divine authority which was

---

[67] IV, vi, 37.   [68] IV, vi, 81–83; 118–20.   [69] IV, vi, 95–98.
[70] IV, vi, 147.   [71] IV, vi, 121–23.

attached to the state structure by Renaissance theorists, and indicates why disregard for the principles of divine and natural law must bring disaster to the guilty civil society:

No, in such a case the gods will not be good unto us. When we banish'd him, we respected not them; and, he returning to break our necks, they respect not us.[72]

Although rebellion among the lower classes is made to bear the chief responsibility for these disasters, it should be recalled that just at this point in the play Aufidius reminds us of Coriolanus' share in the matter. For, as he says, it was the nature of the man "Not to be other than one thing, not moving From the casque to the cushion," which gave occasion for rebellion against him and his subsequent banishment.[73] Thus in this last political crisis the negligence of each degree in its vocation is shown to be responsible for endangering the welfare of the whole Roman state.

The principal political lesson embodied in the legendary history of Coriolanus has now been conveyed. Departure from the pattern of society prescribed by natural law has been portrayed, and the dire consequences of such action depicted. In Act V, devoted chiefly to the denouement of the personal drama, the political theme is swiftly resolved. In the hour of crisis the tribunes realize that the only salvation of the state lies with its naturally ordained aristocratic leaders. Thus Sicinius beseeches Menenius:

> But, sure, if you
> Would be your country's pleader, your good tongue,
> More than the instant army we can make,
> Might stop our countryman.[74]

Not long thereafter the tribunes as political leaders are rejected by their own constituents. Sicinius is told:

> Sir, if you'd save your life, fly to your house.
> The plebeians have got your fellow-tribune
> And hale him up and down, all swearing, if
> The Roman ladies bring not comfort home,
> They'll give him death by inches.[75]

---

[72] V, iv, 34–37.   [73] IV, vii, 42.   [74] V, i, 35–38.   [75] V, iv, 38–42.

So the tribunes come to learn the full meaning of the warning that he who bases political power on the will and voice of the people, *domum ex luto facit*. The democratic process which they represent is discredited by their fall, as it had been by their conduct. The disruptive political influence of Coriolanus is also brought to an end, in the first place by those qualities which made him a noble Roman, loyalty to family and country, and in the second place by that quality which principally rendered him unfit to exercise the specialty of rule, "his own impatience."

The political atmosphere of the play throughout its course is that of an organized society disrupted and rendered chaotic by subversive democratic forces on the one hand, and on the other by an individual temperamentally unfit to function in the capacity of natural governor of the state. But the drama remains in the final analysis the tragedy of the title figure himself, although I cannot fully agree with Swinburne's conclusion that "it is from first to last . . . rather a private and domestic than a public or historical tragedy." It is rather the tragedy of an heroic and essentially noble character brought by an element in his own make-up into inevitable and disastrous conflict with universal laws of political and social conduct. In its broadest aspects the drama presents, then, the clash between passion and reason which lies at the heart of almost all Shakespearean tragedy. Reason in this instance is the political philosophy which lies implicit in every scene of the play and which it has been the purpose of the foregoing analysis to describe. Passion is the pride which most critics have recognized to be the tragic flaw in the character of Coriolanus. His intense loyalty to self, to family, and to party make Coriolanus unable to act in conformity with the divine pattern and purpose of the state. The individual cannot subordinate himself to the commonwealth. As MacCallum explains the problem of Coriolanus' allegiances, "They are primarily the products of nature, instinct and passion; and may exist without being raised to the rank of rational principles; . . . for that reason their relative importance may be mistaken, and one that is the stronger natural impulse may usurp the place of one that is of more binding moral authority." [76] Coriolanus can justly condemn the dangerous democratic activities of the plebeians, but he cannot see his own re-

[76] MacCallum, *op. cit.*, p. 598.

sponsibility in the matter. He is unaware of the public obligations which he and the other aristocrats carry as fathers of the commonwealth. The popular uprising, subversive as it is, is a direct consequence of the conduct and attitude of Coriolanus and his class. In the play the action of the governing class is symbolized and intensified in the person of Coriolanus. The passion of pride blinds his political reason and produces thereby the chaotic situation in the Roman state which leads, in a direct sequence of events, to his own downfall and death.

CHAPTER IX

The Monarchic Cycle in *Julius Caesar* and *Antony and Cleopatra*

I n *Coriolanus* Shakespeare demonstrated that conformity to those
principles of order, degree, and vocation which govern the welfare of all states was requisite to the health of the Roman body
politic. He condemns democracy as a violation of these principles and
accepts aristocracy as more nearly approaching the form of government naturally ordained for a commonwealth. But the tragedy of the
consul and the conduct of the sovereign Senate, with its lack of authoritative vigor and decision, indicated that Rome had not yet
achieved the most desirable political organization. For according to
universal example, "the specialty of rule" must be exercised by a
single authority, not divided among several. The political content of
Julius Caesar and *Antony and Cleopatra* is to be read, I think, as an
illustration of this fundamental principle of Renaissance thinking
about the nature and structure of states. In *Julius Caesar* we see, in the
successful government of the title figure, the advantages of monarchy,
and in the disastrous consequences of his assassination the evils of
multiple sovereignty. In *Antony and Cleopatra,* secondary as the political theme is in importance, we witness the inevitable restoration of
monarchy in the process of elimination which singles out the one man
naturally qualified to exercise supreme authority in a political society.

Roman history from Julius Caesar to Augustus, the period substantially covered by the two plays under consideration, was on more
than one occasion employed by Renaissance political thinkers to confirm the argument for monarchy. In the stability which Caesar
achieved under his dictatorship, in the civil strife which followed his
assassination, and in the peace which returned under the imperial rule

of Augustus, Tudor theorists found proof that under monarchy states flourish, under divided authority they decline. Sir Thomas Elyot, defending monarchy as the only natural form of government in a political society, wrote:

> Finally, untill Octavius Augustus had distroyed Anthony, and also Brutus and finisshed all the Civile Warres (that were so called by cause they were betwene the same selfe Romane citizens) the cite of Rome was never longe quiete from factions or seditions amonge the people: . . . so moche discorde was ever in the citie for lacke of one governour.[1]

Thomas Craig cited the same period of history to prove a similar contention. In the answer which he wrote to Parsons' arguments for popular sovereignty he says of his opponent:

> How many dreadful miseries follow'd [Caesar's] death? The Slaughter of both the Consuls, *Hirtius* and *Pansa*, in the Battle at *Mutina*, the arms of the *Romans* were turn'd against themselves to their own destruction, then the *Triumvirate* of *Antonius, Lepidus,* and *Octavius,* the proscribing of almost all good men, the fatal battle at Philippi, where *Brutus* and *Cassius* being kill'd, the very name of Romans was almost blotted out by their own hands, soon after that the Famine in the land over all *Italy,* and the *Triumvirate* of *Antonius, Octavius* and *Sextus Pompeius,* the fight at *Actium;* Finally, the Commonwealth was so distress'd and torn in pieces and so tired with its Liberty and Democracy, that all consented to have a Monarchy, which all the people formerly had in great abhorrence, and chose to rest there only, as in a safe and fortified harbour against all Storms, Seditions and Tumults of the people. These were the fruits of *Democratic Government,* these were the *prosperous Successes* after the killing of *Caesar?*[2]

For Renaissance political thinkers, therefore, these events in ancient Rome were of more than purely historical interest. Something of this interpretation and use of history is apparent in Shakespeare's two plays on the period.

---

[1] Elyot, *The Boke Named the Gouernour,* p. 13, Everyman's Library.

[2] Craig, *Concerning the Right of Succession to the Kingdom of England* (1703), p. 173. Cf. also Hayward, *An Answer to . . . R. Doleman* (1603), Sig. I, i r: "In your example of Caesar I never saw more untruthes crowded together in fewer words: you say he brake all laws, both humane and devine, that is one; his greatest enemies did give him a most honorable testimonie. . . . You say that Augustus was preferred in his place. . . . But Augustus, Antonius, and Lepidus did first knit in armes by the

I

It is nothing new to assert that the central political thesis in *Julius Caesar* is the practical and theoretical necessity for monarchy. A critic of the last century wrote:

Die Tragödie spielt eine grosse Staatsaction vor uns ab, deren Inhalt sich kurz so summiren lässt: "Die Fortdauer der römischen Republik ist unmöglich geworden. Der ächte Römersinn, der sie bedingte, lebt nur noch in einem Häuflein römischer Bürger, die den gewaltigsten Feind der alten Freiheit umsonst aus dem Wege räumen. Die Zeit ist da für die Monarchie. Rom hat verlernt, sich selbst zu beherrschen, darum verdient es nichts Besseres als——einen Herrscher." [3]

MacCallum's essay on *Julius Caesar* similarly concludes that "Shakespear makes it abundantly clear that the rule of the single mastermind is the only admissible solution for the problem of the time." [4] Few critics could disagree with this conclusion, and few have disagreed.[5] There is, however, some justification for reëxamining the play at this point. In the first place it can do no harm to confirm established conclusions by a new approach to the problem and by new evidence. In the second place, it remains to be shown how the ideas on monarchy embodied in *Julius Caesar* are not only consistent with the monarchic principle expressed in other works by Shakespeare, and particularly in his *Antony and Cleopatra,* but are also an integral part

name of Triumviri, to revenge the death of Julius Caesar, whereupon a long cruell and doubtfull warre was set up; . . . first, betweene these three, and the murtherers of Caesar; then, betweene Lepidus and the other two; lastly, betweene Augustus and Antonius; and this was the sweet success of the murther of Caesar."

[3] A. Lindner, "Die dramatische Einheit im Julius Caesar," *Shakespeare Jahrbuch,* II (1866), 91.

[4] MacCallum, *Shakespeare's Roman Plays and Their Background* (1925), p. 214.

[5] Wolfgang Keller, "Zwei Bemerkungen zu 'Julius Caesar,'" *Shakespeare Jahrbuch,* XLV (1909), 228: "Es ist deshalb wohl verständlich, dass Shakespeare der Sitte seiner königsfrommen Zeit gemäss das Geschichtsdrama nach dem Herrscher nannte und nicht nach dem Revolutionshelden"; H. M. Ayres, "Shakespeare's *Julius Caesar* in the Light of Some Other Versions," *PMLA,* XXV (1910), 187: "It is rather the story of the events that group themselves around the murder of Caesar, from which Shakespeare, setting them forth in something approaching the chronicle method, strove to win what tragic unity he could by emphasizing the unavailing struggle of Brutus to bolster a corrupt aristocracy against the growing power of a debased populace, swayed and informed by a spirit of triumphant Caesarism."

of that larger pattern of political thinking, concerned with the nature and structure of organized society, which he shared with the majority of his contemporaries.

The action of the play opens with the return of Caesar from his final triumph over the forces of Pompey in Spain in 45 B. C. This victory was of double significance to the Roman commonwealth, for it not only marked the consolidation of Caesar's power as a dictator, but suppressed the last of those factions which had made Roman civil life under the Republic so turbulent.[6] Except for a few nominal vestiges of their former republican power the citizens have no longer any part in the government of Rome. Moreover, with the fall of Pompey the Senatorial party lost its chief representative and was reduced from its position as sovereign power in the state to the role of an advisory body. As one historian concludes, Caesar

showed in every possible way that the old officers of the state were to be his nominees, and that they were to be looked on in the future as mere ornamental dignitaries or as magistrates of the municipality of Rome rather than as governors of the Empire.[7]

And with regard to the Senate the same writer remarks that Caesar "showed but little respect for its traditions and let all men see that it was to play a purely subordinate part in the new government." [8]

Thus under the sovereign authority of Caesar the political society of Rome was brought into conformity with that pattern of civil organization which the Renaissance considered ordained by universal law; the aristocrats functioned in their degree and vocation as advisers and counselors, and the citizens in theirs as obedient subjects. Shakespeare suggests this same order in the course of his play. In the first part of the drama the common people are portrayed quietly following their respective vocations and displaying nothing but loyalty and obedience to their sovereign. As Sir Mark Hunter observes, "They seem to be quite happy and fairly prosperous; only eager, like the good fellows they are, 'to get themselves into more work.' There is no sign that they feel themselves to be victims of any sort of oppression. . . ." [9] As usual in Shakespeare the plebeians are described as totally unfit to participate in government; their instability and fickle-

[6] J. Wells, *A Short History of Rome* (1896), p. 280 *et seq.*
[7] *Ibid.*, p. 283.   [8] Wells, *op. cit.*, p. 282.   [9] Hunter, *op. cit.*, p. 117.

ness is recalled in the opening scene, in Casca's account of Caesar's refusal of the crown, and at Caesar's funeral. But there is no indication before the assassination that they either claim or seek to exercise any such democratic authority. They are completely subject to the will of the dictator. The tribunes forbid them to participate in Caesar's triumph, but they fail to heed the admonition and it is "a great crowd" which follows Caesar when he first appears on the stage. Caesar makes no concessions to popular sovereignty when he refuses the crown, although this is a shrewd move to obtain popular sympathy for the monarchic power which is now his in everything but name. As Stapfer suggests, "if Caesar had been only bold enough to set the crown upon his head, the same rabble that applauded his respect for the law would have been equally ready to applaud his violation of it." [10] Caesar is their natural master, and it is only after his death that they seek to function out of their degree and do violence to the state by taking justice into their own hands.

The officers of the republic appear in the play, but it is made clear that Caesar's authority has rendered them purely nominal. The tribunes, aware that the dictator will "keep us all in servile fearfulness," are actually deprived of their function in the course of the play. As Casca relates it, "Marullus and Flavius, for pulling scarfs off Caesar's images, are put to silence." [11] The Senate, too, once sovereign authority in the Roman state, fares only slightly better under Caesar, who regards it as an advisory body completely subservient to his will. This relationship is indicated in the message which he originally plans to send back with Decius:

> Tell them that I will not come today.
> Cannot, is false, and that I dare not, falser;
> I will not come today. Tell them so, Decius. [12]

He scorns the necessity of lying to a body to which he feels no obligation or responsibility. To Calpurnia's suggestion, "Say he is sick," Caesar answers:

> Shall Caesar send a lie?
> Have I in conquest stretch'd mine arm so far,

---

[10] Paul Stapfer, *Shakespeare and Classical Antiquity*, translated by E. J. Cary (1880), p. 315.

[11] *Julius Caesar*, I, ii, 289.   [12] II, ii, 62–64.

To be afeard to tell greybeards the truth?
Decius, go tell them Caesar will not come

. . . .

The cause is in my will; I will not come;
That is enough to satisfy the senate.[13]

This may be a boast unbecoming in a man of Caesar's position, as many critics have protested, but it is a statement of political truth, confirmed by his remark before the Senate itself, "What is now amiss that Caesar and his senate must redress?" [14] The personal pronoun leaves little doubt as to how Caesar regarded the position and function of the Senate in the Roman state as he had reorganized it.

Thus all Rome stands under one man's awe, for Caesar is left to bear the palm of government alone. And in the character which he gives Caesar as a ruler, Shakespeare makes it clear that such autocracy was a blessing to the state. For Caesar is represented as ably qualified, according to Renaissance standards, to exercise "the specialty of rule." There are, to be sure, personality weaknesses which may, as Professor Ayres suggests, represent the influence of an Elizabethan stage tradition regarding the character of the hero.[15] Such traits remind us that we do not see the dictator at the highest point in his career or in the full perfection of his abilities, but rather after those failings which signaled his decline and downfall had already begun to make themselves manifest. Considered from a purely dramatic point of view they prepare the way for the fall of Caesar and, together with the omens and portents, the signs and wonders, give the first part of the tragedy the character and atmosphere of conventional Senecan drama. But as MacCallum warns, these traits should not be given more emphasis than they demand.[16] Certainly they do not alter the main impression of an able and successful governor, to which Caesar's quali-

[13] II, ii, 65–68; 71–72.   [14] III, i, 31.

[15] Ayres, op. cit., p. 225: "Our study has aimed merely to trace from its fountain head in Seneca a stream of tradition, continuing to Shakespeare's time and beyond, under the baptism of which Caesar has become Hercules and speaks with a braggart voice."

[16] MacCallum, op. cit., p. 228. Cf. Stapfer, op. cit., p. 327: "And yet, when the conspirators put a violent end to this poor exhausted spirit, which was dying of itself, the Republic gained absolutely nothing: the Emperor is no more, but the empire is begun—Caesar is dead, long live Caesar!"

ties and deeds, his friends and his enemies, testify. More important, the elements of weakness and decline in the man do not afford politically reasonable grounds for destroying, as the conspirators do, the successful and beneficial monarchic institution which he represents.

As a military leader Caesar brings victory abroad and peace at home, enriching the state with ransoms from his captives and reducing to ordered tranquility the civil strife in Rome. As an administrator of justice he is governed by reason, not by prejudice or passion. Even Brutus must confess that "to speak truth of Caesar, I have not known when his affections sway'd more than his reason." This characterization is confirmed in the Senate chamber, when Caesar neither softens nor bends before the flattery of Metullus, but rather chides this attempt to sway his judgment and reaffirms his resolution to execute justice according to law. As a governor Caesar places the welfare of the state and his subjects before his own in approved Renaissance fashion. He rejects the paper of Artemidorus with the exclamation: "What touches us ourself shall be last serv'd," [17] and moves on to the cares of state which await him at the capital. Caesar, of course, is not without his personal interest, but Shakespeare never suggests that these clash with the higher interests of Rome, and as MacCallum points out, "Provided that his more selfish aims coincide with the good of the whole, and that he has veracity of intellect to understand, with steadiness of will to satisfy the needs of his time, Shakespeare will vindicate for him his share of prosperity, honour and desert." [18] But that quality which would, perhaps, most endear Caesar as a ruler to the average Elizabethan, is his attitude toward the common people. In direct contrast to the contempt which renders Coriolanus an unfit governor is the fatherly affection with which Caesar regards his common subjects. As Antony expresses it, "When that the poor have cried, Caesar hath wept; . . ." [19] The theatrical refusal of the crown and offer to let

[17] III, i, 8.   [18] MacCallum, *op. cit.*, p. 228.

[19] III, ii, 96. Cf. Plutarch, *Lives:* Vol. V, *Life of Julius Caesar*, p. 270, translated from the French of Amyot by Thomas North (1928): "Now Caesar immediately won many mens good willes at Rome, through his eloquence, in pleading of their causes: and the people loved him marvelously also, bicause of the curteous manner he had to speake to every man, and to use them gently, being more ceremonious therein, then was looked for in one of his yeres." Cf. also p. 334: "But to win him selfe the love and good will of the people, as the honorable gard and best safety he could have: he

the rabble cut his throat does not, of course, truly indicate his feeling, although these are shrewdly contrived devices for displaying his attitude with political effectiveness. A more genuine manifestation of his attitude is the will. Whatever the purposes to which Antony may turn this in his oration, the fact remains that Caesar honestly intended that his care for the common welfare should extend even beyond his death. The character of Caesar as a just and benevolent sovereign of the Roman state is enhanced, moreover, by the suggestion that he is, as Tudor theorists believed all kings to be, the divinely appointed lieutenant of God on earth. There is no direct statement of this in the play, but it is suggested in Calpurnia's interpretation of the omens which preceded Caesar's assassination:

> When beggars die there are no comets seen;
> The heavens themselves blaze forth the death of princes.[20]

MacCallum recognizes something of the same aura around Caesar, and concludes his analysis of the character of the ruler as follows:

Such men are ministers of the Divine Purposes, as Plutarch said in regard to Caesar; and in setting forth the essential meaning of his career, Shakespeare can scorn the base degrees by which he did ascend. . . . With them Shakespeare is not concerned, but with the plenary inspiration of Caesar's life, the inspiration that made him an instrument of Heaven and that was to bring peace and order to the world.[21]

Political references to commoners, tribunes, senators and the governor himself in *Julius Caesar* are brief hints indeed, but they sketch with characteristic Shakespearean deftness the political society of Rome as it was organized under Caesar. In all respects the state conforms to those principles of order which Shakespeare and the majority of his Tudor contemporaries considered necessary for civil health. The Soothsayer in Act II innocently observes a microcosmic representation of the commonwealth when he describes "The throng that follows Caesar at the heels, Of senators, of praetors, common suitors." [22] The head of the Roman politic has been transformed from an aristocracy into a monarchy, and the component degrees of society have

---

made common feasts againe, and generall distribution of corne." Plutarch frequently refers to this quality in Caesar's character as a governor.

[20] II, ii, 30.   [21] MacCallum, *op. cit.*, pp. 229–30.   [22] II, iv, 34.

fallen into the prescribed hierarchical order under the government of one sovereign authority.

The conspirators, particularly as their political ideals are represented in Brutus, sincerely believe that such a civic order is not for the highest good of the commonwealth. In principle and in practice they are opposed to the monarchic concept of government for which Caesar stands. Cassius' feeling against the autocracy of the dictator is unqualified. He believes it to be unnatural: "I was born free as Caesar; so were you," he tells Casca, "And this man Is now become a God . . . ,"

> A man no mightier than thyself or me
> In personal action, yet prodigious grown
> And fearful, as these strange eruptions are.[23]

By interpreting these same "strange eruptions" as divine "instruments of fear and warning Unto some monstrous state" [24] he suggests again the unnatural character of a monarchic political society. But Cassius' antagonism toward Caesar is less political than personal; as MacCallum observes, "It is now resentment of pre-eminence that makes Cassius a malcontent." [25] Brutus' feeling, on the other hand, is founded on a broader political philosophy. Uppermost in his mind is the welfare of the Roman state, and he thinks and acts in terms of sincere convictions regarding the public good. As Antony remarks:

> All the conspirators, save only he,
> Did that they did in envy of great Caesar;
> He only, in a general honest thought
> And common good to all, made one of them.[26]

Consistently his motive is "Not that I loved Caesar less but that I loved Rome more." When Cassius first broaches the subject of the conspiracy Brutus urges him to proceed "If it be aught toward the general good." [27] To Antony he explains that "pity to the general wrong of Rome . . . Hath done this deed on Caesar," [28] and to the people he concludes, "With this I depart, that, as I slew my best lover for the good of Rome, I have the same dagger for myself, when it shall please my country to need my death." [29]

---

[23] I, iii, 76–78.   [24] I, iii, 70–71.   [25] MacCallum, *op. cit.*, p. 278.
[26] V, v, 69–72.   [27] I, ii, 85.   [28] III, i, 170, 172.
[29] III, ii, 49–52.

Brutus is convinced that this welfare of the state demands the removal of Caesar. Beyond that his political reasoning is not clear. It seems evident, however, that he was anxious that ultimate sovereignty in Rome be preserved in the hands of the corporate body of the nobility. The whole implication in his desire to destroy Caesar is the restoration of that order under which Rome was governed before the dictator came to power, and when the Senate possessed final political authority. On the one hand he has no real intention of transferring this power to the citizenry in general, as in a true republic. When the assassination is accomplished he proclaims that "Liberty, freedom and enfranchisement" are restored. But as MacCallum points out:

Of the positive essence of republicanism, of enthusiasm for a state in which all the lawful authority is derived from the whole body of fully qualified citizens, there is, despite Brutus' talk of freemen and slaves and Caesar's ambition, no trace whatever in any of his utterances from first to last.[30]

But, on the other hand, Brutus is convinced that political sovereignty cannot safely be vested in one man alone. His celebrated and much-disputed soliloquy in Act II is illuminating in this respect.[31] As all commentators on the passage agree, Brutus is here distinguishing between what Caesar is and what he might become.[32] It is, I believe, the difference recognized in the Renaissance between a ruler exercising power delegated to him by a superior authority and a ruler who possesses ultimate sovereignty in himself. It is, in a word, the difference between limited and absolute monarchy.[33]

Whatever Caesar's actual power as Shakespeare portrays it in the play, the offices and processes of the republic are retained in name at least. Brutus continues to regard Caesar in relation to this aristocratic concept of the state, in which his power is delegated and limited by the sovereign Senate. His argument is substantially the same as the Renaissance argument for limited monarchy. Ponet wrote that as God ordained ephori, tribunes, councils, parliaments, and similar bodies, "so in all Christian realms and dominions God ordained meanes that

[30] MacCallum, *op. cit.*, p. 203.   [31] II, i, 10–34.

[32] Cf. *Julius Caesar*, p. xxxiii, edited by Michael MacMillan, The Arden Shakespeare (1917): "Caesar as virtual ruler of Rome had committed no excesses, but the title of king [argues Brutus] might possibly transform him into a cruel tyrant. Therefore he must be killed."

[33] See Chapter II, above.

the Heads, the Princes and Governors should not oppresse the poore people after their lusts and make their wills their laws." [34] In this respect it is interesting to note that Stirling in his *Tragedy of Julius Caesar* (1607) causes Brutus to say explicitly that the Senate, not Caesar, possesses "lawful sovereignty" in Rome, and that "The Senate king, a subject Caesar is." [35] In such a position Caesar, according to Shakespeare's Brutus, is thoroughly acceptable as a man and as a political leader; the conspirator has no objection to the limited monarchy which the dictator's government in theory now represents. He admires Caesar as a person and respects him as a ruler; his comment on the rule of reason over affection in Caesar is a high tribute to any governor.[36] Therefore, Brutus is forced to conclude that "the quarrel Will bear no colour for the thing he is." [37]

But, Brutus argues, Caesar has reached the extreme limits of the power delegated to him under the aristocratic form of government. At present the dictator at least formally observes the claims of the old order. Moved by ambition, however, he threatens, in seeking the crown, to reject in theory as well as in fact the system through which he rose to his position of authority:

> But 'tis a common proof
> That lowliness is young Ambition's ladder,
> Whereto the climber-upward turns his face;
> But when he once attains the upmost round,
> He then unto the ladder turns his back,
> Looks in the clouds, scorning the base degrees
> By which he did ascend.[38]

For according to Brutus, the crown which Caesar desires is the symbol which distinguishes an absolute monarch from a governor limited by the final political authority of the corporate body of the nobility. By assuming the crown Caesar will transfer sovereign will in the state from the Senate to his own person, thereby fundamentally altering the theoretical structure of Roman political society. I believe that

---

[34] John Ponet, *A Short Treatise of Politike Power* (1556), edition of 1642, p. 7.
[35] Stirling, William Alexander, First Earl of, *The Tragedy of Julius Caesar*, III, i, 274–76 (in *Julius Caesar*, p. 345, The New Variorum Shakespeare, 1913.)
[36] II, i, 20.   [37] II, i, 28–29.   [38] II, i, 21–27.

Brutus is thinking primarily of this effect of the crown on Caesar's political character and position (not on his private moral character, as does MacCallum) when he says:

> He would be crown'd:
> How that might change his nature, there's the question.
> It is the bright day that brings forth the adder,
> And that craves wary walking. Crown him?—that;—
> And then, I grant, we put a sting in him
> That at his will he may do danger with.[39]

Sir Mark Hunter observes that "To Brutus at one point it would almost seem that the forbidden thing was not so much the actual fact of kingship as the name and symbol of royal rule." [40] That, indeed, is the case. Brutus believes with the sixteenth-century advocate of limited monarchy, Buchanan, that rulers should be constrained "to make use not of their own licentious wills in judgement, but of that right or privilege which the People had conferred upon them." [41] Caesar, now a benefit to Rome, might become a menace when the crown establishes the sovereignty of his own "licentious will" to run unlimited and unchecked to whatever lengths he desires. As Brutus reasons it out:

> So Caesar may;
> Then, lest he may, prevent. . . .
>   . . . .
> Fashion it thus: that what he is, augmented,
> Would run to these and these extremities;
> And therefore think him as a serpent's egg
> Which, hatch'd, would, as his kind, grow mischievous,
> And kill him in the shell.[42]

The use of such violence to preserve the sovereignty of the aristocracy in Rome is justified, Brutus maintains, because the welfare of the state demands it. The major premise with which his soliloquy opens reaffirms the high-principled honesty of his intentions: "I know no personal cause to spurn at him But for the general." [43] Only by pre-

---

[39] II, i, 12–17.   [40] Hunter, *op. cit.*, p. 120.

[41] George Buchanan, *De iure regni apud Scotos* (translated, 1689), p. 13.

[42] II, i, 27–28; 30–34.   [43] II, i, 11–12.

venting the imminent accession of an absolute monarch can the common good be served.

Whatever the interpretation of this soliloquy—and any interpretation of so difficult and disputed a passage must be largely conjectural—the political scheme of the first half of the play seems fairly evident. On one side Shakespeare presents Roman political society flourishing under a *de facto* monarchy, with all of its degrees conforming to the pattern ordained by universal law. Against this he sets a group of men who are sincerely convinced that such political organization is a menace to the commonwealth and who believe that the earlier aristocratic government must be restored. With little prejudice so far manifest in either direction Shakespeare brings these two concepts to test. Brutus' words make clear Shakespeare's intention that the criterion to be kept in mind in judging the efficacy and justice of any system of government is the welfare of the society concerned. With these principles established the resolution of the problem begins.

The conspirators act on their beliefs and Caesar is assassinated. The consequences of their deed prove almost immediately the fallacy of their political reasoning and indirectly reaffirm the monarchic principles of society which Shakespeare seems consistently to have held. Its natural head gone, the Roman body politic begins a mad run toward destruction. As MacCallum phrases it, "Brutus has brought about an upturn of society by assassinating the one man who could organize that society." [44] Shakespeare does not leave to implication the political significance of the action which follows the murder of Caesar. In his soliloquy over the body of the dictator Antony forecasts the violence and strife which will devastate the Roman commonwealth and directly links this chaos with the death of the monarch:

> Woe to the hand that shed this costly blood!
> Over thy wounds now do I prophesy
>
>   . . . .
>
> A curse shall light upon the limbs of men;
> Domestic fury and fierce civil strife
> Shall cumber all the parts of Italy;

----

[44] MacCallum, *op. cit.*, p. 263.

> Blood and destruction shall be so in use
> And dreadful objects so familiar
> That mothers shall but smile when they behold
> Their infants quartered with the hands of war;
> All pity chok'd with custom of fell deeds;
> And Caesar's spirit, ranging for revenge,
> With Ate by his side come hot from hell,
> Shall in these confines with a monarch's voice
> Cry "Havoc," and let slip the dogs of war;
> That this foul deed shall smell above the earth
> With carrion men, groaning for burial.[45]

Later, in his funeral oration, Antony speaks again of Caesar's death in terms of its devastating effect on the commonwealth in general:

> O, what a fall was there, my countrymen!
> Then I, and you, and all of us fell down,
> Whilst bloody treason flourish'd over us.[46]

Whatever his own motives, Antony's observations are sound from a political point of view. He recognizes the association between regicide and social chaos as almost any Elizabethan would recognize it. In fact, at this point in the play, he serves to interpret the events of Roman history exactly as Elyot and Craig interpreted them; he too observes "how many dreadful miseries followed Caesar's death," and suggests how "the commonwealth was so distressed and torn in pieces" as a result of this tampering with the divine structure of the state.

The principal source of these afflictions is the multiple authority under which Rome falls at Caesar's death. Immediately there reappear among the now sovereign aristocracy those factions which had so disrupted Roman political life before Caesar established his unitary authority. The resulting "domestic fury and fierce civil strife" are a poor substitute for the peace and order maintained under the monarchic government of Caesar and form an ironic commentary on the promise of general welfare made by Brutus in defense of his deed. The political philosophy which he represents is completely discredited; its consequences are exactly those against which Elyot warned when he condemned aristocracy:

---

[45] III, i, 258–59; 262–75.   [46] III, ii, 194–96.

Some beinge ones in authoritie, be incensed with glorie; some with ambition; other with coveitise and desire of treasure or possessions, wherby they falle in to contention . . . and bryngeth al to confusion.[47]

What Brutus actually brought about was first a virtual absence of government of any kind as party struggled against party for power, and second, the tyranny of the triumvirate, whose oppressions were far more terrible than those of which the conspirators could accuse Caesar.

From the moment of the assassination every semblance of order and authority is gone. Trebonius reports that "Men, wives, and children stare, cry out, and run, As it were doomsday."[48] Brutus describes "The multitude, beside themselves with fear."[49] The common people, who lived in quiet contentment under Caesar's well-exercised power, become one of the principal instruments of disorder in the hands of the factions now struggling for control of the state. The citizens cry "Revenge! About! Seek! Burn! Fire! Kill! Slay! Let not a traitor live!,"[50] in a terrifying scene of mob rule. Shakespeare has drawn no more horrible picture of the injustice of the uncontrolled masses than in the scene portraying the fate of Cinna the Poet. The episode tragically points the complete perversion of order and justice which the collapse of the political structure has brought about.

There is no less confusion among the upper degrees of Roman society. By the opening of Act IV three rival parties are apparent among the Roman aristocrats: the senators, the three men who will constitute the triumvirate, and the conspirators who precipitated the crisis. The disastrous conflicts among them at the expense of the commonwealth are, according to Renaissance thinking, the characteristic fruits of divided political authority. The proscriptions soon eliminate the senatorial party, Shakespeare stressing particularly those instances in which kin turns on kin and friend on friend, in order to emphasize the unnatural violence of the times. Thus Lepidus consents to the death of his brother and Antony to the death of his nephew. Meantime there is suspicion and dissension in the ranks of the factions which remain. Octavius reveals that among the friends of the triumvirate are some that "have in their hearts, I fear, Millions of mischiefs,"[51] and already the suggestion has been made that Lepidus

[47] Elyot, op. cit., p. 8.   [48] III, i, 97–98.   [49] III, i, 180.
[50] III, ii, 208–9.   [51] IV, i, 50–51.

be dropped by the wayside. Perhaps in its political context the celebrated quarrel scene between Brutus and Cassius is intended to suggest something of this same dissension which must harass those who
overthrow established authority. At any rate, the scene, in spite of its
reconciliation, is not discordant with the general atmosphere of turmoil and conflict among Roman leaders which is brought to a climax
at the battle of Philippi. Here, at the cost of those "wounds of civil
war" which the Renaissance considered the worst of diseases to afflict
the body politic, the triumvirate emerges as the triumphant party and
sovereign authority in Rome.

But in the victory of the triumvirate lies the most bitter commentary on the futility as well as the fallacy of the conspirators' political reasoning and the act to which it led. For at the price of ruinous
civil strife they have succeeded only in making way for a tyranny far
worse than that which they overthrew. In a single scene Shakespeare
establishes the character of this government which now controls Rome.
The unnatural cruelty of the proscriptions has already been mentioned; later the extent of the crime is indicated when Brutus and
Messala set the number of victims from seventy to one hundred
senators.[52] The personal greed of the triumvirate at the expense of the
commonwealth and of the citizenry in particular is suggested by
Antony's expressed intention to "determine How to cut off some
charge in legacies." [53] By flaunting this violation of Caesar's will Antony points the contrast between his attitude toward the common people and that of the dictator. It is made clear in the play, moreover,
that the evil effects of the new tyranny will not end with these meas-
ures, for the seeds of dissension from which continued civil strife will
grow are planted in the triumvirate when Antony attacks Lepidus.
The note upon which the political action of the play ends is, accordingly, at best unpromising.

These effects of the conspirators' act on the commonwealth of Rome
make it evident that as democracy is discredited in *Coriolanus* so aristocracy is discredited in *Julius Caesar*. The reaffirmation of the monarchic principle which this conclusion implies is substantiated by evidence in the play itself, particularly by that "spirit of Caesarism"
which, as many critics have observed, permeates the action of the

[52] IV, iii, 173–78.   [53] IV, i, 8–9.

whole play and is represented in dramatically concrete form by the ghost of Caesar. MacCallum says:

It is really Caesar's presence, his genius, his conception that dominates the story. Brutus is first among the struggling mortals who obey even while resisting their fate, but the fate itself is the imperialist inspiration which makes up the significance of Caesar, and the play therefore is fitly named after him.[54]

This spirit which is "Thy evil spirit, Brutus," [55] and which "walks abroad, and turns our swords In our own proper entrails" [56] is the concept of unitary sovereignty. Reiteration of the idea during the violent action of the last three acts reminds us that violation of it was responsible for these social and political ills. It is, moreover, the nemesis against which Brutus' efforts, however highly motivated, are of no avail. In extending the drama three acts beyond the assassination of Caesar, Shakespeare infuses the tragedy of the dictator's fall with additional meaning and significance. It cannot be denied that the first two acts in many respects tell the story of the fall in conventional Senecan terms. But at the same time Shakespeare is building up the concept of the political virtue of monarchy. His purpose in so doing becomes clear immediately after the murder, and is revealed as the unifying theme in all the scenes that follow. The defeat of the conspirators and the discrediting of the aristocratic principle which they represent suggest that Shakespeare saw the inevitability as well as the necessity of rule by one man. The action of *Julius Caesar* demonstrates primarily this necessity of monarchy; the continuation in the slight but positive political action of *Antony and Cleopatra* demonstrates its inevitability.

2

In *Antony and Cleopatra* the chief interest for Shakespeare, as for everyone since who has encountered the play, is the splendid infatuation which the story presents. But as Professor Boas says, "Shakespeare, even when making an elaborate study of amorous passion, does not isolate it from the wider and more material issues of surrounding civic or national life." [57] In dwelling upon the love affair the dramatist only

---

[54] MacCallum, *op. cit.*, p. 214.   [55] IV, iii, 282.
[56] V, iii, 95–96.   [57] Boas, *Shakspere and His Predecessors*, p. 473.

magnified one link in the chain of political events which runs, consistent and unbroken, through ten acts. For it seems evident that the political thinking of the later play, like the historical narrative, is taken up where *Julius Caesar* ended. MacCallum writes:

The political setting of *Julius Caesar* had been the struggle between the old Order and the New. The Old goes out with a final and temporary flare of success; the New asserts itself as the necessary solution for the problem of the time, but is deprived of its guiding genius who might best have elicited its possibilities for good and neutralized its possibilities for evil. In *Antony and Cleopatra* we see how its mastery is established and confirmed despite the faults and limitations of the smaller men who now represent it.[58]

But it is not, as MacCallum implies, an order which three men can represent. It is a monarchic order which Caesar established, and until the three are reduced to one, who is least faulty and limited, the struggle will not be over. The process of selection by which monarchy will be restored through the reduction of three men to one had already been suggested in the earlier play, in the dissensions within the ranks of the triumvirate and particularly in Antony's anxiety to oust Lepidus. To the completion of this process the political action of *Antony and Cleopatra* is primarily devoted. Here are displayed the qualities of character and ability which determine the outcome. Leveled to this political plane Antony's infatuation and its effect on his character is merely one phase of the evolution toward unitary sovereignty. He and Lepidus are eliminated because they do not possess, as Octavius clearly does, the special qualities which, according to Renaissance thinking, mark a man for the vocation of government.

As has been indicated, *Julius Caesar* does not, politically speaking, end on that note of tranquility and repose for which Shakespearean tragedy is generally celebrated. At the opening of *Antony and Cleopatra* neither the form of government in Rome nor Shakespeare's condemnation of it has altered. So long as the triumvirate exercises "the specialty of rule" the state suffers the social ill-health of an unnaturally organized body politic. For however autocratic in conduct, the triumvirate is essentially an aristocratic form of government, or more accurately, because of its tyrannical nature, an oligarchy. Thus

[58] MacCallum, *op. cit.*, p. 344.

it displays the faults and inflicts the evils generally associated with divided authority in Renaissance political thinking. Even Lepidus is aware of the principal weakness of such government, internal conflict; he warns his fellow triumvirs: "When we debate Our trivial difference loud, we do commit Murder in healing wounds." [59] The disastrous effect of oligarchic administration on the general welfare of Rome is vividly set forth by Antony, who explicitly links the civil chaos with divided rule:

> Our Italy
> Shines o'er with civil swords; Sextus Pompeius
> Makes his approaches to the port of Rome;
> Equality of two domestic powers
> Breed scrupulous faction; the hated, grown to strength,
> Are newly grown to love; the condemn'd Pompey,
> Rich in his father's honour, creeps apace
> Into the hearts of such as have not thrived
> Upon the present state, whose numbers threaten.[60]

But out of the strife engendered by oligarchy, monarchy is gradually emerging through a process of elimination. It had already been established in *Julius Caesar* that in the struggle for sovereignty Lepidus will play a negative part. In fact, he is clearly portrayed as a man completely out of his degree and vocation even as a triumvir, a man, as MacCallum points out, "attempting a part or role that is too big for him." [61] Antony, in *Julius Caesar*, calls him "a slight unmeritable man, meet to be sent on errands," [62] and in the later play the servants scoff at his pretensions:

SECOND SERVANT. Why, this it is to have a name in great men's fellowship. I had as lief have a reed that will do me no service as a partisan I could not heave.

FIRST SERVANT. To be called into a huge sphere, and not to be seen to move in 't, are the holes where eyes should be, which pitifully disaster the cheeks.[63]

Such a man could scarcely be described as "most wise, most continent, most temperate, most manly, and most just, full of liberalitie, majes-

---

[59] *Antony and Cleopatra*, II, ii, 20–22.
[61] MacCallum, *op. cit.*, p. 370.
[63] *Antony and Cleopatra*, II, vii, 12–19.

[60] I, iii, 44–52.
[62] *Julius Caesar*, IV, i, 12.

tie, holinesse and mercy," as Castiglione enumerates the qualifications of a ruler.[64] His credulous acceptance of Antony's stories of the crocodile discredits his wisdom; his incontinence is betrayed by the befuddled stupor in which his drinking leaves him; mercy and justice are denied by his cruelty at the proscriptions, which confirms Octavius' assertion:

> I have told him Lepidus was grown too cruel;
> That he his high authority abus'd,
> And did deserve his change.[65]

But it is the lack of the capacity for government and leadership which principally disqualifies Lepidus and is the character weakness directly responsible for his downfall. Some men are born to rule, the rest to obey, wrote theorists of the Renaissance, and Lepidus is clearly one of the latter. He may indeed, as Octavius says, be "a tried and valiant soldier," but the greater fortitude of will and purpose is not his. His subsequent career testifies to the accuracy of Antony's description of his role as a follower:

> Octavius, I have seen more days than you;
> And though we lay these honours on this man
> To ease ourselves of divers slanderous loads,
> He shall but bear them as the ass bears gold,
> To groan and sweat under the business,
> Either led or driven, as we point the way;
>
> . . . .
>
> He must be taught and train'd and bid go forth;
> A barren-spirited fellow; one that feeds
> On abjects, orts, and imitations,
> Which, out of use and stal'd by other men,
> Begin his fashion. Do not talk of him
> But as a property.[66]

Lepidus maintains his spineless role on into *Antony and Cleopatra*. There such diversified characters as Pompey, Enobarus, and Agrippa

---

[64] Castiglione, *The Courtier*, p. 276, translated by Thomas Hoby (1561), Everyman's Library.

[65] *Antony and Cleopatra*, III, vi, 32–34.

[66] *Julius Caesar*, IV, i, 18–23; 35–40.

all recognize him as little more than a fawning sycophant.[67] To the end he is merely a tool in the hands of more masterful men, for as Eros tells Enobarbus:

Caesar, having made use of him in the wars 'gainst Pompey, presently denied him rivality, would not let him partake in the glory of the action; and not resting here, accuses him of letters he had formerly wrote to Pompey; upon his own appeal, seizes him. So the poor third is up, till death enlarge his confine.[68]

Sextus Pompeius constitutes a threat against the authority of the triumvirate and the monarchic aspirations of the triumvirs, but it is difficult to consider him a candidate for the imperial seat. Neither in what he seeks nor what he accepts is there any suggestion that his thoughts fly so high. As far as his political motivation goes, he seems rather to represent the final recrudescence of aristocratic republicanism. His expressed intent is to halt the course of Roman monarchy by restoring the discredited aristocratic state; this reason he associates with a desire for personal revenge for the death of his father, leader of the senatorial party, at the hands of the Caesarian party:

> What was 't
> That mov'd pale Cassius to conspire; and what
> Made the all-honour'd, honest Roman, Brutus,
> With the arm'd rest, courtiers of beauteous freedom,
> To drench the Capitol, but that they would
> Have one man but a man? And that is it
> Hath made me rig my navy, at whose burden
> The anger'd ocean foams; with which I meant
> To scourge the ingratitude that despiteful Rome
> Cast on my noble father.[69]

These are high-minded and sincere convictions, but Pompeius lacks the resolution necessary to establish them as facts. The treaty to which he agrees ruins the real advantages of power and situation which he possessed and paves the way for his downfall by strengthening further the hand of Octavius. Menas accurately identifies the flaw in the political character of Pompeius: "Who seeks, and will not take when once 'tis offer'd, Shall never find it more." [70] So passes the last aris-

[67] Cf. *Antony and Cleopatra*, III, ii, 5-25.
[69] II, vi, 14-23.
[68] *Ibid.*, III, v, 7-13.
[70] II, vii, 89-90.

tocratic threat to Roman monarchy, the last conflict of the old order with the new.

The contest for empire has resolved itself into a duel between Antony and Octavius. It cannot be said, of course, that Antony is ambitious for sole authority, but he has little active choice in the matter, for Octavius forces the issue on him. It would be futile to argue which is the greater, richer personality, which is more the master of sympathy and compassion, or which held the greater attraction as a dramatic character for Shakespeare. But it would be equally futile to argue which, from a rational political point of view, is destined to exercise monarchic sovereignty in the Roman state. Each possesses in a high degree those qualities and abilities which the Renaissance considered essential to the governor of a state. But Antony suffered a flaw which the Renaissance considered, with equal conviction, fatal to "the specialty of rule." To an analysis of this weakness itself the bulk of the play is devoted; here it will be considered in its political context alone.

In *Julius Caesar* Antony is presented as a far more impressive candidate for the imperial mantle than is Octavius. Political astuteness and military genius make him easily the dominating figure in the triumvirate. He it is who steps at once into the dangerous and difficult situation which follows the assassination, turning the helplessness and blunders of the conspirators to his own purposes. He it is whose uncanny sense of mob psychology effects the rout of Brutus and Cassius from Rome, leaving himself and his fellow triumvirs in power. He it is who controls the triumvirate, planning the fate of Lepidus and outlining the course of action while Octavius answers with little argument, "You may do your will," or, "Let us do so." Finally it is Antony whose ability as a soldier accomplishes the overthrow of the republican forces and the conclusive victory of the triumvirate. It is true that Antony makes use of his opportunities and can sway mobs, but, as Sir Mark Hunter makes clear, he is not merely an opportunist or a demagogue.[71] His deeds and abilities are those of a natural leader of men, and his principles, as the great soliloquy in Act III reveals, are those of an avenger of regicide and revolution. This is the main political impression left by Antony in the earlier play, and there

[71] Hunter, *op. cit.*, pp. 134–35.

he appears to be the logical heir to the imperial authority of Caesar.

But such an impression does not take into account significant details and suggestions which foreshadow Antony's political ruin in the later play. For as Bradley observes, "The first of living soldiers, an able politician, a most persuasive orator, Antony nevertheless was not born to rule the world." [72] Already in *Julius Caesar* the voluptuous and sensuous element in Antony's character, the element which was to render him unfit to govern and was eventually to destroy him, is made evident. There we learn that he is a "masker and a reveller" [73] who "is given to sports, to wildness, and much company." [74] In *Antony and Cleopatra* these tendencies, sublimated and concentrated in the one master passion, form the central and all-embracing interest in the play. Their relation to the political scheme of the drama is clearly indicated, however.

Renaissance thinkers concerned with the welfare of states were particularly insistent that in the head of a body politic reason must always rule over passion. It was argued that a man cannot govern others unless he can govern himself. As Erasmus expressed it:

But you cannot be a king unless reason controls you; that is, unless under all circumstances you follow [the course of] advice and judgment. You cannot rule over others until you yourself have obeyed the course of honor. [75]

This doctrine was based in part on the conviction that the character of a people is determined by the character of a ruler. To quote Erasmus again:

The corruption of an evil prince spreads more swiftly and widely than the scourge of any pestilence. In the same proportion a wholesome life on the part of a prince is, without question, the quickest and shortest way to improve public morals. The common people imitate nothing with more pleasure than what they see their prince do. Under a gambler, gambling is rife; under a warrior, everyone is embroiled; under an epicure, all disport is wasteful luxury; under a debauché, license is rampant; under a cruel tyrant, everyone brings accusations and false witness. Go through

---

[72] A. C. Bradley, "Antony and Cleopatra," *Oxford Lectures on Poetry* (1934), p. 295.

[73] *Julius Caesar*, V, i, 62.   [74] II, i, 188–89.

[75] Erasmus, *The Education of a Christian Prince*, edited by Born, p. 189.

your ancient history and you will find the life of the prince mirrored in the morals of his people. No comet, no dreadful power affects the progress of human affairs as the life of the prince grips and transforms the morals and character of his subjects.[76]

But not only on these grounds of moral influence was passion condemned and the prince exhorted to exercise reason. Passion, and particularly sexual passion, was considered to have a devastating effect on the governing abilities of the ruler himself. Thus Sir Thomas Elyot, who defines continence as "a vertue whiche kepeth the pleasaunt appetite of man under the yoke of reason," places the quality prominently among those essential to a successful governor.[77] George More, writing in 1611, thus warns against passion in any form:

A Prince to be too passionate and too cholerike is dangerous, for choller sometimes burneth and dryeth up the veines and taketh life, sometimes it blindeth the understanding, and taketh away sense and reason . . . for the mind doth not easily see the truth . . . where passion and affection beareth sway.[78]

Specifically he admonishes "a Prince to bee continent in life," for excess of passion "will make him weak and effeminate, and destroyeth both body and soul, losing thereby also sometime both life and kingdom." [79] He goes on to cite numerous historical examples—Locrine, Numidia, and Sophinisba among them—whose political ruin he can trace directly to the debilitating influence of incontinence.

Antony could well have been included among these instances. "For a life like his," MacCallum remarks, "is hardly compatible even in

---

[76] Ibid., pp. 156–57. Cf. also, Chelidonius, A Most Excellent Historie of the Institution and First Beginning of Christian Princes (translated, 1571), Chapter IV: "How that those which shall command others, ought first to master them selves, and so suppresse and moderate their affections and passions, that by their good lives, they may induce those that be subject to them, to vertue and godlinesse"; Buchanan, De iure regni apud Scotos (translated, 1689), p. 28: "The whole world doth act to conform to the Example of a King. The Law of Kings prevail not so much to incline Mens Minds unto Obedience, as the Conversation of the rulers. For the fluctuating Multitude doth always change as their Prince doth."

[77] Elyot, op. cit., p. 246.

[78] George More, Principles for Yong Princes (1611), fol. 42 r, v. Cf. also fol. 42 v: "And knowing himself hee must then labour to command himselfe, and make reason rule nature."

[79] More, op. cit., fol. 47 v.

theory with the arduous functions of the commander, the governor, the administrator; and in practice it inevitably leads to their neglect." [80] Each step in Antony's downward course from political power is explicitly linked with his infatuation for Cleopatra and its effect on his character as a leader of men. His fatal passion leads him to disregard political reason and to commit blunder after blunder; such missteps not only demonstrate his unfitness to govern but eventually accomplish his total ruin. At the very opening of the play his followers describe how infatuation is already destroying those abilities by means of which Antony rose to power; their story is almost a paraphrase of More's warning to incontinent princes quoted above:

> Nay, but this dotage of our general's
> O'erflows the measure. Those his goodly eyes,
> That o'er the files and musters of the war
> Have glow'd like plated Mars, now bend, now turn,
> The office and devotion of their view
> Upon a tawny front; his captain's heart,
> Which in the scuffles of great fights hath burst
> The buckles on his breast, reneges all temper,
> And is become the bellows and the fan
> To cool a gipsy's lust. [81]

The same excess of passion which "o're flows the measure" has driven out all concern for his country and the commonwealth, the first consideration of an acceptable ruler; Antony himself exclaims:

> Let Rome in Tiber melt, and the wide arch
> Of the rang'd empire fall! Here is my space.
> Kingdoms are clay; our dungy earth alike
> Feeds beast as man; the nobleness of life
> Is to do thus. [82]

It is Antony's neglect of office which draws the severest condemnation from Octavius. The latter denounces his co-ruler's voluptuousness and consequent effeminacy principally in terms of their effect on the welfare of the state in time of crisis:

> From Alexandria
> This is the news: he fishes, drinks, and wastes

---

[80] MacCallum, op. cit., p. 395.   [81] Antony and Cleopatra, I, i, 1–10.
[82] I, i, 33–37.

The lamps of night in revel; is not more manlike
Then Cleopatra: nor the queen of Ptolemy
More womanly than he; hardly gave audience, or
Vouchsaf'd to think he had partners.[83]

Lepidus, as usual, would mediate, but Octavius continues, with accurate political insight:

You are too indulgent. Let's grant it is not
Amiss to tumble on the bed of Ptolemy;
To give a kingdom for a mirth; to sit
And keep the turn of tippling with a slave;
To reel the streets at noon, and stand the buffet
With knaves that smell of sweat: say this becomes him,—

. . . .

yet must Antony
No way excuse his soils, when we do bear
So great weight in his lightness. If he fill'd
His vacancy with his voluptuousness,
Full surfeits and the dryness of his bones
Call on him for 't; but to confound such time
That drums him from his sport and speaks as loud
As his own state and ours, 'tis to be chid
As we rate boys, who, being mature in knowledge,
Pawn their experience to their present pleasure,
And so rebel to judgment.[84]

Antony himself is not always unaware of his weakness and of the disaster which it threatens to bring to his position. "These strong Egyptian fetters I must break, Or lose myself in dotage," he exclaims early in the play, and in substance repeats on later occasions.[85] But

[83] I, iv, 3–8.   [84] I, iv, 16–21; 23–33.

[85] I, ii, 120. Cf. also I, ii, 132:
I must from this enchanting queen break off;
Ten thousand harms, more than the ills I know,
My idleness doth hatch.
And III, xi, 56:
Egypt, thou knew'st too well
My heart was to thy rudder tied by the strings,
And thou should'st tow me after. O'er my spirit
Thy full supremacy thou knew'st, and that
Thy beck might from the bidding of the gods
Command me.

these moments of realization, while rational, are for the most part retrospective; in crucial action he is governed by his passion.

In dividing his portion of the empire to gratify Cleopatra, he gives Octavius added excuse to assume complete authority. In abandoning Octavia he commits another political blunder at the dictation of his infatuation, for Octavius seizes upon the deed as the immediate justification for overthrowing Antony. In the battles which follow, the military genius which could have saved him is vitiated by the influence of his passion for Cleopatra. Because of his feeling for her he blunders in planning and in execution. As a soldier says of the first phase, the fatal decision to fight by sea, "our leader's led, And we are women's men." [86] And of the second phase, the disastrous flight from action, Antony himself laments, "My sword, made weak by my affection, would Obey it on all cause." [87] To the end Antony's political failure is consistently described in these terms of Renaissance thinking about passion and reason in princes. Whatever his other qualifications, however brilliant his personality and character, his blunders, the result of his inability to rule himself, demonstrate that he is unfit to rule others. No clearer exposition of the Renaissance political principle involved in his downfall could be desired than that given by Enobarbus when he summarizes the whole situation after the battle of Actium. To Cleopatra's query, "Is Antony or we in fault for this?" he replies:

> Antony only, that would make his will
> Lord of his reason. What though you fled
> From that great face of war, whose several ranges
> Frighted each other? Why should he follow?
> The itch of his affection should not then
> Have nick'd his captainship, at such a point,
> When half to half the world oppos'd, he being
> The mered question. 'Twas a shame no less
> Than was his loss, to course your flying flags,
> And leave his navy gazing.[88]

And so Octavius is left to bear the palm alone. He is perhaps an unappealing figure—if not the "disagreeable, ugly, repulsive, colourless and passive instrument in the hands of destiny" that Stapfer por-

[86] III, vii, 70–71.   [87] III, xi, 67–68.   [88] III, xiii, 3–12.

trays him to be,[89] at least one of those of whom MacCallum says, "The light from heaven never shines on their eyes either to glorify their path or to lead them astray." [90] But political reason is clearly on his side. In critical commentary on both *Julius Caesar* and *Antony and Cleopatra*, inadequate emphasis has been given the significance of the fact that Octavius is the same emperor Augustus who was hailed in the Renaissance not only as the man under whom Roman monarchy was restored and civil tranquility established, but as the paragon of princes. Elyot, for example, cites his achievements to prove the necessity for monarchy, and his magnanimity, nobility, tolerance, frugality, and sobriety to illustrate the qualities of a successful prince.[91] Augustus maintained this position in Renaissance political literature of the monarchic school throughout the century.[92] He and his role in history came to symbolize the inevitability and justice of the monarchic form of the state. Shakespeare tempered the concept with realism, perhaps to set off by contrast the brilliance of his central character, but the essential conception of Octavius and the attitude toward him remain the same. It is evident in both plays that, dramatically uninteresting as he may be, Octavius succeeds over his rivals because he possesses those qualifications which, according to Renaissance political thinkers, make a great ruler.

The very characteristic which deprives him of dramatic appeal is

[89] Stapfer, *op. cit.*, p. 409. [90] MacCallum, *op. cit.*, p. 378.

[91] Elyot, *op. cit.*, p. 13. Cf. also p. 124: "In Augustus, emperour of Rome, was a natiue maiestie. For, as Suetonius writeth, from his eien proceded rayes or beames, whiche perced the eien of the beholders. The same emperour spake seldome openly, but out of a comentarie, that is to say, that he had before prouided and writen, to the intente that he wolde speke no more ne lasse than he had purposed." In Book III, Chapter XVI, Elyot cites Augustus as an example of a ruler free from the sin of ambition; in Chapter XXIV of the same book he praises the understanding of the emperor (p. 279): "Howe moche it profited to the noble Augustus that untill the dethe of his uncle Julius Cesar, he diligently applyed his study in Athenes, it well appered after that the Ciuile warres were all finisshed, whan he, refourmynge the hole astate of the publike weale, stablisshed the Senate, and takynge unto hym ten honorable personages, dayly in his owne persone consulted with them of maters to be reported twyse in a monethe to the Senate; in suche wyse aydynge and helpynge forthe that mooste noble courte with his incomparable study and diligence."

[92] For example, Chelidonius (*A Most Excellent Historie of the Institution and Firste Beginninge of Christian Princes*, translated, 1571, p. 60 *et seq.*) cites Augustus as an instance of wisdom and learning in rulers; More (*op. cit.*, fol. 45 r.) praises the emperor for his moderation and continence.

one of his chief virtues as a governor. Unlike his great rival, he allows his political reason to be swayed by no form of excess or passion. His sobriety is a commonplace in criticism of the plays in which he appears.[93] The bacchanalian revels on shipboard are a source of genuine disgust to him:

> I could well forbear 't.
> It's monstrous labour when I wash my brain
> And it grows fouler. . . .
>
> .   .   .   .
>
> But I had rather fast from all, four days,
> Than drink so much in one.[94]

To one of his temperament affairs of state must be placed before such personal pleasures: "Good brother, Let me request you off; our graver business Frowns at this levity." [95] In a similar way the excesses of Antony's passion, as has been noted, offend not only his private scruples but his political principles. No voluptuousness, no incontinence of this sort "blindeth the understanding and taketh away sense and reason" in Octavius.

There is a certain magnanimity and nobility of character which further qualifies Octavius for the exalted position which destiny holds for him. The virtue is particularly manifested in his attitude toward Cleopatra in the closing scenes of the play. He tells the Egyptian:

> Bid her have good heart.
> She soon shall know of us, by some of ours,
> How honourable and how kindly we
> Determine for her; for Caesar cannot live
> To be ungentle.[96]

Elyot had cited the case of Augustus as an example of lack of vindictiveness in a ruler; [97] Shakespeare's Octavius no less demonstrates the same compassion in victory. He tells the conquered queen:

---

[93] MacCallum, op. cit., p. 378–79: "The most obvious trait, as Kreyssig remarks, in the somewhat bourgeois personality of Octavius is his sobriety, in every sense of the word: a self contained sobriety, which, though supposed to be a middle-class virtue, is in him pushed so far as to become almost aristocratic."

[94] II, vii, 104–6; 108–9.   [95] II, vii, 127–28.   [96] V, i, 56–60.

[97] Elyot, op. cit., p. 142 et seq., relates a long anecdote illustrating mercifulness as exemplified in Augustus, concluding, "O what sufficient prayse may be gyven to this moste noble and prudent emperour . . ."

Take to you no hard thoughts.
The record of what injuries you did us,
Though written in our flesh, we shall remember
As things but done by chance.[98]

And later:

                                    Cleopatra,
Not what you have reserv'd, nor what acknowledg'd,
Put we i' the roll of conquest. Still be 't yours,
Bestow it at your pleasure; and believe,
Caesar's no merchant, to make prize with you
Of things that merchants sold. Therefore be cheer'd,
Make not your thoughts your prisons; no, dear queen;
For we intend so to dispose you as
Yourself shall give us counsel. Feed, and sleep.
Our care and pity is so much upon you,
That we remain your friend; and so, adieu.[99]

MacCallum believes Octavius' anxiety to exhibit Cleopatra in his triumph betrays an insincerity of feeling here, but it should be noted that her frustration of his schemes does not alter his admiration or prevent the funeral honors which he pays her in the end. The quality of magnanimity is again evident in his tribute to Antony. Political expediency and political justice alike demand that Antony be destroyed; Octavius is the instrument of this necessity, as he himself realizes, but he is generous enough in spirit to recognize the greatness of his victim; "The breaking of so great a thing should make a greater crack," he exclaims upon hearing of Antony's death.[100] The most accurate analysis of his attitude is his own:

                            O Antony!
I have followed thee to this; but we do lance
Diseases in our bodies. I must perforce
Have shown to thee such a declining day,
Or look on thine; we could not stall together
In the whole world: but yet let me lament,
With tears as sovereign as the blood of hearts,
That thou, my brother, my competitor
In top of all design, my mate in empire,

---

[98] V, ii, 117–20.   [99] V, ii, 179–89.   [100] V, i, 14.

> Friend and companion in the front of war,
> The arm of mine own body, and the heart
> Where mine his thoughts did kindle,—that our stars,
> Unreconciliable, should divide
> Our equalness to this.[101]

But that which chiefly marks Octavius for "the specialty of rule" is his ability to act consistently with reference to a just and legitimate political cause, the welfare of the state which the restoration of the monarchy will accomplish. Personal ambition on his part cannot, of course, be denied, although explicit reference to selfish motives is significantly slight in both plays. Octavius himself is honestly convinced that his cause is right; he believes that he is directed by a divine destiny working for the highest good of Roman political society, and the political scheme of these plays, demonstrating the inevitability and necessity of monarchy, confirms him in this conception of his role. He describes himself in exactly those terms employed by Renaissance theorists to define the nature and function of the absolute monarch; to the abandoned Octavia he says, "the high gods, To do you justice, make them ministers Of us and those that love you." [102] Each event in his career he interprets in terms of his destiny. Referring to his quarrel with Antony he tells Octavia:

> Be you not troubled with the time, which drives
> O'er your content these strong necessities;
> But let determin'd things to destiny
> Hold unbewail'd their way.[103]

When his position is established he asserts that it was never ordained by these higher forces that Rome should be governed by a dual authority; over the corpse of Antony he says, "We could not stall

[101] V, i, 35–48.

[102] III, vi, 87–89. I follow here, as always, the reading in the Cambridge text; Theobald, Johnson, Knight, and Dyce substitute "their." The Folio reading, followed by the Variorum and Arden editors, is: "The high gods, to do you justice, makes his ministers of us." Rowe, Pope and Collier (1842) read "the high gods . . . make his . . . ," and Keightley, "the high God . . . makes his. . . ." But whatever the reading of this difficult passage, the meaning seems clear enough in essence; Octavius considers himself and his supporters the administrators of divine justice on earth.

[103] III, vi, 82–85.

together in the whole world." And even while lamenting "that our stars, unreconciliable, should divide our equalness to this," he clearly suggests that his own success in establishing monarchic sovereignty was dictated by this same destiny. Such an outcome, Octavius is certain, is for the highest good of the Roman commonwealth, for only under a monarchic government can that civil tranquility, the chief symptom of a healthy body politic, be attained. Thus just before the final and decisive victory which will establish his authority and end the disastrous civil wars, he exclaims:

> The time of universal peace is near.
> Prove this a prosperous day, the three-nook'd world
> Shall bear the olive freely.[104]

Octavius succeeds where others failed not only because he possesses adequate natural qualifications, but because he devotes every energy and subordinates every personal feeling to this political philosophy. His subjection of passion and indulgence to reason in this respect has already been observed. His love for his sister is genuine and profound, but, as he explains to her, her own content must be sacrificed to the higher destiny of Rome. He can break his covenant with Lepidus because the latter has endangered the welfare of the state; "Lepidus was grown too cruel . . . , he his high authority abus'd and did deserve his change." Similarly for political purposes he suppresses his regard for Antony the man and destroys Antony the political figure. Thus relentlessly he fulfills his own destiny and Rome's, so that in the end Thyreus can truly say that he "performs The bidding of the fullest man, and worthiest to have command obey'd." [105]

It must be emphasized in conclusion that the foregoing analysis, for purposes of revealing more clearly a fundamental but oft-neglected aspect of the play, has been developed purely in the perspective of Renaissance political theory. This is by no means to claim that political action occupies a position of more than incidental importance in the play. But it is to claim that subordinate as it is, the political action is an organic part of this drama of splendid passion. Much has been written of the world which Antony well lost for love; little

[104] IV, vi, 5-7.   [105] III, xiii, 86-88.

has been written of the nature of that world, or of the integral structural relationship of that loss to the tragedy as a whole. Certainly the grandeur of Antony's love is enhanced by his forfeit of empire. But the tragedy of his passion for Cleopatra is enhanced because this forfeit was no merely noble gesture, no hollow flaunting of Antony's disregard for worldly power. His loss is the inevitable consequence of his infatuation, whether he willed that loss or not. "Not Caesar's valour hath o'erthrown Antony, But Antony's hath triumph'd on itself." [106] His tragedy in part represents the inexorable working of fundamental laws of political and social conduct which the Renaissance well understood.

With the accession of Octavius as Augustus at the end of *Antony and Cleopatra* the cycle which began with *Caesar* is complete. To repeat in summary the words of Craig, "The commonwealth was so . . . tired with its liberty and democracy, that all consented to have a monarchy, which all the people formerly had in great abhorrence, and chose to rest there only, as in a safe and fortified harbour against all Storms, Seditions, and Tumults of the people . . ." The political action of the two plays, following this pattern, is not only continuous in development, but consistent in philosophy and conformable to the principles of political thinking about the nature and structure of states generally accepted in Shakespeare's day. At the opening of *Julius Caesar* Rome is enjoying the civil health of a naturally organized body politic. The civil strife and social chaos portrayed in the second half of the play, and the brutal tyranny established in the place of the monarch, are portrayed as direct consequences of the violation of normal political order which the assassination of Caesar constitutes. These circumstances completely discredit the concept of aristocratic sovereignty which comprises the political philosophy of the conspirators. The futility and error of their honest intentions is further demonstrated by the inevitable restoration of monarchy, suggested in the last acts of *Julius Caesar* and concluded in the political action in *Antony and Cleopatra*. Out of the welter of divided and conflicting authorities emerges the one man who, according to the political standards of the Renaissance, is qualified to be the natural head of the Roman body politic. With nothing to indicate that the promise

[106] IV, xv, 14–15.

of civil peace and order will not be fulfilled, the political action of *Antony and Cleopatra*, unlike that of the earlier play, can end conclusively and happily, for the normal state-structure has been re-established.

CHAPTER X

Conclusion

IN HIS THREE great Roman plays Shakespeare examines history for evidence on political concepts which he held in common with the majority of his contemporaries. Order, degree, vocation, and "the specialty of rule"—these are the elements which form the philosophical structure of the dramas. Goethe was aware of such a pattern of thought when he wrote:

Thus throughout *Coriolanus* there runs the vexation that the common people will not recognize the pre-eminence of their superiors. In *Julius Caesar* everything revolves about the idea that the upper classes are unwilling to see the highest position occupied, because they vainly imagine that they can be effective as a body corporate. In *Antony and Cleopatra,* it is proclaimed with a thousand tongues that self-indulgence and achievement are incompatible.[1]

One is almost tempted to see a cyclic unity in these plays, a unity which embraces the three principal systems of government recognized in Shakespeare's day. In *Coriolanus* democracy is tried and found wanting, for it fails to conform to the principles of political organization ordained by universal law. In *Julius Caesar* and in *Antony and Cleopatra* aristocracy is in turn rejected, and for the same reason. Thus in the course of the three plays Rome moves slowly but inevitably toward monarchy, the form of the state which the Renaissance considered divinely authorized.

Similar principles of political theory govern aspects of the dramatic action in those plays based on Greek history. In the camp action of *Troilus and Cressida* Shakespeare seeks to explain the degeneration which characterized the Greek military machine as he knew it in the

[1] Goethe, *Shakespeare und kein Ende* (1813), 1, quoted in *Antony and Cleopatra,* p. 491, edited by H. H. Furness, The New Variorum Shakespeare.

literature of his day. The action portrays the consequences to a military organization when one of the higher degrees in the integrated structure forsakes its proper vocation and disrupts the whole intricate mechanism. The demoralized atmosphere of the Greek camp can be clearly understood only when it is recognized to be the product of violation of principles which Shakespeare held to be fundamental truths of political organization and conduct. In *Timon of Athens* a political society which fails to conform to similar principles becomes the force of evil which brings about the tragic downfall of the title figure. In neither play, as in none of the Roman plays, can the political theme be called the center of dramatic interest. That, as in all Shakespearean drama, remains in individual men. But in none of these plays can the drama of men be fully appreciated apart from the social-political setting in which they are placed.

For it is by showing men, dominated by passion or guided by false intellectual ideals, in conflict with these universal rational truths that Shakespeare secures his dramatic effects. It is by so representing the violation of political theories in the history of actual states that the playwright makes abstract concepts dramatically effective. All of the five plays which have been under consideration in the foregoing pages have this characteristic in common. Vocation is neglected in *Troilus and Cressida;* the pride and lasciviousness of Achilles make him forget his function as "the arm our soldier" in the military body. Justice and virtue are forsaken by the political society of Athens; lust for gold usurps the place of the former qualities as the motivating purpose of governor and governed alike in the state. Degree is violated in *Coriolanus;* exorbitant pride in the would-be consul and subversive democratic activities on the part of the unqualified masses bring the entire commonwealth to the edge of destruction. Finally, in *Julius Caesar* and in *Antony and Cleopatra* the principle of unitary sovereignty is disregarded with disastrous results for the state and for individuals. The republican political doctrines of the conspirators are completely discredited in the former play, and in the latter, stupidity and passion eliminate those men not qualified to exercise sovereign authority in the state. The follies and blunders, the griefs and calamities which follow upon these clashes between human passion and universal reason are the stuff from which Shakespeare makes tragedy or satire, as suits his purpose. In *Troilus and Cressida* alone of the five plays under consideration, however, did he regard the violation of natural law as foolish and futile, and accordingly the object of satirical scorn and laughter. Elsewhere it is regarded as a violent and terrifying force of evil which sweeps good and bad alike to destruction, and hence is a subject fit for tragedy only.

To maintain that Shakespeare so employed for dramatic purposes certain political conceptions prevalent in the thinking of his day is not to argue that he was an advanced and original political thinker. Fortunately it is no longer necessary to attribute his plays to Bacon on the grounds that they display too profound a knowledge of a variety of subjects to have been written by a pupil of Stratford grammar school. Recent investigation tends increasingly to show that Shakespeare's learning can be satisfactorily explained as the product of an extremely sensitive and perceptive mind in contact with the prevailing intellectual currents of his day, rather than as the fruit of long and intensive academic training. Thus Sir Edmund Chambers, who says of attempts to attribute vast classical learning to Shakespeare, "The inferences have not always been discreet," goes on to remark that "A saner judgment is that of Professor Henry Jackson, who after a careful survey of the evidence found no exceptional learning, but merely an example of familiarity with classical themes, more widespread in Elizabethan days than in our own." [2] Certainly this is true in the case of Shakespeare's knowledge of political theory. There is little evidence of originality in concepts of the state which appear in his plays. The theory of political organization is consistently that accepted by conservative and orthodox thinkers of his day and made known to the general populace through a variety of channels. He is no Bodin examining and explaining the concept in analytical detail. Certainly he is no Hooker suggesting, in spite of himself, the logical basis for republicanism. He is, rather, a poet able to perceive the simple, fundamental truths at the base of these political concepts and to make of them elements which enhance the dramatic quality of his plays and enrich their moral and philosophical significance.

[2] Sir E. K. Chambers, *William Shakespeare: A Study of Facts and Problems*, I, 22–23.

Bibliography

Several of the items in the bibliography are not referred to specifically in the text but represent valuable reference works on subjects closely related to those dealt with in the present study. Titles of Tudor and Stuart works are given in shortened form.

Adams, P., "Shakespeare als politischer Dichter," *Deutsche Volkstum*, XV (1933), 945–53.

Alexander, William, *see* Stirling, William Alexander, First Earl of.

Allen, J. W., English Political Thought, 1603–1660. Vol. I (1603–1644), London, 1938.

——— A History of Political Thought in the Sixteenth Century. London, 1928.

Aristotle, Politiques, or Discourses of Government. Translated out of the Greeke into French with Expositions Taken out of the Best Authours . . . by Loys Le Roy. . . . Translated out of French into English [by I. D.]. London, 1598.

——— A Treatise on Government, or The Politics of Aristotle. Translated by William Ellis. Everyman's Library, London, 1912.

Aronstein, Philipp, "Das nationale Erlebnis im englischen Renaissance-drama," *Shakespeare Jahrbuch*, LV (1919), 86–128.

Aylmer, John, An Harborowe for Faithfull and Trewe Subiectes agaynst the Late-Blowne Blaste, Concerninge the Government of Wemen. Strasborowe [London], 1559.

Ayres, H. M., "Shakespeare's *Julius Caesar* in the Light of Some Other Versions," *PMLA*, XXV (1910), 183–227.

Bacon, Francis, XVI Propositions Concerning the Raign and Government of a King. London, 1647.

Barnes, Barnabe, Foure Bookes of Offices: Enabling Privat Persons for the Speciall Service of All Good Princes and Policies. London, 1606.

Bekinsau, John, De supremo et absoluto regis imperio. London, 1546.

Bilson, Thomas, The True Difference betweene Christian Subiection and Unchristian Rebellion. . . . Oxford, 1585.

Birchensha, Ralph, A Discourse Occasioned upon the Late Defeat, Given to the Arch-Rebels Tyrone and Odonnell. . . . London, 1602.

Blackwood, Adam, Apologia pro regibus adversus Georgii Buchanani dialogum de jure regni apud Scotos. Poitiers, 1581.

Blakey, Robert, The History of Political Literature from the Earliest Times. 2 vols., London, 1855.

Blandy, William, The Castle, or Picture of Pollicy, Shewing Forth Most Lively, the Face, Body, and Partes of a Commonwealth. . . . London, 1581.

Boas, F. S., Shakspere and His Predecessors. London, 1902.

Bodin, Jean, The Six Bookes of a Commonweale . . . Done into English by Richard Knolles. London, 1606.

Born, Lester K., "Erasmus on Political Ethics: The 'Institutio Principis Christiani,' " Political Science Quarterly, XLIII (1928), 520–43.

———— "Some Notes on the Political Theories of Erasmus," Journal of Modern History, II (1930), 226–36.

Bradley, A. C., Coriolanus. Annual Shakespeare Lecture of the British Academy. London, 1912.

———— "Antony and Cleopatra," Oxford Lectures on Poetry. London, 1934.

Braithwaite, R., A Strappado for the Devil . . . (1615). Edited by J. W. Ebsworth. Boston, Lincolnshire, 1878.

Brandes, Georg, William Shakespeare: a Critical Study. Translated by William Archer, et al. New York, 1935.

Brooke, Stopford, On Ten Plays of Shakespeare. New York, 1905.

Buchanan, George, De iure regni apud Scotos dialogus (1579). Translated by "Philalethes." London, 1689.

Bullinger, Henry, Fiftie Godlie and Learned Sermones, Divided into Five Decades . . . Translated out of Latine into English by H. I. . . . (1587). Edited for the Parker Society. 2 vols., Cambridge, 1849–51.

Calvin, Jean, Institution de la religion chrétienne (1560). Edited by Frank Baumgartner. Geneva, 1888.

Campbell, L. B., Shakespeare's Tragic Heroes. Cambridge, 1930.

———— "The Use of Historical Patterns in the Reign of Elizabeth," The Huntington Library Quarterly, I (1938), 135–67.

Campbell, Oscar James, Comicall Satyre and Shakespeare's Troilus and Cressida. San Marino, California, 1938.

Carlyle, R. W., and A. J. Carlyle, A History of Medieval Political Theory in the West. 6 vols., London, 1903–36.

Case, John, Sphaera civitatis. Oxford, 1588.

Castiglione, Baldassare, The Book of the Courtier. Translated by Sir Thomas Hoby (1561), edited by W. B. Drayton Henderson. Everyman's Library, London, 1928.

Caxton, William, Recueil of the Histories of Troy. Bruges, 1475.

Ceriol, Federico Furio, A Very Briefe and Profitable Treatise Declaring Howe Many Counsells and What Manner of Counsellors a Prince That Will Govern Well Ought to Have. Translated by T. Blundeville. London, 1570.

Chamberlin, Frederick, Sayings of Queen Elizabeth. London, 1923.

Chambers, E. K., Shakespeare: a Survey. London, 1925.

———— William Shakespeare: a Study of Facts and Problems. 2 vols., Oxford, 1930.

Chambers, R. W., "The Expression of Ideas, Particularly Political Ideas . . . in Shakespeare," Shakespeare's Hand in the Play of Sir Thomas More, by A. W. Pollard, et al., pp. 142–87. Cambridge, 1923.

Chapman, George, Works of George Chapman: Homer's Illiad and Odessy. Edited by R. H. Shepherd. London, 1875.

Charlton, H. B., Shakespeare, Politics and Politicians. Oxford, 1929.

Cheke, Sir John, The Hurt of Sedicioun Howe Grevous It Is to a Communewelth (1549). In Raphael Holinshed, Chronicles of England, Scotland, and Ireland (London, 1807), Vol. III, 987–1011.

Chelidonius, Tigurinus, A Most Excellent Historie of the Institution and Firste Beginninge of Christian Princes and the Originall of Kingdomes . . . Translated into French by Peter Bouaisteau . . . and Englished by Iames Chillester. London, 1571.

Clemen, Wolfgang, "Shakespeare und das Königtum," Shakespeare Jahrbuch, LXVIII (1932), 56–79.

Coleridge, S. T., Notes and Lectures upon Shakespeare. London, 1874.

Collins, J. Churton, Studies in Shakespeare. London, 1904.

Cook, Thomas I., History of Political Philosophy from Plato to Burke. New York, 1936.

Craig, Thomas, Concerning the Right of Succession to the Kingdom of England . . . Against the Sophisms of Parsons the Jesuite Who Assum'd the Counterfeit Name of Doleman . . . Written Originally in Latin above 100 Years Since . . . and Now Faithfully Translated into English. . . . London, 1703.

Crompton, Richard, A Short Declaration of the Ende of Traytors and False Conspirators Against the State, and the Duetie of Subjects to Their Sovereigne Governour. . . . London, 1587.

Crowley, Robert, Select Works, edited by J. M. Cowper, 1872. "Early English Text Society," Extra Series, Vol. XV.

———— The Voyce of the Laste Trumpet. . . . London, 1549.

———— The Way to Wealth. . . . London, 1550.

Daniel, Samuel, The First Part of the Historie of England (1612). Vol. IV of Daniel's *Complete Works*, edited by A. B. Grosart. London, 1896.

Dante Alighieri, De monarchia. Translated and edited by Aurelia Henry. Boston and New York, 1904.

Davies, Godfrey, Bibliography of British History: Stuart Period, 1603–1714. Oxford, 1928.

De Sélincourt, Ernest, English Poets and the National Ideal. Oxford, 1915.

Dowden, Edward, Shakespere: a Critical Study of His Mind and Art. New York, 1880.

Draper, John W., "Political Themes in Shakespeare's Later Plays," *Journal of English and Germanic Philology*, XXXV (1936), 61–93.

———— "The Theme of 'Timon of Athens,'" *Modern Language Review*, XXIX (1934), 20–31.

Dudley, Edmund, The Tree of Commonwealth (1509). Manchester, 1859.

Dunning, W. A., A History of Political Theories from Luther to Montesquieu. London and New York, 1921.

———— "Jean Bodin on Sovereignty," *Political Science Quarterly*, XI (1896), 82–104.

Einstein, Lewis, Tudor Ideals. New York, 1921.

Elyot, Thomas, The Boke Named the Gouernour (1531). Edited by Foster Watson. Everyman's Library, London, 1907.

Erasmus, Desiderius, The Education of a Christian Prince (1516). Translated with an Introduction by L. K. Born. New York, 1936.

Farnam, Henry W., Shakespeare's Economics. New Haven, 1931.

Figgis, J. N., "Political Thought in the Sixteenth Century," *The Cambridge Modern History*, Vol. III, Chapter XXII.

———— The Divine Right of Kings. Cambridge, 1914.

Fleay, F. G., "On the Authorship of *Timon of Athens*," *Transactions of the New Shakspere Society*, Series 1, Nos. 1–2 (1874), pp. 130–51.

Floyd, Thomas, The Picture of a Perfit Commonwealth. . . . London, 1600.

Forset, Edward, A Comparative Discourse of the Bodies Natural and Politique. . . . London, 1606.

Fortescue, Sir John, The Works of Sir John Fortescue. Collected and edited by Thomas Lord Clermont. 2 vols., London, 1869.

———— The Governance of England (Alternative title: The Difference between an Absolute and Limited Monarchy). London, 1714.

———— A Learned Commendation of the Politique Lawes of England. . . . Translated by R. Mulcaster. London, 1567.

———— On the Nature of the Law of Nature. (First printed in Fortescue's

Works, edited by Lord Clermont, 1869.)

Fripp, E. I., Shakespeare, Man and Artist. 2 vols., Oxford, 1938.

Froude, James A., The History of England from the Fall of Wolsey to the Death of Elizabeth. 12 vols., New York, 1870.

Fulbecke, William, The Pandectes of the Law of Nations, . . . London, 1602.

Gardiner, Stephen, De vera obedientia oratio. Translated into English. London, 1553.

Gayley, Charles Mills, Shakespeare and the Founders of Liberty in America. New York, 1918.

Gentili, Alberico, De jure belli libri tres (1612). Translated by John C. Rolfe, with an Introduction by Coleman Phillipson. Classics of International Law, No. 6. 2 vols., Oxford, 1933.

Gentillet, Innocent, A Discourse upon the Meanes of Wel-Governing and Maintaining in Good Peace, a Kingdome, or other Principalitie . . . against Nicholas Machiavel the Florentine. Translated into English by Simon Patericke. London, 1602.

Gervinus, G. G., Shakespeare Commentaries. New York, 1875.

Gettell, Raymond G., History of Political Thought. New York, 1924.

Gierke, Otto, Natural Law and the Theory of Society, 1500–1800. Translated by Ernest Baker. 2 vols., Cambridge, 1934.

———— Political Theories of the Middle Age. Translated by F. W. Maitland. Cambridge, 1922.

von Goethe, J. W., Shakespeare und kein Ende (1813). Stuttgart, 1840.

Gollancz, I., "The Name *Polonius*," *Archiv*, CXLII, 141.

Goodman, Christopher, How Superior Powers Oght to be Obeyd (Geneva, 1558). Reproduced by the Facsimile Text Society. New York, 1931.

Goslicius, Laurentius Grimaldus, The Counsellor, Wherein the Offices of Magistrates, the Happie Life of Subiectes, and the Felicitie of Commonweales Is Pleasantly and Pithilie Discoursed . . . , Newlie Translated into English. London, 1598.

Gough, J. W., The Social Contract: a Critical Study of Its Development. Oxford, 1936.

Graves, Thornton, "The Political Use of the Stage during the Reign of James I," *Anglia*, XXXVIII (1914), 137–56.

Grosse, F., "Das englische Renaissancedrama im Spiegel zeitgenössischer Staatstheorien," *Sprache und Kultur der Germanischer und Romanischer Völker*, A, XVIII (1935).

Hall, Joseph, Mundus Alter et Idem . . . (1605). London, 1908.

Harington, John, A Tract on the Succession to the Crown (Written in 1602). Edited by C. R. Markham for the Roxburghe Club. London, 1880.

Hart, Alfred, Shakespeare and the Homilies. Melbourne, 1934.

Hayward, John, An Answer to the First Part of a Certaine Conference Concerning Succession Published Not Long Since under the Name of R. Doleman [R. Parsons]. London, 1603.

Hearnshaw, F. J. C., "Bodin and the Genesis of the Doctrine of Sovereignty," Tudor Studies Presented . . . to Albert Frederick Pollard. Edited by R. W. Seton-Watson. London, 1924.

———, editor, The Social and Political Ideas of Some Great Medieval Thinkers. London, 1923.

———, editor, The Social and Political Ideas of Some Great Thinkers of the Renaissance and Reformation. London, 1925.

———, editor, The Social and Political Ideas of Some Great Thinkers of the Sixteenth and Seventeenth Centuries. London, 1926.

Henneke, Agnes, "Shakespeares englische Könige im Lichte staatsrechtlicher Strömungen seiner Zeit," Shakespeare Jahrbuch, LXVI (1930), 79–144.

Hertzler, J. O., The History of Utopian Thought. New York, 1926.

Heywood, Thomas, An Apology for Actors (1612). "Shakespeare Society Publications," Vol. III (1841).

Holinshed, Raphael, Chronicles of England, Scotland and Ireland. 6 vols., London, 1807.

Homilies, Certayne Sermons or Homilies, Appoynted by the Kynges Maiestie to be Declared, and Redde by All Persones, Vicars, or Curates, Every Sunday in Their Churches, Where They Have Cure. London, 1547.

——— The Seconde Tome of Homelyes. . . . London, 1563.

——— An Homilie agaynst Disobedience and Wylful Rebellion [issued singly]. London, 1571 [?].

——— Certaine Sermons or Homilies, Appointed to Be Read in Churches. In the Time of the Late Queen Elizabeth of Famous Memory. London, 1640.

Hooker, Richard, Of the Laws of Ecclesiastical Polity (1594 et seq.). Edited by Ronald Bayne. 2 vols., Everyman's Library, London, 1907.

Horn, F., Shakespeare's Schauspiele Erläutert. Leipzig, 1823.

Horrocks, J. W., Machiavelli in Tudor Opinion and Discussion. New York, 1908.

Hunter, Sir Mark, "Politics and Character in Shakespeare's Julius Caesar," Essays by Divers Hands, Oxford, 1931. "Royal Society of Literature,"

New Series, Vol. X.

The Institution of a Christen Man, Conteynynge the Exposition or Interpretation of the Commune Crede, of the Seven Sacramentes, of the X
Commandementes, of the Pater Noster, and the Ave Maria, Justification and Purgatorie. London, 1537. [Popularly known as "The Bishop's
Book."]

Isocrates, The Doctrinal of Princes. . . . Translated by Sir Thomas Elyot.
London, c. 1548.

———— A Perfite Looking Glasse for All Estates. . . . Translated from
the Latin of Hier. Wolfius by T. Forrest. London, 1580. [This is a
translation of Isocrates' three treatises, To Demonicus, To Nicocles, and
Nicocles or the Cyprians.]

Jacob, E. F., "Sir John Fortescue and the Law of Nature," Bulletin of the
John Rylands Library, XVIII (1934), 359–76.

James I, king of England, The Political Works of James I, Reprinted from
the Edition of 1616; with an Introduction by C. H. McIlwain. Cambridge, Mass., 1918.

———— The Workes of the Most High and Mightie Prince James. . . .
London, 1616.

Janet, Paul, Histoire de la science politique dans ses rapports avec la morale.
2 vols., Paris, 1887.

John of Salisbury, Policraticus. Edited by C. C. J. Webb. 2 vols., London,
1909.

Kautsky, Karl, Thomas More and His Utopia, with a Historical Introduction. New York, 1927.

Keller, Wolfgang, "Shakespeares Königsdramen," Shakespeare Jahrbuch,
LXIII (1927), 35–53.

———— "Zwei Bemerkungen zu 'Julius Caesar,'" Shakespeare Jahrbuch,
XLV (1909), 219–28.

Kellett, E. E., Suggestions: Literary Essays. Cambridge, 1923.

Knights, L. C., Drama and Society in the Age of Jonson. London, 1937.

Knox, John, The First Blast of the Trumpet Against the Monstrous Regiment of Women. Geneva, 1558.

———— The Works of John Knox. Edited by David Laing. 6 vols., Edinburgh, 1864.

Kohler, Josef, "Die Staatsidee Shakespeares in 'Richard II,'" Shakespeare
Jahrbuch, LIII (1917), 1–12.

Languet, H. [Philip Duplessis-Mornay?], Vindiciae contra tyrannos.
(Basel, 1579.) Translated by H. J. Laski. New York, 1924.

Latimer, Hugh, Seven Sermons before Edward VI on Each Friday in Lent,

1549. Edited by Edward Arber. London, 1895. "English Reprints," 13.

Lauder, William, Ane Compendious and Breve Tractate Concernyng the Office and Dewtie of Kyngis . . . (1556). Edited by Fitzedward Hall. London, 1869, "Early English Text Society," Original Series, Vol. III.

Lawrence, W. W., Shakespeare's Problem Comedies. New York, 1931.

Lee, Sir Sidney, A Life of William Shakespeare. London, 1922.

Lindner, A., "Die dramatische Einheit im Julius Caesar," *Shakespeare Jahrbuch*, II (1866), 90–95.

Lipson, Ephraim, The Economic History of England. 3 vols., London, 1931.

Luther, Martin, An den Christlichen Adel (1520). Translated by C. M. Jacobs. Vol. II of *Works of Martin Luther*. Philadelphia, 1915.

———— Von Weltlicher Uberkeyt (1523). Translated by J. J. Schindel. Vol. III of *Works of Martin Luther*. Philadelphia, 1930.

Lydgate, John, Troy Book. Edited by Henry Bergen. London, 1906–35. "Early English Text Society," Extra Series, Vols. XCVII, CIII, CVI.

Lyly, John, The Complete Works of John Lyly. Edited by R. W. Bond. 3 vols., Oxford, 1902.

MacCallum, M. W., Shakespeare's Roman Plays and Their Background. London, 1925.

Machiavelli, N., The Arte of Warre. . . . Englished by P. Whitehorne. London, 1560.

———— Florentine History. Translated by Thomas Bedingfield. London, 1595.

———— Machiavels Discourses upon the First Decade of T. Livius. Translated by E. D. London, 1636.

———— Nicholas Machiavels Prince. Translated by E. D. London, 1640.

———— The Prince. Translated with an Introduction by W. K. Marriott. Everyman's Library, London, 1908.

Malynes, G. de, A Treatise of the Canker of England's Commonwealth. London, 1601.

Marriott, J. A. R., "Shakespeare and Politics," *Cornhill Magazine*, 1927, 678–90.

Matthews, Brander, Shakspere as a Playwright. New York, 1913.

Mayer, E. W., Machiavellis Geschichtsauffassung und sein Begriff *virtù*. Munich and Berlin, 1912.

Mayer, J. P. (in coöperation with R. H. S. Crossman, P. Kecsckemeti, E. Kohn-Bramstedt, and C. J. S. Sprigge), Political Thought in the European Tradition. London, 1939.

Merbury, Charles, A Briefe Discourse of Royal Monarchie, as of the Best Commonweale. . . . London, 1581.

Mesnard, Pierre, L'Essor de la philosophie politique au XVIme siècle. Paris, 1936.

Meyer, E., Machiavelli and the Elizabethan Drama. Weimar, 1897. "Literarhistorische Forschungen," I.

Mohl, Ruth, The Three Estates in Medieval and Renaissance Literature. New York, 1933.

More, George, Principles for Yong Princes: Collected out of Sundry Authors. London, 1611.

More, Sir Thomas, The Utopia (1516). Edited by W. D. Armes. New York, 1912.

Morgan, R. B., editor, Readings in English Social History from Contemporary Literature. Vol. III, 1485–1603. Cambridge, 1921.

Murray, R. H., The History of Political Science from Plato to the Present. Cambridge, 1929.

———— The Political Consequences of the Reformation. Boston, 1926.

Musculus, Wolfgang, Commonplaces of Christian Religion. . . . Translated out of Latine into Englishe [by John Man]. London, 1563.

A Necessary Doctrine and Erudition for Any Chrysten Man, Set Furth by the Kynges Maiestye of England. . . . London, 1543. [Popularly known as "The King's Book."]

Onions, C. T., editor, Shakespeare's England. 2 vols., Oxford, 1917.

Parrott, T. M., The Problem of Timon of Athens. Published for the Shakespeare Association. Oxford, 1923.

Parsons, Robert ["R. Doleman"], A Conference about the Next Succession to the Crowne of England. . . . Antwerp [?], 1594.

Phillips, W. A., "The Influence of Machiavelli on the Reformation in England," Nineteenth Century, XL (1896), 907–18.

Plinius Secundus, Caius, The Natural History of Pliny. Translated by John Bostock and H. T. Riley. 6 vols., London, 1855–57.

Plutarch, The Lives of the Noble Grecians and Romans . . . Translated out of Greeke into French by Iames Amyot, and out of French into English by Thomas North. 8 vols., Stratford-upon-Avon (Shakespeare Head Press), 1928.

Pollard, A. F., The History of England from the Accession of Edward VI to the Death of Elizabeth (1547–1603). London and New York, 1910.

Pollard, A. W., and G. R. Redgrave, A Short-Title Catalogue of Books Printed in England, Scotland, and Ireland, and of English Books Printed Abroad, 1475–1640. London, 1926.

Ponet, John, A Short Treatise of Politike Power . . . (1556). London, 1642.

Pongs, H., "Shakespeare und das politische Drama," *Dichtung und Volkstum*, XXXVII (1936), 257–81.

Praz, Mario, "Machiavelli and the Elizabethans," *Proceedings of the British Academy*, XIV (1928), 49–97.

Raleigh, Sir Walter, The Cabinet Council. London (Published by John Milton), 1658.

——— The Prince, or Maxims of State. London, 1642.

Read, Conyers, Bibliography of British History, Tudor Period, 1485–1603. Oxford, 1933.

Rollins, Hyder, "The Troilus-Cressida Story from Chaucer to Shakespeare," *PMLA*, XXXII (1917), 383–429.

Ronsard, Pierre, Institution pour l'adolescence du roy tres-Chrestien Charles IX de ce nom. Vol. V of *Complete Works*, edited by Paul Laumonnier. Paris, 1919.

Routh, E. M. G., Sir Thomas More and His Friends, 1477–1535. London, 1934.

Sabine, George H., A History of Political Theory. New York, 1937.

Saint German, Christopher, The Dialogues in English between a Doctor of Divinity and a Student in the Laws of England (1530 *et seq.*). London, 1580.

Shakespeare, William, The Complete Works of William Shakespeare. Edited by William Allen Neilson. The Students' Cambridge Edition, Boston and New York, 1910.

——— Antony and Cleopatra. Edited by R. H. Case. The Arden Shakespeare, London, 1920.

——— Antony and Cleopatra. Edited by H. H. Furness. The New Variorum Shakespeare, Philadelphia, 1907.

——— Coriolanus. Edited by W. J. Craig and R. H. Case. The Arden Shakespeare, London, 1922.

——— Coriolanus. Edited by H. H. Furness, Jr. The New Variorum Shakespeare, Philadelphia, 1928.

——— Julius Caesar. Edited by H. H. Furness, Jr. The New Variorum Shakespeare, Philadelphia, 1913.

——— Julius Caesar. Edited by Michael MacMillan. The Arden Shakespeare, London, 1917.

——— Timon of Athens. Edited by Sir Henry Irving and F. A. Marshall. The Henry Irving Shakespeare, London, 1888–90.

———— Timon of Athens. Edited by K. Deighton. The Arden Shakespeare, London, 1905.

———— Troilus and Cressida. Edited by K. Deighton. The Arden Shakespeare, London, 1922.

Simpson, Richard, "The Political Use of the Stage in Shakspere's Time and the Politics of Shakspere's Historical Plays," *Transactions of the New Shakspere Society*, Series 1, Nos. 1–2 (1874), 371–441.

Sisson, C. J., "King James the First of England as Poet and Political Writer," *Seventeenth Century Studies Presented to Sir Herbert Grierson*, 47–63. Oxford, 1938.

Sleeth, Charles R., "Shakespeare's Counsellors of State," *Revue anglo-américaine*, XIII (1935), 97–113.

Small, S. A., "The Political Import of the Norton Half of 'Gorboduc,'" *PMLA*, XLVI (1931), 641–46.

Smith, Thomas, The Commonwealth of England and Maner of Government Thereof. . . . London, 1589.

Stafford, William [John Hales?], A Compendious or Briefe Examination of Certain Ordinary Complaints. . . . (Alternative title: A Discourse of the Commonweal of this Realm of England.) London, 1581.

Stapfer, Paul, Shakespeare and Classical Antiquity. Translated from the French by Emily J. Carey. London, 1880.

Starkey, Thomas, A Dialogue between Cardinal Pole and Thomas Lupset. . . . (c. 1538), edited by J. W. Cowper and S. J. Herrtage, London, 1878. "Early English Text Society," Extra Series, Vol. XXXII.

———— An Exhortation to the People Instructynge Theym to Unitie and Obedience. London, 1540.

Starnes, D. T., "Shakespeare and Elyot's 'Gouernour,'" *University of Texas Studies in English*, VII (1927), 112–32.

Stephen, Sir Leslie, Studies of a Biographer. 4 vols., New York, 1907.

Stirling, William Alexander, First Earl of, The Poetical Works of Sir William Alexander. Edited by L. E. Kastner and H. B. Charlton. London, 1921–29.

———— A Paraenesis to the Prince. London, 1604.

———— The Tragedy of Julius Caesar. London, 1607.

Swinburne, A. C., Shakespeare. London and New York, 1909.

Tatlock, J. S. P., "The Chief Problem in Shakespeare," *Sewanee Review*, XXIV (1916), 129–47.

———— "The Siege of Troy in Elizabethan Literature, Especially in Shakespeare and Heywood," *PMLA*, XXX (1915), 673–770.

Tawney, R. H., and Eileen Powers, editors, Tudor Economic Documents. 3 vols., London, 1924.

Tolman, Albert H., "Is Shakespeare Aristocratic?," *PMLA*, XXIX (1914), 277–98.

——— "The Structure of Shakespeare's Tragedies with Special Reference to Coriolanus," *Modern Language Notes*, XXXVII (1922), 449–58.

Tschischwitz, Benno, Shakespeares Staat und Königthum. Halle, 1866.

Tupper, Frederick, "The Shaksperean Mob," *PMLA*, XXVII (1912), 486–523.

Tyndale, William, The Obedience of a Christen Man and How Christen Rulers Ought to Govern . . . (1528). London, 1561.

Vennar, Richard, The Right Way to Heaven . . . with an Exhortacion to Continue All Subiects in Their Due Obedience Together with the Reward of a Faithfull Subiect to His Prince. London, 1602.

——— The True Testimonie of a Faithfull Subject. . . . London, 1602 [?].

Vergil, The Georgics. Edited by John Sargeaunt and Thomas Royds. Oxford, 1924.

Waring, L. H., The Political Theory of Martin Luther. New York and London, 1910.

Wecter, Dixon, "Shakespere's Purpose in *Timon of Athens*," *PMLA*, XLIII (1928), 701–21.

Weissberger, L. A., "Machiavelli and Tudor England," *Political Science Quarterly*, XLII (1927), 589–607.

Wells, J., A Short History of Rome. London, 1896.

Wentworth, Peter, A Pithie Exhortation to Her Majestie for Establishing Her Successor to the Crowne, . . . Edinburgh, 1598.

Wilson, John Dover, The Essential Shakespeare. Cambridge, 1932.

Wood, F. T., "Shakespeare and the Plebs," *Essays and Studies by Members of the English Association*, XVIII (1932), 53–73.

Wright, E. H., The Authorship of Timon of Athens. New York, 1910.

Wright, Louis B., Middle-Class Culture in Elizabethan England. Chapel Hill, N.C., 1935.

Index

Absolutism, royal, 24; opponents of, 65; *see also* Monarchy; Sovereignty

Achilles, antisocial conduct, 121 ff., 207

Agamemnon, 117, 121, 124, 126

Agrippa, Menenius, *see* Menenius

Ajax, 122, 123

Alcibiades, contrast in reaction of Timon and, to same situation, 127, 143; triumph over Athens, 129; causes of corruption in Athens described by, 130; charges against Senate, 131, 132, 138; seeks justice, 133; banishment, 143; function in drama, 145

Alexander, William, 30, 182; quoted, 60

Allen, J. W., 19, 26; quoted, 10, 11, 21, 22, 54, 76, 85, 94, 98*n*

Ambition, odium attached to, 86

Amyot, Jacques, quoted, 34

Anabaptists, 56

Analogy, concept of state embodied in, 4, 8; between body of the state and the human body, 6, 8, 9, 11, 12, 28, 55, 61, 62, 64 ff. *passim*, 73, 74, 94, 108, 151, 158; significance of analogical argument, 61-75, 77; analogical argument against plurality forms of government, 106; *see also under* Beehive; Body, human; Natural phenomena

Anatomical analogy, 61, 66, 67, 108; used by Queen Elizabeth, 71; *see also* Body, human

Angels, analogy to hierarchy of, 67

Anglicans, 59

Animal analogy, 61, 66, 68, 109

Answer to . . . R. Doleman, An (Hayward), 26

Antony, 179, 186, 187; soliloquy over body of Caesar, 184; funeral oration, 185; infatuation for Cleopatra, 188 ff.; effect on his character, 189, 196; anxiety to oust Lepidus, 189; description of Lepidus' role, 191; contest for empire between Octavius and, 193; political impression left by, in *Julius Caesar*, 193; Octavius' tribute to, 201; tragedy of his love enhanced by forfeit of empire, 204

Antony and Cleopatra, political content, 4, 10, 113, 172 ff., 188-205; monarchic cycle in, 172 ff.; splendid infatuation the chief interest, 188 ff.; Lepidus' spineless role, 191; aristocracy rejected, 206

Apemantus, 137, 144

Apology for Actors (Heywood), 36

Aristocracy, Shakespeare's use of term, 16; monarchy superior to, 104 ff.; function in Rome, 175; discredited in *Julius Caesar*, 187; rejected in Rome, 206

Aristotle, 29, 54, 55, 57, 62, 104; quoted, 47, 51*n*

"Arm our soldier, the," 151; the true function of Coriolanus, 162, 164, 167; Achilles' function as, 207

Astronomical analogy, 61, 66

Athens, social corruption, 112, 126-46; Timon's outburst against corruption, 128, 135, 137, 138; causes of social disorder, 130; Alcibiades' charges against Senate, 131, 132, 138; Senate, 140, 143, 145

Aufidius, 163, 169

Augustus, 173; role in political literature and in history, 199; lack of vindictiveness, 200; accession of Octavius as, 204; *see also* Octavius

Authority, 23, 24; source and exercise of, 11, 12, 110; of king, 20 ff., 110, 179; secular and ecclesiastical, 25; obedience to, 85; essential to structure of state, 94;